C9012

7.19.95

T5-AXI-463

1949

The Twilight Before The Dawn

by

Jack Fitzgerald

OTHER JACK FITZGERALD BOOKS

The Spring Rice Document
Battlefront Newfoundland
Crimes That Shocked Newfoundland
The Jack Ford Story – Newfoundland's POW in Nagasaki
Legacy of Laughter
Remarkable Stories of Newfoundland
Treasure Island Revisited – A True Newfoundland Adventure Story
Ten Steps to the Gallows – True Stories of Newfoundland and Labrador
Newfoundland Adventures – In Air, On Land, At Sea
Where Angels Fear to Tread
Another Time, Another Place
Amazing Newfoundland Stories
The Hangman is Never Late
Untold Stories of Newfoundland
Beyond the Grave
Beyond Belief
Strange But True Newfoundland Stories
Jack Fitzgerald's Notebook
Ghosts and Oddities
Stroke of Champions
Up the Pond
A Day at the Races – The Story of the St. John's Regatta
Newfoundland Disasters
Rogues and Branding Irons
Convicted
Too Many Parties, Too Many Pals
Ten Steps to The Gallows
Incredible Newfoundland Stories
Newfoundland Fireside Stories

Ask your favourite bookstore or order directly from the publisher.

Creative Book Publishing
430 Topsail Rd.,
St. John's, NL
A1E 4N1

Tel: (709) 748-0813 •Fax: (709) 579-6511
E-mail: nl.books@transcontinental.ca • www.creativebookpublishing.ca

1949

The Twilight Before The Dawn

by
Jack Fitzgerald

St. John's, Newfoundland and Labrador
2012

© 2012, Jack Fitzgerald

 Canada Council **Conseil des Arts** **Canadä** Newfoundland
for the Arts du Canada Labrador

We gratefully acknowledge the financial support of the Canada Council for the Arts,
the Government of Canada through the Canada Book Fund (CBF),
and the Government of Newfoundland and Labrador through the Department of
Tourism, Culture and Recreation for our publishing program.

All rights reserved. No part of this work covered by the copyrights hereon may be
reproduced or used in any form or by any means—graphic, electronic or
mechanical—without the prior written permission of the publisher.
Any requests for photocopying, recording, taping or information storage
and retrieval systems of any part of this book shall be directed in writing to
the Canadian Reprography Collective, One Yonge Street, Suite 1900,
Toronto, Ontario M5E 1E5.

Cover Design by Maurice Fitzgerald
Layout by Joanne Snook-Hann
Printed on acid-free paper

Published by
CREATIVE PUBLISHERS
an imprint of CREATIVE BOOK PUBLISHING
a Transcontinental Inc. associated company
P.O. Box 8660, Stn. A
St. John's, Newfoundland and Labrador A1B 3T7

Printed in Canada by:
TRANSCONTINENTAL INC.

Library and Archives Canada Cataloguing in Publication

Fitzgerald, Jack, 1945-
    1949 : the twilight before the dawn / Jack Fitzgerald.

Includes bibliographical references.
ISBN 978-1-897174-98-2

    1. Smallwood, Joseph R., 1900-1991. 2. Prime ministers--
Newfoundland and Labrador--Biography. 3. Newfoundland
and Labrador--Politics and government--20th century. I. Title.

FC2175.1.S63F58 2012   971.8'04092   C2012-905020-2

1949 The Twilight Before The Dawn was written not only to record and preserve the most important turning point in Newfoundland history but also to provide an insight into the forces at play in the battle that took place while leaving the reader with an appreciation of the very different and difficult life Newfoundlanders experienced before 1949. It is a story to be preserved for future generations. That is the reason why I dedicate this book to my grandchildren Jill Carter and Eva Fitzgerald.

TABLE OF CONTENTS

INTRODUCTION

1949: The Twilight Before the Dawn is a non-fiction, historical record of the most important event in Newfoundland's history; union with Canada. No other event has had the same impact on the New-foundland people. Not only was there an immediate improvement in the lives of Newfoundlanders, but it also opened the door to op-portunities for a future that the ordinary citizen could not imagine. Where else, but in a third world country, would the purchase of new shoes for children or extra cans of milk for infants be consid-ered news items. Yet, in the month following Confederation when people began receiving cheques from Ottawa in the mail these ex-periences were happening all over Newfoundland and were being reported in Newfoundland newspapers.

The story of how Newfoundland became the tenth province of Canada is a most complex story. To tell it involved researching Newfoundland political history, volumes of National Convention and referenda records, volumes of declassified, government se-cret records, parliamentary records, historical publications, archival records, biographical books, newspaper and magazine records, constitutional law books, and the extensive biographical material and books relating to the life of Joseph R. Smallwood.

When Smallwood stood in the National Convention as the only declared Confederate the challenges to his cause were daunting. There was widespread uncertainty throughout Newfoundland after WWII. The temporary prosperity experienced during the war due to the large investments by the Americans and Canadi-ans was not expected to last. There was a dire need to build a country wide infrastructure and no money to do so. The cost of living was high and poverty still widespread. A surplus had been built up on the backs of the Newfoundland people. There were no roads, inadequate schools, few and inadequate hospitals, and a high rate of infectious diseases. Rivalries divided the country with the St. John's and nearby communities against the outports; the merchant class against the working class and there were reli-gious differences. To bring this divided country together in any kind of majority was a monumental task.

Smallwood's personal biography from 1900 to 1949 is crucial to understanding and recognizing how the political and people skills and leadership qualities he quite successfully demonstrated in the battle for Confederation had been shaped by his lifetime work and experiences up to that time. My writings in this regard were helped by the fact that I knew the man from 1965 to 1990 during which time I had many conversations with him about his role in the coming of Confederation to Newfoundland. Particularly helpful were Smallwood's writings: *I Chose Canada, To You With Affection, No Apology From Me, The Time has Come To Tell* and his first book published in 1931 *The New Newfoundland.* I also consulted his *Encyclopaedia of Newfoundland* and *The Books of Newfoundland* (6 vols); Richard Gwyn's, *Smallwood the Unlikely Revolutionary,* and Harold Horwood's, *Joey, The Life and Political Times of Joey Smallwood.* I participated in a series of conversations in a group setting with Smallwood, Greg Power, Joe Ashley, Herb Wells and Ted Garland. More recently I was able to interview Jack Ford concerning the attack on Smallwood at the CLB Armoury during the referendum battle. Ford served as a bodyguard for Smallwood at that event. I was also fortunate in being able to interview Mike Critch, the only surviving reporter to have covered the National Convention.

The story of Newfoundland's road to Confederation is told in fifteen chapters beginning with the truth about life in Newfoundland prior to 1949, the backwardness, the poverty, the isolation and the lack of opportunities for its people.

Chapters two, three, four and five continue with the unfolding story of how the National Convention and referendum came about and the emerging of an unlikely leader from the working class in a society dominated by a merchant class. These include an amazing biographical background of Joseph R. Smallwood which details the events and experiences of his early life that prepared him well for the role which fell upon him as leader of the Confederate movement and Newfoundland's first Premier.

Chapters six, seven, eight, nine, and ten chronicle the, sometimes raucous, National Convention that included a physical confrontation, threats, and much backroom intrigue and political back stabbing. It was indeed a 'knock down and drag 'em out' battle and these chapters show how Smallwood made a difference in the outcome.

Chapters eleven and twelve reveal what happened when the anti-confederate majority in the Convention included only Responsible Government, with its twenty-nine votes, and Commission of Government, with zero support, in their recommendation for ballot choices while completely excluding Confederation, which recorded sixteen votes. This effort was publicly dubbed 'The decision of the twenty-nine dictators.' All legitimate political forms with substantial public support deserved a place at the table and as choices in a referendum. Also revealed is Mackenzie King's reluctance at first to accept the Confederation majority in the second referendum and the factors that influenced his choice.

Chapter thirteen records the attempts by some prominent members of the establishment to prevent Smallwood from becoming interim Premier and even their backroom lobbying to replace him as leader of the Confederate movement. This chapter also deals with the conspiracy charges that have lingered over the decades.

Chapters fourteen and fifteen reveal the background of Smallwood's choice to go with the Liberal Party, the socialists who joined with him and soon after abandoned the party, as well as his discussions with Canada's socialist party (CCF) leader. It also covers the behind the scenes political wranglings just weeks before the new Premier and Lieutenant Governor were chosen and sworn in. In addition, this chapter briefly discusses the question of whether Newfoundland was a colony or dominion in 1949.

Throughout the book there are many insightful testimonials, from those involved behind the scenes, to the amazing political skills used by Smallwood to win the battle. Hon. R. A. Mackay, a top level official in External Affairs, who was assigned to block Smallwood's access to political leaders in Ottawa in 1946, twenty years later while referring to the role of Smallwood in bringing about Confederation commented, "Who else but Smallwood could have done it?"

– Jack Fitzgerald, author

CHAPTER 1

Newfoundland Fifty Years Behind

"During the past 100 years, I do not think there was any doubt of the fact that the Water Street merchants are very largely to blame for the backwardness of the economic development of Newfoundland. Their system of control of the fisheries, which was set up by them, was really an extension of the feudal system, with all its faults. The fishermen of this country were practically serfs to the Water Street merchants of St. John's."

- Quote from a secret memo to the Canadian Government from Canada's High Commissioner to Newfoundland, C. Burchill, 1943

From the time of its discovery in 1497 up to 1933, New-foundland was a handicapped country. It did not grow, develop and advance like the rest of North America, primarily because of the obstacles placed in its way by elite and powerful groups whose only vision of the colony was motivated by greed. To them Newfoundland was simply a source of accumulating great personal wealth.

The main obstacle which kept Newfoundland fifty years behind the rest of North America, and in poverty, were the merchants. At first, it was the merchants of the west coast of England who dominated over the colony for more than three centuries. They were then replaced by the Water Street merchants of St. John's who dominated for another century.

As late as the years just prior to Confederation, a very large part of Newfoundland's population existed on little or no actual cash from January to June. Historian Herbert L. Pottle in his book *Newfoundland Dawn Before Light* stated, "For a large proportion of the year, as of old, they were dependent upon "credit" by the local merchant and, in the case of the very dependent, a mere pittance of government "relief."[1]

'TRUCK SYSTEM' CONDEMNED IN ENGLAND

The fishing industry in Newfoundland operated on the 'truck system.' The Amulree Royal Commission leveled a blistering attack on that merchant operated system in 1933. It pointed out that the system, "...is sapping the energy, initiative and moral sense of the people and, instead of building them up into an independent and self-reliant race, is reducing them to a state bordering on servitude." The report noted that Britain had abolished this outrageous system 100 years before. However, according to the report, the Newfoundland merchants persisted in maintaining the

---

[1] Pottle was a member of the six-man Commission of Government which governed Newfoundland frugally, and also a member of the first provincial cabinet in 1949.

same credit system. The report recommended, "This is a system so vicious in theory and so damaging in practice that a determined attempt must be made to alter it."[2]

One hundred years of Responsible Government had upheld this system. This was perhaps the major cause of the political division in the referendum between the Avalon Peninsula, which was under the influence of merchants and the fishermen of the outports.

Another historian, A.H. McLintock described it as a subtle system, "because it impoverishes and enslaves the victims, and then makes them love their chains."[3]

Bert Butt, a St. John's delegate to the National Convention, also referred to the causes of Newfoundland's backwardness. He explained:

If we go back into Newfoundland's history far enough we have, on the authority of McLintock, (historian) a clear picture of how in her struggle to establish herself, Newfoundland had to grow up in an atmosphere where the whole power of great nations tended to depress the struggling colony. The Island of Newfoundland and the potential and actual wealth of her fisheries were treated as just another source of producing wealth for the Mother Country, as well as being used as a training ground for the defence of Britain which at that time was looked upon as the chief preoccupation of Government.[4]

G.H. Shakespeare, the Parliamentary Under-Secretary of State for Dominion Affairs in Britain, was taken aback by the poor conditions he found in Newfoundland in December 1941. He reported to his Government:

---

[2] *The Amulree Royal Commission Report*, 1933, 103,106, 115.

[3] A.H. McLintock, *The Establishment of Constitutional Government in Newfoundland, 1783-1832. A Study of Retarded Colonization* (London: Longman-Green and Co. 1941).

[4] GN10/A/1 File #10.

I only got the impression of an Island with primitive road conditions which would disgrace a cannibal island in the Pacific and of a complete lack of telephone and modern communications. I couldn't even telephone from Gander to St. John's without going through three different systems, one of them being a teleprinter.

He recommended that, after the war, building a road system across the Island connecting smaller communities would be the first essential program to be carried out.

Early in 1941, *Collier's Magazine* assigned journalist Alexander Davenport to travel across Newfoundland to write an article about Britain's oldest colony and its people. Interest in Newfoundland had been sparked by the Americans moving to the Island to set up military bases. His writings were anything but complimentary. He revealed to millions of Americans the picture of widespread poverty and backwardness. Davenport wrote:

Almost 50,000 Newfoundlanders are on relief at six cents a day. And the six cents is in food warrants, not money, not that it makes much difference. The waiting list for the microscopic dole is a thing to shudder at, not to count. The American 'Oakie,' the poorest of the share-croppers, the most wretched of our slum-dwellers, know no such poverty or neglect.

Futility in government offices, a fantastic lack of sanitation, an almost complete absence of medical care and all the other murdering corollaries of poverty have reduced the morale of a once hardy people to a melancholy level.[5]

Some people over the years expressed the opinion that the first settlers to Newfoundland chose isolated bays and

---

[5] Jack Fitzgerald, *Battlefront Newfoundland*. By 1949 the six cents a day dole had increased to twenty-five cents a day.

coves to be near the fishing grounds. However, the truth of this issue is related to British policy. Mr. Butt explained:

> The main cause of our having done so may be ascribed to the fact that the repressive measures taken against settlement in the Island were the main cause of our having to hide away in places where we could not be found. In addition, because of our actual settlement in isolated places and our preoccupation with the fisheries, there came down through the years a feeling that agriculture which in most countries formed the basis of a stable economy should not be pushed so far as it could have been in this Island.[6]

The lifestyles and choices forced upon early settlers by British merchants inspired government policies, built an unstable economy resulting in a series of constant depressions in Newfoundland. When industrialization came and progressed in North America, Newfoundland was left behind.

While advocating union with Canada in 1946, Joseph R. Smallwood described the backwardness of his country in comparison to others in North America:

> We are fifty years behind the times and in some cases 100 years. We have one of the highest rates of tuberculosis in the world, one of the highest infant mortality rates in the world, one of highest maternity mortality rates in the world, and one of the highest rates of beriberi and rickets in the world.[7]

Prior to 1949, visitors to Newfoundland were immediately struck by its poverty and backwardness. The poverty was widespread and deprived generations of even a basic education. Had it not been for the denominational system, as

---

[6] GN 10/A/1

[7] Department of External Affairs, *Documents on Relations Between Canada and Newfoundland*, Vol. 1, 1940-1949.

desperate as it was for funds, the education system would have been even more destitute. Colin G. Jones, delegate from Harbour Grace to the National Convention, told fellow delegates:

> Many of our outport schools were scarcely fit to herd cattle into and in such buildings we compelled our children to spend five or six hours a day. These were poorly lighted and inadequately staffed. A large percentage of children had defective eyesight due to strain. Many schools contained long benches on which five or six children sat with no support to their backs and with chests cupped in so they could reach the desk which was either too high or too low. Is it any wonder we have such a high percentage of tuberculosis in this country. To teach in anyone of the schools on the Island the government only required Grade XI plus five weeks summer training.[8]

NEWFOUNDLAND EXCLUDED FROM NORTH AMERICAN GROWTH

When Canada and the rest of North America were being colonized, building cities, nations and generally progressing, similar growth in Newfoundland was almost at a standstill. At first, it was the west county merchants of England who used their political clout to have the British Parliament bar permanent settlement in Newfoundland.[9] These merchants feared that a growing population in Newfoundland would threaten their dominance of the Newfoundland fishery. They also persuaded Parliament that the Newfoundland fishery was a great training ground for the British Navy.

After escaping the shackles of the British merchants, a new group stepped in and implemented its own controls over Newfoundlanders and retarded progress for another

---

[8] PANL National Convention, GN/10/A-Box 1-File 7.

[9] There were several exceptions where colonies were allowed but did not last. St. John's was issued a charter in the 16th century, but there is no evidence that it resulted even in a temporary colony.

100 years. These were the Water Street merchants who controlled the political and economic structures to their own advantage. They developed an economic system that exploited Newfoundlanders and treated them like feudal serfs. These circumstances worsened in 1933. In that year, despite the wishes of the Newfoundland people, which were made known in a general election, the government of the day surrendered political independence for the promise of economic security.

In an address to the National Convention in 1946, Major Peter Cashin, delegate for Ferryland, referred to an article in the *Canadian Journal of Economics and Politics* by Professor A. S. Plumtre of the University of Toronto, in which he stated that in the same year Newfoundland lost its independence, Britain defaulted on a loan to the United States without losing its independence. He argued that Newfoundland's case for an honorary default was stronger than Britains.[10]

For more than 400 years while the rest of North American was progressing politically and economically, Newfoundlanders remained in bondage to the British and Water Street merchants. It was not until 1815 that the laws against permanent settlement were repealed. Although historically, Newfoundland is recognized as Britain's oldest colony, colonial status was not officially recognized until 1824.[11]

Canada's High Commissioner to Newfoundland, C. Burchill, in a secret memo to the Canadian Government in 1943, recognized the causes of Newfoundland's backwardness and pointed out:

> During the past 100 years, I do not think there was any doubt of the fact that the Water Street merchants are very largely to blame for the backwardness of the economic development of the country. Their system of control of the fisheries, which was set up by them, was really

---

[10] PANL National Convention 10/A/1/5.
[11] *Documents Relating to Canada and Newfoundland*, Vol.1, 62.

an extension of the feudal system, with all its faults. The fishermen of this country were practically serfs to the Water Street merchants of St. John's.[12]

Addressing the National Convention, Smallwood referred to the uphill battle forced on Newfoundlanders. He said:

Newfoundland's present population is something less than a third of what it ought to be, thanks to the callously selfish policy of those old English West Coast merchants.

Long after we had got away from Fishing Admiral rule, and were administrated a little less crudely by a series of naval captains sent out as governors, and after the Island had become comparatively well populated, Newfoundland was for many valuable years denied the right of governing herself; and while nearly every other constituent part of the Empire–all of them comparatively recent arrivals among the fold–were governing themselves in their own interest, Newfoundland was put to the necessity of agitating for decades for the simple right of self-government. It was not until 1855, that right was finally won."[13]

EXPECT MERCHANT OPPOSITION

As early as 1943, Burchill was advising Ottawa that the strongest opposition to Newfoundland's Union with Canada would come from the merchants because of their fear of having to pay a greatly increased direct taxation, particularly Income Tax. He explained:

They are living in a happy paradise at the present time, because about 75% or 80 % of the total revenue of Newfoundland is from the Customs Revenue, which they

---

[12] Ibid.
[13] PANL National Convention 10/A/1/5

pay, but pass immediately to their customers, plus a profit of at least 30% on the amount of Customs duties, which they consider to be part of the cost of the commodities in which they deal.[14]

MORAL AND ECONOMIC COLLAPSE

In April 1932, Newfoundlanders had lost faith in their country's political system, and they were in a hostile and angry mood. An editorial in the *Daily News* noted that destitution in Newfoundland was beyond parallel in North America, and the qualities of integrity, honour and justice no longer existed there. Regarding the collapse of the Newfoundland Government in 1933, Richard Gwyn wrote, "A government of geniuses could not have prevented it, small minds in a small colony hastened the inevitable."[15]

Newfoundland's surrendering of its independence in 1934 stemmed from the country's disastrous economic collapse between 1929-1930. In 1933, the Newfoundland Government and legislature fully supported the setting up of a royal commission by the British Parliament to inquire into Newfoundland's failed economy.

The Amulree Commission, as it was named, studied Newfoundland's economic crisis and recommended how to deal with it.

The end result of the inquiry was the recommendation to suspend Responsible Government, and give legislative and executive authority to a commission which would be responsible to the government of the United Kingdom until Newfoundland again became self-supporting. It also recommended that the United Kingdom should assume financial responsibility for the government of Newfoundland.

The Newfoundland Legislature and the British Parliament agreed to accept these recommendations and proceeded to suspend the Newfoundland constitution. This

---

[14] *Documents on Relations Between Canada and Newfoundland*, 1940-1949, Vol. 1.

[15] Richard Gwynn, *Smallwood the Unlikely Revolutionary*, 1968.

process included the following steps: first, there was the report and recommendations of the Amulree Commission; second, there was the Address presented to the King by the Newfoundland Legislature, praying the suspension of the existing Letters Patent;[16] third, was the enactment by the Imperial Parliament of the Newfoundland Act of 1933, authorizing the necessary change in the Letters Patent; fourth, was the new Letters Patent, dated January 30, 1934, suspending the operation of the Letters of 1876 and 1905 and constituting the Commission of Government.[17]

The citizens of St. John's continued to elect a city council, but only property owners were given the privilege of voting.

THE LEGAL OBSTACLE TO REGAINING INDEPENDENCE

The new Commission of Government was appointed by the British Government in 1934. However, the Amulree Commission did not make it plain as to how Newfoundland independence was to be restored. This led to much political debate in later years.

Hon. Harry A. Winter, KC, an appointed member of the Commission who later became a Justice of the Newfoundland Supreme Court, observed a weakness in the new system from the beginning. While the legislation promised the restoration of Responsible Government, it added: "...at the request of the Newfoundland people." Yet the Act neglected to provide a mechanism to enable the people to make that request when the opportunity arrived to do so. Winter asked, "Would they do it by petition, or by the holding of numerous public meetings, or by sending a delegation to Westminister?"[18]

---

[16] Letters Patent are official documents granting a right or privilege.

[17] Jack Fitzgerald, *Battlefront Newfoundland* (Creative Publishers, 2010).

[18] Winter's speech to the Newfoundland National Association was published in the *Express* in 1941 and in *Battlefront Newfoundland* by Jack Fitzgerald, 2010. Winter's position as appearing in next few pages is based these sources.

Another problem was how to determine when Newfoundland had become self-supporting. Some argued that Newfoundland became self-supporting during the war, even though it was predicted that the economic progress made during that time would not continue and Newfoundland would return to a slumping economy.

Winter drew attention to these problems as early as 1941. He interpreted the legal issues surrounding the event:

> The Letters Patent provided for the means of Newfoundland returning to a democratic form of government. Sec XXII states, 'And we do hereby reserve to ourselves, our heirs and successors, full power and authority from time to time to revoke, alter, or amend these our Letters Patent as to us or them shall seem met.'

> It is absurd to imagine that in practice anything of the sort would be done without consultation in some way with the people of Newfoundland and some expression, however made, of their feelings and desires. We therefore look, among the documents listed above, for an appropriate reference to that factor in the situation. We find only one. It is at the very end of the extract from the Amulree Report which was annexed to the Address of our Legislation. It read as follows:

> It would be understood that, as soon as the Island's difficulties are overcome and the country is again self-supporting, Responsible Government, **on request from the people** of Newfoundland, would be restored.

When the time came for a National Convention and the opportunity was given to the Newfoundland people to have its say, some public figures either were not aware of such a condition, or else deliberately tried to muddle the political waters. Winter focussed on the problem. He asked:

12

Who and what, for this purpose, are the people of New-foundland? All the people, including infants in arms? Or can we assume, for want of anything more definite, that those are meant who would have been entitled to vote in a general election? If so, is there to be a sort of referendum? And must a new voters list be compiled? Would the bare majority rule apply?

If the most unpardonable sin of all had not been committed and we had been left some sort of representative House, these questions could not arise. For this purpose such a House would be accepted as standing for the people and it could easily ascertain their will. But the very act, which professed to provide for the expression of that will, destroyed the only simple and obvious means of expressing it!

Winter asserted that the Newfoundland people themselves, rather than the elite few wanting a return to the good old days when they were the political bosses of the colony, were the ones to make that choice. He said:

Now, I firmly believe the majority of Newfoundlanders competent to judge the matters at all, do not approve or desire a return to complete self-government. Not immediately, at any rate. And certainly it can hardly be desired by any English government which holds the financial bag. If that is so, we have the strange situation that both parties desire neither A nor B but C, but they have no apparent means of getting to C.

Not a Simple Matter

Mr. Winter suggested that it was not a simple matter of starting over from the beginning as we did with Responsible and then Representative Governments. He said:

It was far easier to work from the ground up. We should

13

now be looking, not for something new, but for something for which, on the face of it, we have been deemed unworthy. And we are saddled with a very large debt which did not exist in 1832 and 1855. Even disregarding this, it would still have to be settled in advance just what kind of government was desired, just to what extent the Imperial government would continue to exercise control. And who is to decide it?

It now stands, if I were asked to make my own request, I should certainly vote for Responsible Government, but merely as the lesser of two evils and as a stepping-stone, backwards again, to the status really desired. And could absurdity go further than the prospect thus opened up?

What ministry, vested with full powers, would forthwith legislate itself out again and go through the same humiliating experience, differing only in degree from that of 1933?

It is only when we get down to it and envisage the practical steps necessary to be taken that we see the full absurdity of what was done by the Baldwin government, an absurdity arising out of their own premises.

As I see it, the whole of this strange, unparalleled, ill-considered experiment in government can be thus bluntly summed up. If the Commission of Government were competent, and proved it by balancing the budget, they would be replaced by local administrators, who are ex-hypothesis incompetent. If the Commission of Government prove incompetent, there is apparently nothing to be done about it.

Evidently, it is not only in Newfoundland that people are illogical, ministers incompetent, and legislators careless.

Smallwood agreed with the points made by Winter but felt they should have been made as clear in 1934 as they had been later in 1945. He felt that the two basic conditions had to be met before Responsible Government would be restored. Smallwood noted that these conditions would be met, "...when Newfoundland is again self-supporting and 'on request from the people'."

BLACK PERIOD FOR NEWFOUNDLANDERS

This was a black period in Newfoundland history which contributed to the apparent anxiousness to follow what then seemed like the only sensible course. Later, describing the challenges facing the people in the 1930s, Joey Smallwood recalled:

A hundred thousand people, ⅓ of our population were starving on the dole of six cents a day for each person. The cod fishery had dropped from being worth $11¼ million in 1929 to $4¾ million in 1931. The Seal Hunt dropped from a total catch in 1929 of 201,000 seals to just 48,000 in 1932, Newfoundland's iron ore worth $4 million in 1929 was down to ½ million in 1932. Two hundred and twenty thousand passengers used the railroad and coastal steamships in 1930, but this dropped to 113,000 in 1933.

Newfoundland revenues which depended on ad valorem customs duties on imports fell disastrously to $7½ million of which $5 million went out of the country in annual interest to Newfoundland's bond holders. (Ad valorem based on estimated value) This left $2½ million to pay civil servants, pensions, military pensions, police and courts, roads, bridges, all government services for one-year.[19]

---

[19] PANL NC 10/A/1/5.

Once empowered, the Commission of Government acted swiftly in accepting its responsibilities. Newfoundland's debt in 1934 was about $100 million, with relatively high interest rates. The new Government had this debt converted to a sterling issue at three per cent with both principal and interest being guaranteed by Britain. Considerable sums of money were advanced to Newfoundland for development purposes, and budget deficits up to 1939, totalling over $16 million, were paid by England.[20]

SWEPT UNDER THE CARPET

It was incredible that during this low ebb in Newfoundland fortunes, that some politicians found a last way to pocket public funds for themselves. Just before the findings of the Amulree Royal Commission were made public, Newfoundland's $100 bonds had dropped to sixty dollars, an unmarketable price at the time. In the White Paper that was released after the Royal Commission Report, Britain agreed to honour the bonds at $100 each. However, among the limited small circle of insiders who had prior knowledge of Britain's intention to guarantee the bonds were some who were unscrupulous enough to purchase the bonds at sixty dollars and soon after sold them at $100 each, making hefty profits. Nobody was ever brought to justice for this crime.[21]

By 1941, Newfoundland was making a remarkable recovery. However, this was not stable growth, but rather improvements due in large part to the heavy defence expenditures in Newfoundland and Labrador by the United States and Canada. By the end of the war the Americans had spent $300 million in Newfoundland and the Canadians $100 million. There were also benefits from the increased prices of Newfoundland's chief exports, fish and newsprint.

---

[20] Department of External Affairs, *Documents on Reglations Between Canada and Newfoundland 1940-1949*, Vol. 1.

[21] Ibid.

By 1941, Newfoundland's economic situation was improving. The country was holding an annual surplus amounting to about $29 million. Its debt had been reduced to about $74 million, and the public services had been expanded and improved. Revenues had grown from just over $12 million in 1939 to $37 million in 1946. Yet, when the Commissioners wanted to put more money into health and welfare to ease the problems caused by widespread poverty, they were blocked by Britain. The British argued that such a move would increase the annual cost of operating Government and pointed out that the surplus would be needed to build infrastructure after the war.[22]

But Choosing Confederation was no option!

In 1890, Canadian politicians became the third major contributor to Newfoundland's backwardness in the twentieth century. They also gave Newfoundlanders a tangible reason to foster a hatred and suspicion of Canadians for the next sixty years.

It was in 1890 that the historic Bond-Blaine Treaty was negotiated between Newfoundland and the United States. If it had stood, it would have had a great impact on economic growth in Newfoundland. The Treaty got its name from the two men who negotiated it. Sir Robert Bond, who was Newfoundland's Colonial Secretary at the time, and James G. Blaine, Secretary of State for the United States. The agreement reached covered mutual trade between Newfoundland and the United States and gave the Americans fishing rights in Newfoundland waters.

A.B. Morine, a Nova Scotian politician who later moved to Newfoundland, learned of Bond's success and wasted no time notifying the Canadian Government. Ottawa was furious because it had failed in its own attempt to negotiate a similar treaty with the Americans.

---

[22] Herbert Pottle, *Dawn Without Light.*

The Canadians felt the Treaty was not in Canada's best interest because it still held high hopes to bring Newfoundland into union. Canada feared that the Treaty would strengthen Newfoundland's economy and destroy all hopes of the colony entering Confederation. The enthusiasm that greeted the Treaty in Newfoundland was short-lived after Canada, aided by Great Britain, lobbied successfully to squelch it.

Some felt that the Bond-Blaine Treaty accommodated Newfoundland because Blaine was deliberately trying to cause a strain between the two British possessions. This, he felt, would enhance the American sphere of influence. It did have the affect of raising Bond's stature at home and abroad. Journalist Charles Dana of the *New York Sun* wrote, "The Newfoundland Commissioner is a comparatively young man, but his tact and ability enabled him to rank with the leading statesmen of the time."

MARITIME PROVINCES ON VERGE OF REBELLION

Canada aggressively pursued Britain's support to overturn the treaty. They overwhelmed the Colonial Office in London with telegrams from its officials who presented strong arguments against the Treaty, which Canada viewed as an assault on Canadian independence. They argued that the Maritime provinces were on the verge of rebellion because of their desire for the same agreement negotiated by Newfoundland.

Ottawa argued that the treaty would cause Newfoundland to develop a dependency on the United States and the issue would destroy any chances of Newfoundland becoming a province of Canada. Instead, Newfoundlanders would be more receptive to union with the Americans.

The pressure on London to lobby Washington against Newfoundland was powerful enough to bring the British into the debate. Bond responded by accusing Canada of interfering in Newfoundland affairs, but the British gave in to Ottawa and refused to ratify the Treaty on the grounds it was clearly to the detriment of Canadian interests.

Newfoundland's negotiations with the United States, traditionally, were merged with those of Canada. It was likely memories of this conflict that gave Americans cold feet in 1948. Bond held a different view. He saw the Treaty as an assurance of the colony's political independence. If the Treaty had been ratified, there is little doubt that Newfoundland's history would have been different.[23]

Newfoundlanders were outraged by Canadian interference in the Bond-Blaine Treaty, and much of the animosity towards Canadians lasted into the 1940s. Any effort to persuade Newfoundlanders to join Canada appeared to be doomed.

BURIN TEACHES CONFEDERATE A HARD LESSON

The general election of 1873 exemplifies the intense feelings regarding union with Canada when James Winter was elected to the House of Assembly in the Burin District under the leadership of pro-Confederate Sir Frederick Carter. Before he had a chance to celebrate victory with his supporters, he was surrounded by an angry mob of anti-Confederates who demanded to know his position on union with Canada.

Winter replied that he would only support Confederation if the issue was put to the people in a national referendum and obtained a majority vote. Shouts of "Traitor! Traitor!" echoed through the mob as they seized their MHA and forcibly escorted him to the court house where they locked him inside a cell like an ordinary criminal.

After leaving the building, and discussing their action among themselves, they had second thoughts about the prison being able to hold him if his supporters tried to set him free. They went back to the court house, removed their prisoner from the building and forced him onto a boat. He was

---

[23] Karl Samuelson, *Fourteen Men* (St. John's, NL: Robinson-Blackmore Printing and Publishing, 1984)88. Joseph R. Smallwood, *Encyclopedia of Newfoundland and Labrador.*

taken to Beau Bois, twelve miles away, where they arranged to have him imprisoned under guard in a private residence.

The new MHA escaped in the darkness of night and walked back to Burin.[24]

NEWFOUNDLANDERS DISLIKE FOR CANADA LASTED TO 1949

The strong anti-Confederation sentiment that took hold in Newfoundland and lasted for almost a century was reflected in "The Anti-Confederation Song," author unknown:

Hurrah! for our own native isle, Newfoundland,
Not a stranger shall hold one inch of its strand,
Her face turns to Britain, her back to the Gulf,
Come near at your peril, Canadian wolf.

Ye brave Newfoundlanders, who plough the salt sea,
With hearts like the eagle, so bold and so free,
The time is at hand, when you'll all have to say
If Confederation will carry the day.

Cheap tea and molasses they say they will give,
All taxes take off that the poor man may live,
Cheap nails and cheap lumber our coffins to make,
And homespun to mend our old clothes when they break.

If they take off the taxes how then will they meet.
The heavy expenses on the country's upkeep?
Just give them the chance to get us in the scrape,
And they'll chain you as slaves
with pen, ink and red-tape.

Would you barter the right that your father's have won,
Your freedom transmitted from father to son?

---

[24] Joseph R. Smallwood, *Encyclopaedia of Newfoundland and Labrador.*

For a few thousand dollars of Canadian gold,
Don't let it be said that your birthright was sold.

INSURGENCY BACKFIRED ON MERCHANTS

Ten years after accepting the Commission of Government, widespread dissatisfaction was growing, especially among the merchants, who had lost their influence over government. Insurgency is not a word often heard throughout Newfoundland history, but C.J. Burchill used it in his secret memo to the Canadian External Affairs Department in 1943. Burchill, Canada's High Commissioner to Newfoundland, kept Ottawa informed on politics and politicians in Newfoundland during the early 1940s.

In response to the Commission of Government's decision to implement a small increase in taxes, the St. John's Board of Trade passed a resolution to stop the move and called for public support to get rid of the Commission and replace it with some form of Responsible Government.

Burchill informed Ottawa that the action was "an insurgent move, against the Commission of Government, which was asinine from the beginning."[25] The issue backfired on the merchants by making the public aware of how they had manipulated the tax policies of Newfoundland for their own advantage. He explained that the merchants were responsible for the very high tariffs which were a major contribution to the high cost of living. Burchill reported to Ottawa:

> They also have had brought home to them the fact that the Water Street merchants are paying a very slight percentage of the revenue through income taxes, but are getting enormously wealthy because of the fact that they are adding a large profit margin on the Customs duties, as well as on the cost of the commodities which they import. The higher the duties, the more profit the

---

[25] Department of External Affairs, *Documents on Relations Between Canada and Newfoundland*, Vol. 1, 1940-1949 Part 1.

merchant makes. Viewed in their proper background, the resolutions of the Board of Trade are really an expose of the Water Street merchants of the City of St. John's. The Water Street merchants are to this day the strongest opponents of Confederation with Canada, and not only that, but with the possibility of only one or two exceptions they would have no dealings with Canada at all if they could avoid it.[26]

The announcement that most Newfoundlanders were waiting to hear came in December 1945 when Britain proclaimed that a National Convention and referendum would be held in Newfoundland in the spring of 1946. This would allow the people of Newfoundland to make an informed and free decision on their future form of government.

---

[26] Ibid, 61.

CHAPTER 2

A Leader Steps Forward

"Smallwood's vivid personality, his self-assurance, his firm belief that Newfoundlanders could be converted to union, had created a favourable impression on the Canadian political leaders-the Prime Minister and the prospective Prime Minister St. Laurent, included. Neither Newfoundland nor Smallwood were any longer unknown politically in Ottawa. Henceforth, when memos or dispatches about Newfoundland matters were sent up to our political masters, they were read.

Joey returned to Newfoundland convinced Canada would accept Newfoundland on satisfactory terms, if the people of Newfoundland made it clear they wanted to come in. As for the decision by Newfoundlanders, Joey had no doubt about his ability to convince them to decide the right way."

- Quote from Professor R. A. McKay,
Dalhousie University and Adviser to the
Department of External Affairs, 1946 after
Smallwood made his first visit to Ottawa
to research Confederation

THE FORD HOTEL

When Prime Minister Clement Atlee's announcement was made in December 1945, Joseph R. Smallwood was having breakfast at the Ford Hotel on Dorchester Street in Montreal. It was the last day of a business trip to the city. In 1941, he had participated in the Newfoundland National Association's public forum in St. John's, which lobbied for a change in how the Commission of Government operated. Many people were questioning the right of the six-man commission to rule Newfoundland without any democratic input by its people, especially at a time when Newfoundlanders were shedding blood in Europe in defence of freedom. The Commission was even publicly described as "A dictatorship of six."[1]

Smallwood's attention was drawn to the front page headlines of the newspaper on his table. After thirteen years of living under a non-democratic government, Newfoundland was on the verge of regaining the political independence it had lost in 1933. The story reported that a National Convention and a national referendum would be held on June 21, 1946, as the first steps in the return of independence to Newfoundland. The National Convention's mandate would be to determine if Newfoundland had reached the status of being self-supporting financially and to recommend to the United Kingdom the form or forms of government to be placed before the Newfoundland people in a referendum.

SMALLWOOD MOVED BY ATLEE'S ANNOUNCEMENT

The legal process in returning independence to Newfoundland, discussed in Chapter One, was far more complex than some observers had maintained. In fact, the legislation had a condition attached to the returning of Responsible Government. That condition was that Responsible Government would be returned, "at the request of the Newfoundland people." However, it failed to provide a legal mechanism for implementing this commitment. It was this

---

[1] Jack Fitzgerald, *Battlefront Newfoundland*.

very failure that made the Convention and referendum necessary. Smallwood had long been aware of this shortcoming due to his participation in the Newfoundland Nationalists Association (NNA) forum held at the CLB Armoury in St. John's in 1941.

He needed time to consider Atlee's announcement and the part he would play in it. Having lost his appetite, he left his breakfast and went out into the streets of Montreal where he walked for hours in deep thought. He considered the role he expected to play in the days ahead and the implications it would have on Newfoundland. He reflected:

> Now it would be in our hands, and now Britain had provided the answer to the puzzle that Harry A. Winter, prominent Newfoundland lawyer, had put forward publicly in 1941, 'How were the Newfoundland people to make their decision?'[2]

He recalled the NNA's public forum when Harry A. Winter, gave a legal analysis of the 1933 agreement to surrender independence and accept Commission of Government. Winter had pointed out that the document was flawed, and it failed to provide the legal mechanism for Newfoundland's return to self-government. Smallwood immediately recognized in Atlee's announcement the solution to the absurdity reflected in the 1933 legal documents.

VOICE OF LIBERTY RADIO BROADCASTS

Six months earlier in June 1945, Peter Cashin was one of the first old-time politicians off the mark in what was to become the political battle of Newfoundland's history. Cashin had served as a Finance Minister in pre-Commission days. He was well aware that after the war Britain would move towards restoring Newfoundland's independence and was anxious to participate. Cashin did not intend to wait for the British

---

[2] Joseph R. Smallwood, *I Chose Canada*, 226.

announcement. His first action was to launch a series of radio broadcasts referring to himself as the "Voice of Liberty."

Governor Sir Humphrey Walwyn was not impressed with Cashin and viewed him as a typical old time politician who, "...hurled abuse at everybody." Walwyn told British officials that Cashin was the type of politician the public could expect if Responsible Government was returned. Even though he was convinced that Cashin was already so discredited that he would be a detriment to the Responsible Government cause, he did recognize an advantage to his public involvement in the National Convention. Walwyn explained:

> By and large it is not a bad thing that somebody – even a man of his stamp – should be taking the field, since his campaign if continued ought to do something to stir Newfoundlanders out of their present apathy and draw some of the better type into the arena.[3]

Cashin, who became an arch foe of Smallwood was, in 1925, a Tory member of the Newfoundland Legislature, and serving in the cabinet of Prime Minister Sir Walter S. Monroe. Smallwood later described Cashin as, "... one of the most colourful men ever to sit in the chamber. He was fluent, rough and direct. Peter was inclined to deliver slashing and altogether unparliamentary speeches, for which the Speaker ought to have dealt with him."[4]

When Prime Minister Atlee announced that the Newfoundland people would decide Newfoundland's political future in a National Referendum, Peter Cashin, a confirmed Responsible Government advocate, was outraged. He condemned the idea for a National Convention and Referendum. He believed no such provision had been made in the 1933 agreement to surrender independence. Cashin asked, "How can any thinking Newfoundlander, honestly

---

[3] Department of External Affairs, *Newfoundland Documents 1940-1949 Vol. 1* .

[4] Joseph R. Smallwood, *I Chose Canada*, 160.

and conscientiously, give his moral support and endorsement to a thing which is not alone illegal but even ethically improper."[5]

CHES CROSBIE

Another Newfoundlander destined to play a role in the great political drama beginning to unfold in Newfoundland was Ches Crosbie. Crosbie was the most respected and best liked of the Newfoundland merchants, and when the time came, he topped the polls in the district of St. John's West to get himself elected as a delegate to the national convention. However, those closest to him knew that he was not a pro-Confederate, but committed to playing a key role in the process.

One of several secret memos among Canadian External Affairs Department records revealed an insight into Crosbie's intentions. It stated:

> Ches Crosbie, businessman, contended Newfoundland could be made self-supporting and favoured Responsible Government–provided that he and his friends could control it, but, failing that, would, I think, work for a more efficient Commission.[6]

IMMERSED IN RESEARCH

Unlike Cashin, Smallwood concluded that the decision to hold a National Convention followed by a referendum corrected the original legal problem. He returned to his hotel still uncertain over what form of government would be best for Newfoundland. Fresh on his mind was a comment his friend F. Gordon Bradley had made twenty years earlier, "You mark my words Joe! Confederation with Canada is our only salvation." He was not impressed with Bradley's argument then, but since that time, Newfoundland had gone

[5] PANL GN10/A Box 1, File #5.
[6] Ibid.

broke, surrendered its independence and despite the temporary improvement brought by the war, still faced a challenging future. Smallwood ended his soul searching with the firm decision that he would be a candidate for election to the National Convention. He recognized that the Convention offered a real opportunity for Newfoundland and its people to advance and escape the poverty to which it seemed to have been condemned, but he was undecided as to which form of government would best serve Newfoundland's interests. As he walked back to the Ford Hotel, union with Canada was on his mind, but he knew little about the Canadian system of government or how it might benefit Newfoundland. Smallwood concluded that he would carry out a thorough study of how Canadian Confederation worked.

Later that evening, he met with Ewart Young, an old friend and journalist from home who was now living and working in Montreal. Young was a passionate Confederate and the two conversed for hours. Joey left Ewart Young, still uncommitted, but a little more enthusiastic towards Confederation.

The next morning he caught a ride back to Gander aboard a RAF plane. Smallwood was able to hitch the ride to and from the mainland through David Anderson, the RAF Commanding Officer at Gander. Anderson had enticed Smallwood to set up a pig farm there to supply fresh meat to the military. Some speculated that Ches Crosbie was Smallwood's secret partner in the venture and had financed the deal. That same night Joey penned letters to Canada's Prime Minister and the Premier of each province of Canada. Without committing himself to Confederation, he requested their help in educating him on how the Canadian Government operated.

In response, he received stacks of information including: budgets, speeches, estimates of revenue and expenditures, annual reports, books and magazines. Joey recalled:

> I buried myself in a small mountain of printed material, working at it day and night. Often I had pulled down the blinds to shut out the dawn before I turned in for a

few hours of sleep. For several weeks, I continued this intensive study and made innumerable notes.[7]

THE CONFEDERATION CAMPAIGN BEGINS

The more Smallwood read, and the deeper his research took him, the more passionate he became towards Confederation. He became convinced that union with the Canadian Dominion offered the best future for the Newfoundland people and was the solution to Newfoundland's problems.

Joey had already established a good basis on which to launch his campaign to get elected to the Convention. In addition to the notoriety he gained through his popular *The Barrelman* radio show, Smallwood had made political inroads in the Gander-Bonavista area. His lifetime interest in politics and community activism had led him to organize a union of low paid airport workers in Gander, as well as establish a fund for the family of a pilot friend who had died in a plane crash. His pig farm operation brought him in contact with Gander's business community.

THE SMALLWOOD LETTERS

In 1946, despite subtle suggestions from London, there was practically no interest among Canadian politicians to have Newfoundland become its tenth province, or even a territory. Neither was there any significant support for such a move among Newfoundlanders, who harboured a strong dislike for Canadians since Canada scuttled the Bond-Blaine Treaty in 1890, which had promised some great advantages to Newfoundland.[8]

Smallwood knew his country's history well and realized that it would be an uphill battle to convince Newfoundlanders to

---

[7] Joseph R. Smallwood, *I Chose Canada*, 229.

[8] That is not to say that the federal cabinet had not previously discussed the possibility of union with Newfoundland. However, there was little enthusiasm towards such a move.

support union with Canada. First, he had to get elected to the Convention. Gander was in the district of Bonavista Centre and, historically, the people of Bonavista Bay had been opposed to Confederation since 1869. It might have been easier to run as an uncommitted delegate, as many did, but Joey was not one to run away from a political battle. He accepted the challenge and set out to change voters' minds.

Joey undertook two initiatives which set the seeds of change in the anti-Confederate sentiment throughout his country. The first of these efforts took place in March 1946 when Joey Smallwood stepped into the office of Sir John Currie at the *Daily News* on Duckworth Street in St. John's. He held in his hands a file containing eleven articles he had written explaining what union with Canada would mean for Newfoundlanders. Joey had already publicly declared himself a Confederate and Currie was a known anti-Confederate. Currie told Smallwood he was willing to publish all eleven items as letters to the editor, and on consecutive days, as Joey had requested.

THE LETTERS HAD POSITIVE AFFECT

By the end of March 1946, the effectiveness of Smallwood's efforts was recognized by Canada's External Affairs Department. The Department, while monitoring the current political attitudes in Newfoundland during March, detected a changing trend in political thought towards Canada. Canadian officials had anticipated some improvement due to Canada's role in the war and the fact that Canada had made loans to Britain. However, the changes detected in March were described as favourable, if not spectacular, and attributed mostly to the efforts of one man– Joseph R. Smallwood. In a secret letter to the Secretary of State for External Affairs for Canada from the Canadian High Commissioner to Newfoundland, J. S. Macdonald, Macdonald wrote:

Influential, also, in helping this trend has been a remarkable series of letters in the press from the pen of

31

Mr. J. R. Smallwood, the popular historian and journalist, in which he attempts, with such information as he can gather from blue-books and periodicals, to discuss the advantages and disadvantages of Confederation with Canada.[9]

By the process of question and answer, he demolishes, very effectively, arguments often put forward in anti-Confederate circles and sweeps away many of the misconceptions to which local prejudice was strongly attached. Taken all in all Mr. Smallwood's letters have proved to be the most powerful propaganda in favour of Confederation that has so far been brought to bear on the subject.[10]

Up to this point the Canadians had been underestimating Smallwood as a political lightweight who was considered a rabble rouser and potential troublemaker by the St. John's Establishment. Canadian bureaucrats were speculating that F. Gordon Bradley, a prominent lawyer who had served in the cabinet of Sir Richard Squires, would be the delegate to emerge as the pro-Confederates strongest advocate.

Joey had run in Bonavista South in 1932 as a Liberal and lost. Although Joey and Bradley had been close friends since the days of Sir Richard Squires, Joey had not been aware that his friend had been the source of undercover police attention towards him at that time. Smallwood's support of socialists in the United States and England was a source of discomfort for some people in St. John's. Undercover police even attended his public rallies and submitted reports on his speeches. Bradley, while serving in the federal cabinet in the first years of Confederation, frequently undermined Joey's policies in Newfoundland.

THE LETTERS IGNITE DEBATE
From the first in the series of "Smallwood Letters" he emphasized that his purpose was to inform the public regarding

---

[9] *Documents on Relations Between Canada and Newfoundland Vol. 1.*
[10] Ibid, 233.

the pros and cons of Confederation. He wrote:

> I am not writing a case for Confederation; or a case
> against Confederation. I am writing the case concerning
> Confederation. To the best of my ability, I am setting
> down all the arguments I know in favour of Confedera-
> tion, and all I know against it.[11]

Referring to Newfoundland's failure to join Confederation in 1867, Smallwood pointed out that Newfoundlanders
were poorly informed, misguided, and possessed very little
knowledge of Canada, nor any understanding of the
concept of how Confederation worked. He observed, "Less
than 500 Newfoundlanders had even visited Canada in
those times. That is not the case in 1946." He wrote:

> Newfoundlanders were now prepared to hear the case
> for Confederation. He felt that people were better edu-
> cated and informed than in the previous century and
> pointed out: radio is almost universal, newspapers were
> widely circulated, tens of thousands of Newfoundlan-
> ders had visited Canada and every Newfoundland family
> had a relative or friend working in Canada. Thousands
> of Newfoundlanders had worked with the Canadians in
> Newfoundland during the war.[12]

Smallwood acknowledged that most Newfoundlanders
favoured Responsible Government but wanted it under conditions that would assure its success. He firmly believed that
Newfoundlanders realized the imprudence of going it
alone. He explained:

> Arguments to the effect that they must shape their own
> destiny without consulting anyone else; pleas that they

---

[11] *Daily News*, March 1, 1946, 4.
[12] Ibid.

must paddle their own canoe; and sink and swim by their own unaided efforts–all these left Newfoundland cold and unmoved. An insistence deep down within tells them that we must spare no effort to seek extra help.[13]

HOW CONFEDERATION WORKED

Smallwood's first letter provided some geographic background and a brief explanation of how the Confederation system of government operated. He told readers that Canada was the third largest country in the world, made up 27% of the total British Empire and it was also the third greatest trading nation.

In explaining Confederation, he wrote that Confederation is another federal system of government in which any two or more self-governing countries, states or provinces may set up an additional government with areas of responsibility defined in a constitution.

He noted the United States and Canada as examples of federal systems. In the case of the United States, each state had self-government with one central government in the role of federal government. Canada was a union of nine provinces, some of which were colonies before Confederation. In Canada's case, each province had its own legislature and the Federal Government had a parliament and an appointed senate. The division of authority in Canada was set down in the British North American Act. Smallwood advised, "Our provincial government would be master in all matters that affected Newfoundland alone."

WHY SHOULD CANADA PAY MORE THAN SHE GETS?

In another letter, Smallwood confronted an opposing viewpoint against Confederation that was widespread and gaining credibility. He began the letter:

A point that puzzles many Newfoundlanders is this: Why should Canada be willing to accept Newfoundland? If

---

[13] Ibid.

as I shall show Canada would pour much more money into Newfoundland than she would take out. Why would Canada ever consider accepting this?

Smallwood informed readers that some people were already using the argument, "You can bet your boots that if Canada accepts us, it is because she sees a way of getting the best of the bargain." He quickly countered this by pointing out that it was a form of reasoning that, if true, would see Canada get rid of its three Maritime provinces and the Prairie provinces and have only Quebec, Ontario and British Columbia. He explained:

> Over half of Canada's revenues, at that time, were coming from these three provinces. On the basis of this argument, by uniting only the have provinces, Canada would be the richest country in the world with lower taxes and its people living like lords. We must remember Canada is not a private business enterprise seeking a cash dividend each year and concerned only with a favourable balance sheet.

Smallwood advised Newfoundlanders to approach the question of future government with caution and be confident that there will be a net gain for the colony if they decide to choose union with Canada. He reasoned:

> Twenty million dollars seems big money to us, but what does it mean to Canada which deals in thousands of millions? The Dominion of Canada pours more money into the three Maritime provinces and the three Prairie provinces than it gets back. This is what Confederation means. Real Canadian statesmanship demands that all Canada shall be prosperous and healthy, not merely the wealthier parts. Canada's share the wealth movement has received less attention than it deserves.

NEW FACTS PUBLISHED ON DAILY BASIS

Other letters dealt with the gains and losses of union with
Canada. Smallwood told readers that although it was impossible to determine all gains and losses, it was possible to assess some. His problem in this area was related to the
unavailability of up-to-date accounting figures which, by
their nature, were constantly changing.

Included among the immediate gains Confederation offered Newfoundland was an estimated 33% reduction in the
cost of living. In addition, there would be increased income
that would benefit all Newfoundlanders. Included in this
were: family allowances for children up to sixteen years of
age; increased old age assistance available at lower ages;
availability of unemployment insurance for the unemployed
and veteran's pensions and rehabilitation programs which
were the envy of Newfoundland veterans. Smallwood said
the income benefits from union would make a great contribution to the general commerce of the colony as well as
to the Newfoundland Government.

In explaining the immediate benefits stemming from the
elimination of customs duties on imported goods from
Canada, Smallwood reminded readers of the long-time
abuse of Newfoundland customs by the merchants. He referred to the outrageous practice of merchants adding a
profit to the duty collected from the people of the colony,
in addition to the profit on the goods being sold.

JOEY CONTINUED TO MAKE CASE

Smallwood included an extensive list of other advantages
that union with Canada had to offer Newfoundland. For the
youth of the country, Canadian programs included: pre-em-
ployment training programs, vocational training schools
and apprenticeship programs. All of these programs would
benefit Newfoundlanders in developing skills expected to
be in demand with the development of the country's natural resources.

Newfoundland stood to gain financially because Canada would relieve it of the operating and maintenance costs of operating non-American bases on Newfoundland soil. In addition, all civil aviation would be integrated with the Canadian system already considered the best in the world.

An advantage to Newfoundland's fishermen, not apparent at the time, was the 33% reduction in the cost of living. This saving significantly reduced the costs to fishermen in preparing for the fishing season. Newfoundland fishermen would also benefit from Canadian fish research and experimentation programs. As a province of Canada, Newfoundland would continue to export fish to "current" and new markets with Ottawa, supplying trade agents in all foreign markets.

Other benefits Confederation would bring to Newfoundland, according to the Smallwood Letters were:

• The Canadian Government taking over responsibility for the experimental farm near St. John's.

• The implementation of Canadian agricultural polices to benefit Newfoundland farmers.

• All federal work and projects in Newfoundland to come under the "Provision of Fair Wages and Hours of Labour Act."

• Newfoundlanders would be free to move anywhere in Canada to seek employment.

• Newfoundland would benefit from the position held by Canada after the war to make strong trade treaties with other nations.

• Newfoundland workers would benefit from Canada loaning billions of dollars in Europe to enable those countries to spend in Canada. Especially advantageous because Newfoundland was in a poor financial and trade position to bargain with great nations in the matters of trade.

• All our banking services were already provided and were Canadian and all our life insurance was already supplied by Canadians.

• Many Newfoundlanders were already going to Canadian schools and universities to better their education.

SMALLWOOD STEPS INTO THE POLITICAL ARENA

By the end of March, Smallwood had established himself as an authority on Confederation and had sparked interest among voters in the district he had chosen to contest–Bonavista Centre. Election campaigns require more than time and hard work, they need money. Joey found a creative way to raise that money without soliciting public support. His plan involved blankets, 3000 military blankets to be exact and a call to an old friend, Ches Crosbie, a prominent St. John's businessman and candidate himself in the district of St. John's West.

Joey succeeded in borrowing $3000 from Crosbie which he used to purchase 3000 military blankets from the Royal Canadian Air Force, at a cost of one dollar per blanket. He then sold the lot to the Woods Department of the Bowater Pulp and Paper Company for three dollars each. He repaid the loan from Crosbie along with a $1500 profit. When he repaid the $3000, he added $1500 as profit to Crosbie for his investment. Joey told Crosbie, "If you ever want advice on making any more financial investments, give me a call."

A friend of Joey's, Anthony Mullowney, who had planned on running as a Confederate with him, was to share in the campaign fund, but he decided not to run and allowed Joey to keep his share. Smallwood paid off some bills and put the remainder into his campaign.

CHAPTER 3

National Convention's
First Confederate

Professor R.A. McKay, External Affairs, after Joey's first
visit to Ottawa to discuss Confederation, said:

"I recall a meeting about this time in the office of the Un-
dersecretary of the Department, Norman Robertson. There were
five of us present in all. Norman's comment was 'I suppose we
have here all the people in Canada interested in having Newfoundland join Canada.' By the time Joey left Ottawa, feelings
among the federal cabinet had changed."

After deciding himself to seek election to the National Convention, Smallwood visited St. John's to persuade Ches Crosbie to seek election as well. In fact, Joey had hoped that Crosbie would embrace the Confederate cause and, with Joe's full backing, become the Province of Newfoundland's first Premier.

Crosbie considered running and held a series of private meetings with friends, Smallwood in attendance, at his home on Rennies Mill Road. Despite Crosbie's popularity among Newfoundlanders, he was a poor public speaker. Joe tried to correct this by using the broadcast facilities of the radio station where he had once worked after it closed down each night. There in a completely private setting, Crosbie recorded speeches, written for him by Smallwood who then helped him with delivery and pronunciation. Smallwood recalled in his autobiography:

> I was convinced that Crosbie wanted to be Premier and throughout a large part of the life of the convention, I did everything in my power to persuade him to support my motion for terms. 'You don't have to be a Confederate, Ches, to be willing to get the terms. And even after we get the terms, you don't have to support them if you don't like them.'

Crosbie and Smallwood continued to hold secret meetings late at night in Joe's Duckworth Street apartment which was owned by Dick Chalker, Crosbie's cousin.

With the problem of campaign funds taken care of and an extensive knowledge of Canada and its system of government, Smallwood set out on an aggressive, gruelling campaign that took him from settlement to settlement, cove to cove, and house to house, always followed with a political rally in whatever hall was available to him. By the time of each rally, Joey had befriended someone in every household in the community, and there was always an enthusiastic crowd to hear his pitch for Confederation.

Smallwood's first meeting took place at the LOL Hall in Middle Brook on April 6, 1946. The soon-to-become-leader of the Confederate movement took to the stage dressed in a dark suit, vest, white dress shirt and tie. He met every question from the audience head on and, by the end of the meeting, four hours later, with sweat rolling down his face, in rolled up shirtsleeves, he was given a long standing ovation with voters leaving the hall comparing him to Winston Churchill. Word of the successful Middle Brook meeting spread rapidly to other districts and sparked encouraging support for his campaign.

At his next meeting, which was in Greenspond, the enthusiasm continued. Out of the 500 votes cast in the election from that community, Joey received 495. From there he repeated his efforts in Fair Island, Silver Hare Island, Bragg's Island and on and on until he had covered the entire district. Smallwood had lost an election in Bonavista in 1932, but he was in a far more advantageous position for this battle.

SMALLWOOD'S GOOD FORTUNE BEGINS!

Fortune smiled upon Joe Smallwood from the start of Newfoundland's journey back to democracy and to its becoming Canada's tenth province. In announcing the holding of a National Convention, a basic eligibility requirement which had a profound affect on the eventual outcome of the whole process was that candidates had to be resident of the district where he or she intended to seek election. In 1943, Smallwood moved to Gander, part of the Bonavista Centre District, where he operated a pig farm. He later recalled:

> Whatever chance I might have of being elected to the National Convention for Bonavista Centre, I would have no chance whatsoever if I were reduced to running in the constituency that contained my home on Kenmount Road, St. John's West Extern–that is, if I ran as a Confederate.[1]

---

[1] Joseph R. Smallwood, *I Chose Canada*, 232.

Canada's High Commissioner J. Scott Macdonald, like most Newfoundlanders, saw this rule as providing for a more democratic representation of the Newfoundland people. He explained:

> Unlike in Responsible Government days when a large number of outport candidates were parachuted in from St. John's, rules had been set to avoid that practice. The requirement for residence of nominees in the constituencies for which they chose to stand had probably resulted in better representation of local opinion than was normally the case.[2]

MAXIMUM ADMINISTRATIVE DELAY (MAD)

Macdonald reporting on Smallwood's intensive campaign told External Affairs in Ottawa, "I was struck with the energy he is putting into the campaign and the wide knowledge he has accumulated, though I think I was able, on a number of points, to give him a rather clearer understanding of some of the factors involved."[3]

However, Macdonald questioned the appropriateness of Canadian officials corresponding with Smallwood, and he asked that he be given copies of all correspondence going to him. Ironically, Smallwood's expertise on Confederation could not have been achieved had he limited himself to the direction and influence which the High Commissioner had attempted to heap upon him through what bureaucrats knew as the "Maximum Administrative Delay" policy known well in bureaucratic circles as MAD. Simply put, this is what was described in pre-Confederation Newfoundland as, "Send the fool farther."

Smallwood's energetic and dynamic campaign brought him victory with 89% of the vote and the biggest margin of all candidates. Some reported a low turnout for the

---

[2] *Documents on Relations Between Canada-Newfoundland*, Vol 2, pt. 1, 263.

[3] Ibid, 242.

countrywide election, and others said it was larger than expected. No doubt the voting was affected by several factors.
Most fishermen and woodsmen were working away from
their district in June and no provision was made for them
to vote. The fact that Newfoundlanders had lost the right
to vote thirteen years earlier and traditional political parties
had been abandoned did not help. The exception to the
loss of democracy was St. John's, which continued to elect
its own city council. However, as stated earlier, only those
who owned property were eligible to vote, and were only
given one vote for each property owned. This was just one
more example of the control the merchant class had in
Newfoundland prior to 1949.

Although most delegates did not declare the option they
favoured for Newfoundland's political future, Canada's External Affairs Department assessed that 25% were in favour
of a return to Responsible Government and another 25%
wanted to examine all the facts and study the evidence before making a decision. About 33% felt that Newfoundland
was not yet ready to return to Responsible Government.
This left 17% who favoured Confederation.

DID CORRUPTION BRING
NEWFOUNDLAND DOWN IN 1933?

Joey Smallwood did not agree with the Amulree Report's
claim that widespread political corruption brought about
Newfoundland's downfall in 1933. Smallwood explained:

> There wasn't as much corruption in a decade in New-
> foundland as there would be in any six months in many
> Canadian provinces, or in a week in any American state.
> The difference lay in the fact of the Newfoundland par-
> ties' intellectual bankruptcy. Lacking deep-seated and
> strongly held views on vital matters, the two parties slan-
> dered each other, each trying to convince the people
> that its opponent was a dirty embezzler or pick-pocket–
> that was the sum of their propaganda. That kind of

propaganda convinced a lot of Newfoundlanders, and a lot of others, that Newfoundland politics was corrupt and rotten.[4]

Smallwood wasted no time after being elected to the National Convention. The Smallwood Letters had opened peoples' minds to the alternative of Confederation. In his next step, he changed minds at the highest levels of the Canadian Government. This came about due to his one-on-one meetings with federal cabinet ministers.

After his election to the National Convention as the only declared candidate supporting union with Canada, he sought to deepen his knowledge of Confederation. The most effective way of doing this, he thought, was to go to Ottawa and interview Canada's top political officials. His first move was to seek the help of the Canadian High Commissioner to Newfoundland in opening the doors of power in Ottawa.

He approached Hon. J.S. Macdonald while the High Commissioner was visiting Gander on June 29, 1946. Smallwood informed him that although he was the only confirmed Confederate elected, there were eight or nine others ready to support union. Macdonald thought that it was too early in the process for any delegate to have declared himself for Confederation. At this period in time, Canada had little interest in making Newfoundland its tenth province. The High Commissioner felt that a visit to Ottawa by Smallwood, in his delegate capacity, would be a public embarrassment to Canada. He stalled Joey by suggesting that he drop in to visit him during a trip to St. John's, which he had scheduled for early July. The High Commissioner expressed his concerns to Ottawa and noted that caution be used in dealing with him because he might become a valuable ally to Canada.

---

[4]Joseph R. Smallwood, *I Chose Canada*, 196.

TRIED TO HOODWINK JOEY

Joey had already collected volumes of information on Confederation but was now focusing on the Department of Fisheries and the Department of Public Health. Both departments had concurrent jurisdiction with the provinces and he wanted to study how this would work with Newfoundland as a province.

The High Commissioner strongly attempted to discourage him from making the trip. Prior to Joey's visit in 1946, the Canadian Government had never gone beyond publicly stating that if Newfoundland clearly wanted union, Canada would be sympathetic to their desire.

In a letter to the External Affairs Department, Macdonald stated, "Smallwood's mere presence in Ottawa at a time like this would undoubtedly lead to a good deal of publicity that would be embarrassing for Canada."[5]

He suggested that a visit to Ottawa would not be necessary because Joey could collect much of the published material available in Ottawa by mail. Senior bureaucrats in Ottawa shared Macdonald's viewpoint.

The problem was passed on to the Associate Under Secretary of State for Canada, H.H. Wrong, for direction. Wrong agreed that Smallwood should be discouraged from visiting Ottawa, but commented, "On the other hand, if he insists, we cannot prevent him from doing so, and he may be too valuable a friend to risk antagonizing." In the case that Smallwood proceeded with his visit to Ottawa, Mr. Wrong recommended that it be arranged in such a way that the public would not view it as Ottawa involving itself in a decision belonging to the people of Newfoundland.

Instead of Smallwood travelling directly from St. John's to Ottawa, Wrong suggested he hitch a plane ride from Gander, where he resided, to New York. He could then drop in and visit Ottawa on his return trip. Wrong advised that External Affairs bureaucrats should make every effort to block

[5] *Documents on Relations between Canada-Newfoundland*, Vol 1.

Smallwood from the halls of political power in Ottawa. The man chosen to run interference in the scheme was Dr. R.A. McKay, a professor at Dalhousie University and an author, who was serving as a senior adviser in the External Affairs Department. Wrong argued that this meeting should not arouse suspicions in Newfoundland because Smallwood, a writer, was simply visiting McKay, who was also a writer.

McKay puts MAD into effect

The problem with the entire Canadian MAD scheme was that Joey was shrewd enough to detect exactly what they were doing. He decided to play along, but only to a point. He kept his appointment with Professor McKay who treated him courteously during his visit. The two met for dinner where the professor set out to lower Joey's expectations about his visit to Canada's capital. He gave a lengthy explanation of the difficulty of getting certain figures. He felt he had gained Newfoundland confidence by arranging visits to several bureaucrats, who would be willing to provide helpful information about the Canadian system of government.

Part way into the charade, McKay began feeling guilty about his role. Although Smallwood was amused by the situation, he gave no indication that he was aware of the game being played by McKay. He had been around the block politically and understood how the game of MAD operated. Joey reversed the roles of the game's participants and went ahead with his own plans for sidetracking the bureaucrats. He smiled, expressed his gratitude to the senior official for his help, and then went off on his own to do what he had come to Ottawa to do.

Several days later, the High Commissioner in Newfoundland heard rumours that Joey was successfully meeting with cabinet ministers. He sent an immediate warning to McKay to keep a closer eye on the Newfoundland politician. His memo stated:

In view of the care that has been taken to direct his (Smallwood's) activities to purely factual matters having to do with the details of federal administration, I can scarcely believe there is any truth in such rumours, but I think it would be desirable if I could have an outline of his activities while in Ottawa.[6]

By the time McKay read the message, Joey was on his way home to Newfoundland feeling pleased with the success of his visit. On his own initiative he had circumvented the bureaucrats and gained access to the office of Prime Minister Mackenzie King, who was out of the country. There he met and befriended King's adviser, Jack Pickersgill, held meetings with Deputy Prime Minister Louis St. Laurent and members of the Federal Cabinet. When the Hon. Robert (Bob) Winters was advised by the Prime Minister's office to meet with Smallwood, he begrudgingly allowed for a fifteen minute visit. He was so captivated and impressed with Smallwood's presentation that the meeting lasted more than ninety minutes. Joey also received a warm welcome from Trade Minister C.D. Howe, one of King's most powerful ministers.

Before leaving Ottawa, Smallwood had thanked Professor McKay for his courtesies. External Affairs officials in Ottawa and in Newfoundland were by then quite aware that they had been out manoeuvred.

Contrary to what some have written about this era, Canada was not overly enthusiastic about the possibility of union with Newfoundland. Professor R.A. McKay described the attitude running through the top echelons of power in Ottawa after being told of Smallwood's pending visit in 1946:

I recall a meeting about this time in the office of the Under-Secretary of the Department, Norman Robertson. There were five of us present in all. Norman's comment was 'I suppose we have here all the people in

---

[6]*Documents on Relations Between Canada and Newfoundland 1940-1949, Vol. 1* Department External Affairs, 285.

Canada interested in having Newfoundland join Canada.' The main reason was financial. It was clear that Newfoundland would need proportionately much more financial assistance than any existing province, and if this was granted it might touch off demands from other provinces–especially the Maritimes–for better terms.[7]

An official at the American Embassy told a Canadian diplomat, "If Newfoundland became a province, Canada would have a little Ireland on its hands, a disgruntled people no matter what is done for them."[8]

If Smallwood was ready to embrace the cause for Confederation, he had to be ready to take on Canada's politicians as well as public opinion in Newfoundland. Reflecting on the success of his trip, Joey recalled:

I realize now that the Canadian government were probably holding their breath just a little while when I was in Ottawa. I think that perhaps they all breathed a sigh of relief when I was safely out of Ottawa again. For my part, I came away from there feeling reasonably sure that we were wanted.[9]

However, Professor McKay was quick to notice a positive shift in the attitudes of the federal cabinet towards Newfoundland. He advised Macdonald in St. John's of Smallwood's effectiveness in dealing with the political leaders.

External Affairs documents record that Smallwood had been quite persuasive in his round of meetings. Some years later, Professor McKay recalled his 1946 Ottawa meeting

---

[7]James R. Thoms, *Call Me Joey* (Cuff Publications, 1990).

[8]Other references claim the statement originated several years earlier from the Premier of Nova Scotia.

[9]*Documents on Relations Between Canada and Newfoundland 1940-1949, Vol. 1.*

with Smallwood which turned out to be an embarrassment to several senior diplomats, including himself. He wrote:

> We had a long and rather academic discussion over lunch on how Newfoundland might fit into the Canadian federal system. I found he had already done his homework and was quite familiar with the federal system. This was typical of the man–he usually knew what he was talking about, or if he didn't, he asked penetrating and sometimes disturbing questions.

> I was on more embarrassing ground when he asked for assistance in meeting the Prime Minister and other ministers who might be influential. The politicians had shown little interest in union. Prime Minister King had made sympathetic noises in Parliament some months earlier when asked a question by the Opposition, but he had been emphatic that Newfoundlanders must decide the issue themselves. Other ministers, and especially the Minister of Finance, were something less than lukewarm toward union.

> There was no indication that any political leader wanted to meet Smallwood–for although he was elected to the constitutional convention as an avowed Confederate, he had no party or political organization behind him and apparently no funds to build one... nor had he ever held public office. The Prime Minister and colleagues were apprehensive of appearing to back a probable loser.

> I was, therefore, instructed to resort to what the British civil service used to label MAD tactics (maximum administrative delay) in passing Smallwood on to higher authority. I, accordingly, explained to him how busy the PM and ministers were, how difficult it was to arrange interviews on short notice, how I would do the best I

could, but could not promise, and so on and so on. Mr. Smallwood, of course, saw through the facade and went his own way. With sure political instinct, he turned to the politicians rather than the bureaucrats.[10]

Two days before leaving Ottawa, Joey dropped in on McKay to tell him he had enjoyed a very satisfactory visit and was leaving for home that afternoon. But before departing, he let the senior bureaucrat know how he succeeded in gaining access to the political leaders. On his own, he had approached an old acquaintance, Senator McLean and arranged to bypass the bureaucratic route and MAD to go directly to the offices of real power. This led him first to Frank Bridges, Minister of Fisheries. He had discovered that the Prime Minister had an office in the House of Commons to which he normally returned after the question period in the House. Smallwood had seen the door open, walked in and introduced himself to Jack Pickersgill, then Secretary to the Prime Minister. Deputy Prime Minister Louis St. Laurent came in shortly thereafter and Pickersgill introduced Joey as "Mr. Smallwood from Newfoundland."

"Come in Mr. Smallwood I am so glad to meet you," said the DPM, and they went to his private office where they talked for over half an hour. This opened many doors to Smallwood including, that of C.D. Howe, whom Joey found to be really interested in union. He also met Cauldwell of the CCF party, whom he found to be a kindred socialist spirit. McKay explained the Smallwood impact in Ottawa:

> Smallwood's vivid personality, his self-assurance, his firm belief that Newfoundlanders could be converted to union had created a favourable impression on the Canadian political leaders: the Prime Minister and the prospective Prime Minister, and Mr. St. Laurent, included. Neither Newfoundland nor Smallwood were any

---

[10]*Documents on Relations Between Canada and Newfoundland, Vol.1.*

longer unknown politically in Ottawa. Henceforth, when memos or dispatches about Newfoundland matters were sent up to our political masters, they were read.

Joey returned to Newfoundland convinced Canada would accept Newfoundland on satisfactory terms, if the people of Newfoundland made it clear they wanted to come in. As for the decision by Newfoundlanders, Joey had no doubt about his ability to convince them to decide the right way.[11]

THE FINAL WORD FROM TOP DIPLOMAT

In true diplomatic fashion, Lester B. Pearson, Under-Secretary of External Affairs, described Smallwood's political coup in circumventing the bureaucrats' MAD ploy in the Department's usual tactful language. He stated:

I might add, also for your information, that officials of this Department saw very little of Mr. Smallwood during his visit. He called on Mr. MacKay the day after his arrival and the day before he left and, although Mr. Mackay made arrangements for him to see certain officials, he did not keep these appointments, apparently preferring to make his contacts with officials through the Minister of Fisheries (Frank Bridges) or other members of Parliament.[12]

Smallwood recalled, "I expected to have a warm welcome in Ottawa. If the plague had descended on them, I didn't think they would have been any more scared. They were scared. They were really scared; I was almost an untouchable."[13] The MAD episode marked the end of the bureaucratic attitude that Joe Smallwood was a pushover. Thereafter, Smallwood had the ear of the Prime Minister and cabinet.

---

[11] *Documents on Relations Between Canada and Newfoundland, Vol. 1.*
[12] Ibid.
[13] Joseph R. Smallwood, *I Chose Canada*, 564.

Smallwood's autobiography published in 1974, ten years before the secret External Affairs documents were published, did not reveal that he had any awareness of how the MAD plan had worked out in External Affairs between Scott Macdonald in Newfoundland and H. H. Wrong, senior official in External Affairs and later Ambassador to the United States, with Professor R.A. MacKay participating.

The federal documents, published in two volumes containing a total of 2100 pages revealed that Smallwood had positively affected attitudes towards Confederation both in Newfoundland and in Ottawa even before the National Convention had gotten underway.

The "Smallwood Letters" published in the *Daily News* in March 1946, and described earlier in this chapter, had a positive effect in Newfoundland. The other even more significant success was that Smallwood had changed attitudes in the federal cabinet during his July 1946 visit to Ottawa. This is verified in the writings of MacKay.

Over the years, Smallwood believed that Jack Pickersgill had played a much bigger role at that time than he actually did. In his autobiography, he showed his unawareness of his own success when he wrote, I have often wondered what St. Laurent, [Deputy Prime Minister] and other ministers thought of me at the time."[14] This was a question answered by Professor R.A. MacKay much later and detailed earlier in this chapter.

Smallwood's unawareness of who instigated the MAD plan is also reflected in his autobiography when he said, "I did have two staunch supporters in Pickersgill and Scott Macdonald, [instigator of the MAD plan] and probably R.A. MacKay."[15] MacKay was the first of the diplomats in Ottawa to realize that Smallwood had been underestimated.

---

[14] Ibid.
[15] Ibid.

CHAPTER 4

The Road to Confederation

"Joey Smallwood led the movement to make Newfoundland a province and then directed a social revolution which has changed the ideas, aspirations, and attitudes of the people for the rest of time."

— I.F. Perlin, Editor *Daily News*, 1969

Newfoundlanders had lost faith in their country's political system in April 1932, and they were in a hostile and angry mood. An editorial in the *Daily News* noted that the destitution in Newfoundland was beyond parallel in North America. The qualities of integrity, honour and justice no longer existed here.[1] It was in this atmosphere that events got out of hand. This led to rioting and the Prime Minister running for his life from the Colonial Building on Military Road.

In April, the opposition called a public meeting which was held at the Majestic Theatre in St. John's. A thousand people turned up for the event which was chaired by prominent Water Street merchant Eric Bowring. When Smallwood became aware of this, he initiated his own response. He rushed to the Department of Finance and, after researching records over the previous twenty-five years, compiled a list of the large sums of money paid from public funds to the Bowring firm. The information gathered formed the basis for an article critical of Bowring which he published in the *Watchdog*, a Liberal Party newspaper, and passed out free of charge to those going into the meeting.

The crowd inside the hall was in an angry mood and left no doubt to whom the target of their bitterness was– Prime Minister Sir Richard Squires. It was no place for Squires or his supporters. Part way through the meeting Smallwood, an adviser to Squires, made his way to the middle of the hall and standing on a chair was shouting, "Question!"[2] Once recognized by the crowd as a supporter and colleague of the Prime Minister, the cry went throughout the hall, "Throw him out!" A few people demanded to, "Let him speak!"

Eric Bowring, who sensed a problem was developing, defused the situation temporarily by inviting Smallwood to join him on the stage. Joey agreed, and made his way through the crowd and onto the platform facing the

---

[1]Richard Gwyn, *Smallwood the Unlikely Revolutionary.*
[2]Edited by James R. Thoms, article by Herb Wells, *Call Me Joey.*

multitude. Joey recognized that the crowd was made up of mostly the unemployed and the hungry and felt that if given the chance, he could influence them.

He began his address, "Beware of the Greeks when they come bearing gifts, and I say, beware of Water Street merchants when they come with political advice." The noisy crowd had settled down, but only momentarily. Joey felt comfortable in the situation, and began pacing back and forth across the stage while delivering a bitter attack on the merchants of Water Street. When he neared the northern stage exit for the third time, two hands extended out from behind the curtains, pulled him into the wings and out of sight of the audience. It was there he was beaten by several men and tossed out into the street.[3]

The opposition was now in full control of the hall, the meeting resumed and was going well until a muffled sound was heard originating from the back of the hall. A bruised, but not in the least deterred, Joey Smallwood had returned and was pushing his way towards the stage. He didn't quite make it. He was again seized by a couple of men and tossed out through the front door. Guards were placed on all doors to assure he stayed out.

Smallwood's feistiness that night became legend for decades afterwards in old St. John's. Aubrey MacDonald, once Dean of Newfoundland Broadcasters, recalled:

Joey was forever engaging someone in an argument. Politics, of course. The more opposition he had, the more he'd argue, and I can't recall him ever using filthy, vile, obscene language. The word 'fear' was not in his lexicon, and many times he was threatened physically. One man, a politician, a physical giant, approached Joey one day, peered down at him and yelled, "You little rat, I'll kill you with one hand!" Joey looked up at the enraged Goliath and yelled right back, 'Go on, hit me. Hit me!'

[3]Ibid.

Something, perhaps respect for the courage of such a tiny man, stayed the hand of his huge tormentor.[4]

Joey Smallwood was just thirty-two years old in 1932. Only a few people were aware of the experience he had already gained at public rallies in the United States and in England, which well prepared him for the battles he faced on the road leading Newfoundland into Confederation.

BORN TO LEAD

. Joseph R. Smallwood may have had a moment of prophetic vision, when as a student at Bishop Feild College on Bond Street in St. John's, he wrote across the top of the inside cover of his history book "The Right Honourable Joseph Roberts Smallwood, K.C. M.G. P.C." The letters K.C.M.G. referred to Knights Commander of St. Michael and St. George and the P.C. represented Privy Counsellor."[5]

Joey Smallwood, the son of Charles Smallwood and Mary De Vanna, was born on December 24, 1900 in Gambo, Newfoundland, . His grandfather David operated the sawmill in Gambo for forty years. Charles worked as a surveyor at the same mill after David Smallwood moved to St. John's. The Smallwoods moved to St. John's soon after Joey marked his first birthday. They rented a two room flat in Murphy's Range above a store located on the corner of LeMarchant Road and Lime Street. In the 1940s and 1950s the store was known as Walsh's Store. The original Murphy's Range was destroyed by the Great Fire of 1892 and was one of several 'ranges' of houses rebuilt after the fire to meet the demand for housing.[6]

---

[4]Edited by James R. Thoms, *Call Me Joey*.

[5]Harold Horwood, *Joey: The Life and Political Times of Joey Smallwood* (Stoddart Publishing Co. Ltd., 1989).

[6]Murphy"s Range ran along the south side of LeMarchant Road from Cookstown Road to Lime Street. It was constructed by Joseph Murphy, a shipwright with Baine Johnson Ltd., after the 1892 fire that destroyed St. John's. The entire range was sold in 1953. Murphy emigrated from Ireland in 1872.

Having lived there for a year, the family moved to the north side of Bond Street several doors east of Cathedral Street.

When young Joey was approaching three years of age and had not spoken a word, Charles and Mary Smallwood became concerned. This concern was alleviated after his third birthday and speech soon became his major asset. Of equal concern to them was that Joey had been born bow-legged, which interfered with his walking. Fortunately, his grandfather, who had opened a boot manufacturing company in St. John's, came to his rescue. David Smallwood made a special pair of high laced boots which corrected this problem over time. A strong bond of affection developed between Joey and his grandfather, and Joey spent as much time as he could puttering around the boot factory, chasing David Smallwood wherever he went. The Smallwood Boots Factory was managed by Joey's uncle Fred, who came up with a novel way of advertising his product. On the side of a cliff at the Narrows he installed an iron bar fixed into the cliff from which hung a huge black boot and a large sign with "Buy Smallwood's Boots" inscribed on it in white letters.[7]

St. John's had 19th Century Character and Charm

The St. John's of Joey's youth was little different than the St. John's of the 19th century. The city was built to meet 19th needs: narrow unpaved roads, rows of wooden houses, each with a basement coal pound fed through an outside chute, or a small coal pound near the kitchen stove. There were stables for horses, hen houses and blacksmith operations. Houses were lit by kerosene and gas lamps, and streets dimly lit by gas-lamps hanging from street poles.

Residential areas were mostly row type wooden houses built along unpaved dusty streets, lanes and walkways shooting out in all directions. Horse-drawn carriages served as

---

[7]Joseph R. Smallwood, *I Chose Canada.*

taxis and horse-drawn slovens did the work trucks do today.

The harbour was a busy port. Ships from many countries visited daily. The water was then clean enough for people to swim in, and there were several memorable harbour swimming races. Most merchants had their own wharfs and some owned a fleet of ships. It was a beehive of activity where children often played amid much danger, and over the years many lost their lives after falling into the harbour. Dogs, chickens, cows, and goats roamed the streets. The goats were a major problem when allowed to wander the city. To deal with them the City hired its own goat catcher. There were many taverns and hop beer shops. In addition to the stores on Water Street and Duckworth Street, every neighbourhood had several stores which sold groceries, meats and vegetables. These stores were in addition to many other smaller convenience stores. After the 1892 fire, Water Street was rebuilt similar to those main streets found in English and Irish cities. A few merchants owned cars, and trams (electric street cars), true marvels of the 20th century, were introduced as public transportation.

Very few homes had water and sewerage. A system of night carts, honey-wagons, as they were called, operated after dark collecting night soil, house by house, from honey buckets left out in front of the house. These were taken to a couple of sites in the city and dumped into French sewers (underground stone tunnels) which carried the sewerage into the harbour. One such sewer ran from the top of Adelaide Street, now part of City Hall, down through Bishop's Cove and into the harbour. During a heavy rainstorm in the early 1950s, the part of the French sewer in the Cove caved in from the weight of a truck. The truck had to be towed out.

Garbage collectors for the city were called 'ashmen' because there was little garbage to collect. Every house filled its ash bucket from ashes taken from the kitchen stove and other fireplaces, and placed it outdoors for the ashman to collect. Paper bags, cardboard and wooden cartons were burned in kitchen stoves. There were several small dumps around town, some privately owned, where the ashes were dumped. Red painted cast iron fountains were placed around town to water the horses. Some citizens depended on cast iron, dark blue street tanks for their water needs. Houses were painted in dark colours because of the dusty streets and the constant flow of smoke from the house chimneys of the town. Added to this was the billowing smoke from the local industry and manufacturing plants which were also fuelled by coal. It was only after Confederation when street paving was carried out that home owners were able to use brighter paint colours. There were only about 130 miles of paved road in all Newfoundland before Confederation. Some of the paved streets in St. John's prior to 1949 included Water Street, Waterford Bridge Road, LeMarchant Road, Topsail Road, Duckworth Street, New Gower Street, parts of Pennywell Road, and Freshwater Road.

SCHOOL DAYS

Growing up in old St. John's was a delight for young Joey. He had lots of friends and found many an adventure along the St. John's harbour front, as well as on the streets in summer and winter. One winter, while living on Bond Street, Joey was involved in a daring childhood escapade that left him with a head scar that lasted a lifetime. Joey and his sister Marie were with neighbourhood friends, doing what kids in every neighbourhood of the city often did in winter– sliding down hills on a sled or slide as they were also called.

Joey and Marie took their sled to the top of Garrison Hill to race against friends in a contest to prove who among the gang had the fastest sled. Picking up speed as they moved down the hill of packed snow and ice, Joey tried unsuccessfully to bring his slide to a stop in time to avoid crashing into the front wall of the Parker residence on the lower western corner of the Hill. Marie, apart from being shook up, was unharmed, but Joey suffered the head cut which scarred him for life.

It was while living on Bond Street that Smallwood began school. His parents registered him at the British Hall, a Church of England school opposite the old Imperial Tobacco factory.

MOVED TO CORONATION STREET

In 1905, the Smallwoods moved to Coronation Street, a new residential area of town, and Joey was transferred to the nearby Methodist school. He delighted in living there because his grandfather David lived nearby on Springdale Street. The Methodist Church was located between Pleasant Street and Larkin Street, adjacent to the Horwood Lumber Yard. The lumberyard was known as "the Battlefield" for over half a century.[8]

The area between Coronation Street and Springdale Street had been part of Casey's Farm.[9] The soil in the area was fertile and David made good use of an acre of open land behind his property, which was almost joining the backyard of Joey's house. Both Springdale and Coronation Street had backyards that were separated by a long laneway, which included the one acre meadow which David had converted into farmland. The senior Smallwood also kept two horses with a carriage for each horse. It was here that Joey developed an interest in farming and animals.

The Smallwood family's fourth household move came in 1907, when they moved from Coronation Street to the lower part of Southside Road, just a few doors east of where Hans

[8]According to oral tradition, this was the area where sealers fought over the right to be first in loading a fresh water supply for their vessel before heading for the annual seal hunt. The field was near where a fresh water stream entered the harbor near Springdale and Water Streets. Its name, "Battlefield," was still being used in the early 1950s. (Springdale Street from Water Street to New Gower Street was then known as Flower Hill.)

[9] Casey's Farm was north of Gilbert Street to LeMarchant Road. It was converted to residential area which allowed Springdale Street to be extended from Gilbert to LeMarchant Road to enable coal deliveries to the LeMarchant Road neighbourhoods. The Methodist Guards had a building near David Smallwoods house.

Noseworthy operated a neighbourhood store in the 1960s-1970s. At first he attended St. Mary's School near the Long Bridge, but this was too far to walk twice a day, so his parents arranged for his transfer to the Roman Catholic School at Littledale.[10] Harry Murphy, who in 1967 was living on Flower Hill, was a friend of Joey's when they both attended the little one-room school operated by Roman Catholic nuns. Harry lived on Angel Place but had to walk to and from Littledale because the west end did not have a Catholic school. In 1967, after learning of this, I arranged for Harry and his wife Mary to visit Joey at his Roche's Line home.

Joey was most gracious and obviously delighted to see Harry after so many years. While relaxing and sharing a glass of wine with Joey in his library, the two reminisced about their days at Littledale. Harry began to recall an incident of mischief at the school which sparked a grin and a wink of the eye by Joey. Murphy had managed to say, "Remember Joe, out behind the school when the Sister caught us!" when Joey interjected. "Now Harry, let's not tell tales out of school." Harry, returning the wink, said, "Saying the Angelus."[11] When the laughing subsided, Harry went on to recall another childhood adventure he shared with Smallwood that involved raiding chestnut trees along Waterford Bridge Road. Harry got caught by the property owner because he wasn't as fast as the other boys. On our return drive to St. John's, Harry remembered Joey as adventurous and a leader among the boys in their class.

A STUDENT AT BISHOP FEILD

At Bishop Feild, Smallwood was already displaying some of the qualities of leadership which proved so valuable to him when he began his political career. In response to the dry molasses puddings being served, Joey led students in boycotting the dining room. He made up posters to use and

---

[10]Harold Horwood, *Joey, The Life and Political Times of Joey Smallwood.*
[11]The Angelus is a Catholic prayer traditionally said at noon.

came up with the slogan "More Lassey, Less Pudding." The boycott was successful and a little more molasses was added to the pudding.

On another occasion he defied the school's rules regarding Sunday attendance at church. He held a deep respect and curiosity about the Salvation Army and after leaving the school residence to walk to St. Thomas' Church nearby with other students, he persuaded them to go with him instead to the Salvation Army Services at their Citadel in the centre of town. Later, after returning to the College, Smallwood and friends were grounded for two weeks for disregarding school rules.

This matter did not sit right with Joey who persuaded the others to join him in boycotting the dining hall. As a result, the two week punishment was reduced to three days following which Joey and friends returned happily to the dining hall.

Years later, when Joey was Premier of Newfoundland, Malcolm Hollett, leader of the opposition in the Legislature, and Oxford graduate, confronted Joey over lassy bread. Joey was recalling his youth and praising the baking skills of his mother and especially her homemade bread which, like most young boys, he loved to coat with lassy (molasses) and butter.

The Opposition Leader interjected, "But if you put butter on the bread, the lassy will run off!"

Joey jumped to his feet in faked astonishment saying, "Oh no! Oh no! The Honourable Leader of the Opposition obviously knows nothing about 'lassy bread.' You put the lassy on first and then spread the butter on top."[12]

JOEY'S CIRCULATING LIBRARY

Joey had a voracious appetite for reading as a young boy which lasted throughout his life. In 1973, he estimated he had read about 20,000 books. To finance keeping up with all the latest periodicals and magazines while at Bishop

[12]Harold Horwood, *Joey, The Life and Political Times of Joey Smallwood.*

Feild College, he set up a little business he described as 'a circulating library' which met with some success. He rented newspapers and magazines to fellow students for a penny each. In his memoirs he recalled, "I made no profit for myself and did not want to, but I did manage to do a lot of reading."

Joey's interest in the political life of Newfoundland emerged while he was attending Bishop Feild College. It was while there that he developed a keen interest in the legislative and political processes. He spent most of his free time at the Newfoundland Legislature in Colonial Building which was just a few minutes' walk from his school. The knowledge he gained of parliamentary procedures and politicians there served him well in later years.[13]

Dr. Fred Rowe, who after Confederation served in the Smallwood cabinet, drew a comparison between Smallwood and Winston Churchill in respect to both of their school days. He pointed out:

> It was at school that Smallwood became a voracious reader, and it was perhaps this habit which affected his subsequent years more than anything else. Like Winston Churchill, he was in some respects an indifferent student, however, his taste for reading was destined to offset the deficiencies of his limited formal education, and, in time, was to make him (again like Churchill) a master in the use of the English language.[14]

DOWN MEMORY LANE

On an occasion in 1973, while Smallwood led the Liberal opposition, Nelson Oates, his nephew and driver, had taken Joey's car for servicing. Joey was in a nostalgic mood and asked me if I would drive him to several places around the city. It turned out to be a trip down memory lane. Joey sim-

---

[13]Interview by Jack Fitzgerald with Smallwood in 1984.
[14]Frederic W. Rowe, *The Smallwood Era*, 1985.

ply wished to visit the places that had meant so much to him in his youth. The first stop was Bishop Feild College, then to the streets where he once lived: Bond Street, LeMarchant Road-Lime Street, Coronation Street and Springdale Street. Throughout the drive, Joey reminisced about his memories of each place and the friends he made growing up. When we stopped on Coronation Street, Joey recalled the Bromleys who had lived next door to him, and he described his grandfather's farm on Springdale Street which adjoined his backyard. I pointed out that in the mid-1950s I had lived around the corner at 48 Charlton Street, which bordered on the Smallwood farm, and by then the neighbourhood boys were using the old farm as a soccer field. Among them were Dennis (Doc) O'Keefe who later became Mayor of St. John's; Andy Churchill and Billy Smith who became famous soccer players across the province. The trip down memory lane had to be interrupted because of time, and we didn't get to visit the site of his Southside Road home or Littledale School.[15]

Neither was there time to visit Balsam Street where he and Clare, in the late 1920s, rented a four-room apartment to which he brought Sir Richard Squires and Sir William Coaker to a secret-meeting in an unsuccessful attempt to reconcile their political differences. Still in his twenties, Joey was an astute politician and was promoting his strongly held conviction that only Sir Richard Squires, supported by Coaker, could defeat the ruling Tories in the coming general election.

DROPS OUT OF SCHOOL

When Joey dropped out of school in 1915, very few students in Newfoundland were completing high school, and it was not difficult for him to find a decent job with any one of the several newspapers operating in the city. In his

---

[15] Author Jack Fitzgerald recalling one of many anecdotes regarding his own friendship with Smallwood.

autobiography, Joey recalled, "A career in journalism was one of the normal routes into politics." Many journalists and editors of that era began their writing careers working as printers. Joey was certainly filled with enthusiasm and a willingness to learn as he embraced his first job as a "printer's devil" with the *St. John's Plaindealer* at $1.50 weekly. Apprentices were called devils because their hands, face and clothes were so often black with printer's ink. From there he spent a brief period at *The Spectator* on Theatre Hill before accepting a position with the *Daily News*. There, in addition to printer's duties, he was given the responsibility of bill collecting. He was also able to squeeze some time into his schedule to venture into writing. Joey's first articles were for the *Fishermen's Advocate* published by Sir William Coaker whom he keenly admired. His reputation as a journalist grew rapidly and landed him a job at the *Evening Telegram* with a weekly salary of twelve dollars, well above what he was being paid at the *Daily News*.[16]

SMALLWOOD JOINS LABOUR PARTY

While employed with the *Plaindealer*, Smallwood joined the first trade union in Newfoundland, the Newfoundland Industrial Workers Association with offices on New Gower Street at the foot of Flower Hill in St. John's. Smallwood's introduction to political activism came in 1919 when a Labour Party was formed in St. John's to contest that year's General Election. Joey, a socialist, joined the party and became one of its most active campaigners. At that time Joey felt the Liberal Party was intellectually bankrupt. The Labour Party ran only three candidates: William Linegar, John Cadwell and Mike Foley. The Labour Party failed to elect a member. The successful candidates were: Sir Michael Cashin, Liberal; Sir Richard Squires, Liberal Reform; and John R. Bennett, People's Party.

The *Evening Telegram* owners, who supported the Liberal Party, had no problem with Smallwood's political allegiance

---

[16]Joseph R. Smallwood, *I Chose Canada*, 97, 98.

to the Labour Party. They respected his journalistic abilities and gave him a salary of $25 weekly, which was almost on par with the editor's salary.

He continued his career as a journalist when he moved to Nova Scotia and found work as a reporter with the *Halifax Chronicle*. While there, he also contributed to the *Atlantic Leader*. About a year later, he sought and found employment in the United States. First, he moved to Boston where he became a reporter with the *Boston Herald,* and then to New York where he became reporter for the popular socialist newspaper *The Call*. His fascination with socialism was growing, and he spent long hours in New York libraries reading everything he could find on the topic. He developed his oratorical and debating skills by going to Central Park where the city's soap-box speakers frequented and challenged any and all on the topic of socialism.

SMALLWOOD WITH MOVIE COMPANY

Smallwood gave up his job at *The Call* to return to Newfoundland where he found work as legislative reporter for the *Daily Star*. When the legislature closed, he worked for a short while with another St. John's newspaper the *Evening Advocate* after which he returned to the excitement and challenges of New York.

Soon after his arrival there, he landed a job at the prestigious *New York Times* with help from Sir Robert Bond's nephew F. Fraser, executive assistant to the editor. However, Smallwood was broke, sleeping on park benches and the job would not be available for several weeks. Out of desperation, he sought and was hired by the movie producer Ernest Shipmen. His duties with Shipmen involved the setting up of movie companies in Nova Scotia, Prince Edward Island and Newfoundland to make films for an international market. Smallwood later recalled, "The nearest we got to the actual making of a film was at Charlottetown."

Not one to waste energy or time, Smallwood returned to
New York and over a period of several years held journalist
positions with several publications. First, he applied to and
was rehired by *The Call*. Around the same time, he became
a speaker for the American Socialist Party. He then moved
onto an editor's job with McGraw-Hill publishing house and
was assigned to edit one of their many magazines the *Elec-
trical Merchandiser*. This was a job he thoroughly disliked. By
then he had little problem finding work and became employed writing weekly features for *Gilliams Editorial Syndicate*,
which were supplied to newspapers across America for their
Sunday editions.[17]

IMMERSED IN STUDIES ON SOCIALISM

Author Harold Horwood, a colleague of Smallwood in the
Battle for Confederation, wrote in 1989 that Joey's knowledge of the meaning of socialism was gained from his reading of a magazine that was little better than a comic book.[18]
Well, it was a fact that Joey's introduction to socialist read-
ings was in the form referred to by Horwood, but that was
long before he left Newfoundland to live in New York. It
was in New York that Smallwood studied socialism, befriended many American socialists, became a member of
the American Socialist Party, was a public speaker for the
party in New York during the 1924 US Presidential elections
and in 1928 was a British Labour Party speaker on the same
platform with Prime Minister Ramsay McDonald. In his autobiography, Smallwood recalled:

What a glorious opportunity there was in New York for
a young man to resume and vastly improve his interrupted education. For years, I went night after night to
classes and lectures at the Rand School of Social Science
on 15th Street off Union Square in New York City.[19]

[17]Ibid.
[18]Harold Horwood, *Joey*.
[19]Joseph R. Smallwood, *I Chose Canada*, 134.

There were also countless opportunities to attend lectures given by prominent socialist writers at the time, and Joey spent most of his spare time attending them. Most of these were held at the Cooper Union Institute in Cooper Square, and the Labour Temple, both in New York City. Many lectures delivered by author Will Durant were published in Durant's book the *Story of Philosophy*. Smallwood recalled, "Wherever there was an outstanding speaker, if I knew about it, I was there."[20] Among the lectures he attended was one given in New York by the world famous author and philosopher Bertrand Russell. Recalling the lecture, Smallwood said:

> Russell spoke for three-quarters of an hour, and if he had spoken in Aramaic, I would have understood him as readily; for, in fact, I didn't understand a single, solitary sentence of his speech and I was not alone. [21]

This was evident, according to Smallwood, when Russell interrupted his lecture to comment, "That's all clear to you of course," which caused the audience to respond with laughter. Later, Smallwood got to interview Russell in his private home as he prepared to leave for England and continued the interview in the taxi ride to the New York pier where Russell boarded his boat for England.

While in New York, Joey began research on a book containing a collection of biographies of some of the world's great liberators. He spent several years gathering material from the New York Library at Fifth and Forty-Second Street. The book was never completed and over the years what he had completed was lost.

JOEY'S PUBLIC DEBATES IN UNITED STATES

Joey Smallwood's readiness to take on anyone, any crowd whether in the parks or on public platforms in the town squares of New York and New Jersey, proved to be valuable

---

[20]Ibid, 148.
[21]Ibid, 149.

training for the man destined to lead his country into union with Canada, and to become its first Premier as a Canadian province.

It was at some of these rough-and-tumble public meetings where Joey developed the art of handling hecklers and influencing large crowds. Smallwood gained a reputation within the socialist movement for his public speaking and was enrolled as one of the movement's able speakers in its New York speakers' bureau.

In his role as a socialist speaker, he became popular in certain communities. The bureau would receive specific invitations for Smallwood to speak in Jewish communities and in Harlem. During the Presidential Election of 1924, the Socialist Speakers' Bureau played an active role in the campaign which they viewed as an opportunity to spread socialist ideals. The bureau sent its speakers to about twenty cities in New York and New Jersey.

In later years, Smallwood attributed his self-confidence to his years at Bishop Feild College, where he mingled with students from the Colony's richest families, and refused to allow himself to be intimidated by anyone. His experiences with the American socialist movement allowed him to tone and improve upon this skill.

JOEY ESCAPES KU KLUX KLAN

In Buffalo, New York, a stronghold of the Ku Klux Klan (KKK), Smallwood shared the stage with America's best known black labour organizer, Frank R. Crosswaithe. Smallwood's job was to warm up the crowd for Crosswaithe, the main attraction. About 10,000 people, most of them black, turned up in the public square to hear the speakers. Smallwood, still in his twenties, stepped onto the stage displaying courage and confidence as he began his speech. The crowd was impressed. However, his message shocked them, and caused a quick response by civic leaders in the city.

While the black people surrounded the stage, the KKK was moving in behind them, and paying close attention to the young speaker. Smallwood had launched into an attack on the hostile KKK. Referring to the patriot John Brown, Smallwood told the crowd, "John Brown said that he would prefer to hold a black baby in his arms to holding the baby Jesus." The remark and tone of Smallwood's speech signalled the start of trouble.

Not deterred, Joey continued to talk while the civic leaders gathered with Crosswaithe off stage to plan the speedy exit of both Smallwood and Crosswaithe from the town square. As soon as Smallwood left the stage, there was an uneasiness bordering on fear among the crowd. Crosswaithe and Smallwood were hustled into a waiting car which rushed away from the open square and sped through the streets of Buffalo putting as much distance between them and the KKK as speed would allow.

Smallwood could not go back to his hotel because authorities feared the KKK would go there, so he spent the night with Crosswaithe in an all-black hotel in the black section of town. In his memoirs, Smallwood recalled, "I learned a lot that night of what it felt like to be a black in the United States in the 1920s."[22]

Years later, as Premier of Newfoundland, Smallwood had a scheduled meeting with officials at Rockefeller Plaza in New York which was related to development in Labrador. After arriving in New York, he tracked down Crosswaithe who then held a powerful position with the New York Housing Commission. The two had much to talk about including their memories of the KKK incident and the 1924 Presidential Election. Crosswaithe drove Joey to his meeting at the Rockefeller Plaza in a chauffeur driven Cadillac owned by the Housing Commission.

CONFRONTING NEW YORK DEMOCRATS

Smallwood's next speaking engagement, following his confrontation with the KKK, was in Poughkeepsie, New

---

[22]Joseph R. Smallwood, *I Chose Canada*, 1973, 144.

York, where the socialists had arranged for a rally in the town square. When he arrived in Poughkeepsie, he was given the royal treatment by the multi-millionaire socialist Frank King who had worked his way up from pushing a cart in a New York ghetto to owner of the King Court Hotel and other businesses and property in the state. King had sent a Rolls Royce to pick up Joey and bring him to the King Court Hotel where he was provided with a room at no charge.

This proved to be a memorable visit for Smallwood because of his encounter with Eleanor D. Roosevelt, wife of Franklin D. Roosevelt. In his hotel room, Joey was reading a front page newspaper story of Mrs. Roosevelt's scheduled rally, and on the same page a report that the socialists had scheduled Joseph Smallwood to speak in the same square at the same time. The newspaper speculated that a clash over who had the right to hold a rally was sure to erupt.

Joey took the newspaper and walked down to socialist headquarters. He approached the manager waving the newspaper in his hand asking, "What's all this about?"

The manager responded, "Pay no attention to it. We have the permit–look here it is, see? –so the other crowd will have to take a backseat."[23]

Smallwood countered that they should not create a major issue over the matter. He pointed out that Roosevelt would attract a large gathering, far more than he could,. "Let them speak. They won't take long, and the crowd will be eager to hear our answer to them, and we can make it a tremendous propaganda victory for the cause." The manager agreed. Smallwood's strategy was proven to be correct when 12,000 people turned up, and Mrs. Roosevelt expressed her gratitude to Smallwood before and after her address.

When Joey began his speech, the crowd had not left the Square. Mrs. Roosevelt had ended her address with an announcement that Al Smith, Governor of New York, was supporting the prominent industrialist John W. Davis for

---

[23]Ibid, 146.

President. Joey began his speech by reciting the names of seventy-two industrial and financial companies of which Davis, the Democratic presidential candidate, was a director. At the end of the list, he commented:

> Mrs. Roosevelt tells us that Al Smith is for John W. Davis. And she asks us to believe that if Al Smith is for John W. Davis, then John W. Davis must be all right. I suggest to you, on the contrary, that it may only show that there's something wrong with Al Smith!

In 1961, Eleanor Roosevelt was special guest at the official opening of Memorial University. Joey had gone to her Manhattan apartment to personally invite her. He asked her if she remembered the meeting at Poughkeepsie, and she replied that she did, and she recalled the nice, young man who spoke for the other side. At this point, Joey informed her that he was that young man.[24]

While campaigning as a socialist in New York, Smallwood came to know Fiorello La Guardia who later became Mayor of New York and visited St. John's during WWII.

JOEY INTERVIEWS US LABOUR LEADER

With Smallwood's involvement with socialists in the United States and being a reporter for the socialist magazine the *Call*, it was inevitable that he would land an interview with a labour leader making national headlines in the United States. Bill Haywood, nicknamed "Big Bill," had been arrested over a labour matter and was out on bail when Joey interviewed him. Big Bill's story became sensational next day when he jumped bail and ended up in Moscow. Haywood passed away in the Russian capital sometime later.

A half century later, Richard Nixon travelled with Premier Smallwood to Moscow. During the visit, the Premier

---

[24]Ibid, 146,147.

pointed to a plaque erected by the Russians to honour the memory of "Big Bill" Haywood which was near the plaque to another American, John Reed, author of *Ten Days that Shook the World,* the first book written on the Russian Revolution.

C.H. Burchill, one of several of Canada's High Commissioners to Newfoundland during the 1940s, holding an object retrieved from Bay Bulls Harbour during WWII which is believed to have been from Sir Humphrey Gilbert's ship when he claimed Newfoundland in 1583. This is the only known photo of that object which has since disappeared. (Jack Fitzgerald)

Judge Harold Winter

Joseph R. Smallwood in his days as *The Barrelman Radio* personality. (Evening Telegram)

Duckworth Street in St. John's in Smallwood's days growing up in the city. Young boys, using birch brooms, made money by sweeping off the board-walks across the street for pedestrians for a penny. (City of St. John's Archives)

When the Smallwood family moved to St. John's from Gambo, they lived in the apartment above the store on the corner of LeMarchant Road and Lime Street. (PANL)

A one room school in pre-1949. (PANL)

The old Memorial University on Parade Street. (PANL)

CHAPTER 5

Joey: Socialist and Labour Organizer

A 1931 Vision of Newfoundland's Future.

"The Railway would be a thing of the past, having been replaced by countrywide paved roads that would handle all transportation, both cargo and passenger. Newfoundland will be one of the great summer playgrounds of America, with as many as 50,000 tourists visiting the Island each year. New hotels and road-houses will have been built in various parts of the country. Many tourists will have built summer cottages and camps in Newfoundland. There will be a large university at St. John's. Education will be free and compulsory. Illiteracy will be abolished. There will be technological colleges. Newfoundland literature would be full of creativeness and significance."

- The New Newfoundland,
Joseph R. Smallwood, 1931

While living in New York, Joey befriended John P. Burke, a giant of the American labour movement, who was then President of the International Brotherhood of Pulp, Sulphate and Paper Mill Workers. The two often walked for long hours along Fifth Avenue discussing labour and socialism. Burke was concerned over the disintegration of Local 63 at the Grand Falls Pulp and Paper Mill where the membership had dropped from 1700 to less than a hundred. When Joey told him that he was returning to Newfoundland, Burke offered him $45 a week to rebuild the Grand Falls local. Joey accepted the offer and returned home in 1925. He tackled the job with enthusiasm, and by the time he was finished, he had not only reorganized the workers at the Grand Falls Mill, but, on his own initiative, also organized a new local at the recently opened Corner Brook Mill.

He started from scratch in signing up members at the Corner Brook Mill. He was aggressive in his efforts and never missed an opportunity to recruit a member. He used oil barrels as speaking platforms and even ventured inside the mill during working hours to communicate the virtues of unionism. He selected the local train station as a productive site to enrol members. It seemed that the whole population turned out at the station on Sundays to greet arriving trains or bid farewell to departing ones. It was here that he mounted the oil barrels to speak to a ready-made audience.

While building up the two unions, he saw that labour in Newfoundland lacked the strength that a countrywide organization would give it, and he set out to organize the first Newfoundland Federation of Labour. Burke was not pleased with this move and reminded Smallwood that he was being paid to work for the Pulp and Paper Workers International. However, Burke agreed that Joey could organize the NFL on his own time. Smallwood succeeded in bringing unions in Grand Falls and St. John's into the new NFL and was elected its first president. Joey had to abandon the federation due to lack of funds and staff to help him.

A REMARKABLE YEAR

The year 1925 was a memorable year for Joey Smallwood, not only for his success in labour organizing, but also, because he got engaged and married Clare Oates of Carbonear. Joey met Clare while working in Corner Brook and staying at the boarding house of her cousin, a Mrs. Baggs. The boarding house was six miles from Corner Brook and Joey walked the distance twice daily. Clare, the daughter of a Carbonear sea captain, was spending her summer vacation in Corner Brook. It was love at first site. Two weeks later, they became engaged and planned their wedding for the fall.

One day, he was approached by a group of section workers with the Newfoundland Railway who complained that they were already the lowest paid workers with the railway and were going to have their pay reduced even more in November. Joey sympathized with their plight and accepted their request to organize them, the same as he had done for the paper workers in Grand Falls and Corner Brook. This was an especially challenging job for Smallwood to accept because the section workers were spread across Newfoundland.

Smallwood succeeded in his commitment by walking across Newfoundland, signing up members as he went. He started at Port aux Basques and by the time he finished he had walked 780 miles, which included walking branch lines and a side trip to and from Carbonear where he and Clare made arrangements for their wedding. He walked eighteen to twenty miles daily and rested and ate wherever he found the opportunity. He slept outdoors, in shacks and on kitchen couches and floors. By the time he arrived at Avondale, he had recruited 600 members.

During his journey, Joey made it a point to stop and visit Sir Robert Bond at his Whitbourne Residence. He had met Bond once before when he was a reporter for the *Evening Telegram* in 1919. Bond had retired from politics and Joey, as hard as he tried, was unable to persuade him to return.

After bidding farewell to Sir Robert, Joey continued his walk.

It was a stroke of good fortune that Smallwood met three top railway officials at Avondale. They were Herbert Russell, General Manager, whom Joey already knew; Colonel Michael Sullivan, Chairman of the Railway Commission; W. F. Joyce, the railway's Chief Engineer. This encounter led to a discussion about Joey's involvement in organizing the section workers union.

Joey decided, then and there, to advance the cause of his union's members. After discussing the pros and cons of the labour dispute, Joey told them:

> We can close down the railway, gentlemen, because you know the condition of the rails, and the section men know it; and what's more important, the locomotive engineers and firemen on the railway who would not be willing to take his train over any length of track that he knew the section men had not attended to for so much as a week.[1]

Russell, appealing to Smallwood's political views, reminded him that as a socialist he believed in nationalization and the Newfoundland Railway was the biggest example of nationalization in Newfoundland. Joey agreed and emphasized that he wanted the nationalization to succeed. However, he added, "Nobody had the right to expect the railway's success to depend on cutting the pay of the few hundred men who were already the lowest paid group in the system. They knew I had all the trump cards."

The end result of the impromptu meeting was that the decision was made not to cut the section men's salaries as had been planned. Joey celebrated by catching a ride on the freight train from Avondale to St. John's.

---

[1] Joseph R. Smallwood, *I Chose Canada*, 159.

Within a week after arriving in St. John's, Joey started up a weekly newspaper that he called the *Labour Outlook*, which he mailed free of charge to the 600 members of the new union. In that edition, Joey provided a detailed account of his chance meeting with the top railway executives and its successful outcome. The first issue was welcomed by the section-men because of the great news it contained for them.

While operating this newspaper, Joey was offered the job of editor of the *Daily Globe* where he replaced Dr. Harris Mosdell who had been fired by Dick Hibbs, the paper's owner. Hibbs, a friend of Smallwood's from his days at Bishop Feild College, enticed him by offering to send a daily copy of the paper, free of charge, to all 600 members of Joey's union. Joey accepted the deal and ended publication of his labour newspaper.

JOEY GETS POLITICAL

Following the defeat of Sir Richard Squires in 1923, Sir William Coaker withdrew his support and that of the Fishermen's Protective Union from Squires. The two did not speak to each other after that, and it appeared that there was no possibility of reconciliation.

After walking across Newfoundland, and day after day speaking with people from every area of the Island, Joey, already an astute politician, was convinced that Squires could win the next general election, but only if he had the backing of Coaker. He discussed this strategy with Sir Richard and Lady Helena Squires at Cherry Hill Lodge, their summer home at Midstream Manor.[2] Both Richard and Helena had developed a strong dislike for Coaker, and the meeting failed to bring about any positive move towards reconciliation.

---

[2]Cherry Hill Lodge deteriorated over the years and despite efforts to save it, it was allowed to be torn down in the early 1970s. The area is now part of Bowring Park. The Lodge was located in the area of the park now occupied by an open air theatre.

Yet, Smallwood remained determined that the Liberals could only win the next election with the combination of Squires and Coaker. A year or so later, Joey and Clare Smallwood were living in a rented four room flat on Balsam Street in St. John's. Joey once more pursued his idea and invited Sir William Coaker and Sir Richard Squires for a meeting at his flat. It took skilful persuasion on Joey's part to bring about the meeting. After several hours, it had gotten nowhere, and Squires and Coaker left the meeting as far apart as ever.

In late 1926, while at the *Globe*, Joey began compiling a "Who's Who of Newfoundland". However, when the *Globe* went out of business, he sold the project to its owner. He got enough money from the sale to pay his fare to London and the remainder he gave to his wife who returned to live with her parents in Carbonear.

ON PLATFORM WITH BRITISH PRIME MINISTER

Smallwood's passion for politics found an outlet in London. He sought out and attended a district meeting of a prominent Labour MP where he wasted no time in jumping into the fray. Several known communists tried to disrupt the meeting, and when they attacked the MP, Joey jumped to his feet and delivered a lively and effective defence of the incumbent. It was a night Smallwood never forgot. The impression he made as a speaker led to his sharing the political stage, in that same district, with Sir Ramsay Mc Donald, Prime Minister of England.

Joey sought out British parliamentarians to discuss Newfoundland and the condition of its people. One of those, Dr. L. Haden-Guest, a London Labour Party Member of Parliament, invited Joey to write an article for a new Labour Party magazine. Joey did a feature item on Premier Greenfield of Alberta. Haden-Guest became involved in a dispute with his party's leader, J. Ramsay MacDonald, and resigned causing a by-election.

He ran again as an independent constitutional candidate. Joey's appetite for politics drew him into that election on the side of the Labour party's candidate, a George Isaacs, who did get elected. When Prime Minister Ramsay MacDonald visited the London district to campaign for Isaacs, Joey was one of several Labour speakers on the podium to precede MacDonald's address. A relay of public speakers were arranged to keep the crowd's interest while awaiting the arrival of the Prime Minister.

During his stay in London, Joey demonstrated a great appetite for politics and made it a point to attend every political meeting that he could regardless of the political party involved. This included Socialist, Liberal, Tory, and Communist, including the founding of Leon Trotsky's Fourth International. In addition, he attended debates on religion and philosophy and spent a great deal of time in the British House of Commons and visiting the British Museum. In his memoirs he recalled, "If there was an '-ism' to be explained or debated anywhere in London, I tried to get to it–it was like living New York all over again in the English atmosphere."

While in London, he wrote his first book, a biography of Sir William Coaker, written in three days. Lady Helena Squires had moved to London for the winter, and she and Joey often dined together and accompanied each other on long walks. When Coaker visited London, Joey used the opportunity to pursue his effort to bring Coaker and Squires together. He persuaded Lady Squires to invite Coaker for dinner where Smallwood successfully convinced her to arrange a meeting between her husband and Coaker when they returned to Newfoundland.

After returning to Newfoundland, Joey moved to Corner Brook where he started up the tabloid newspaper, the *Humber Herald*. Joey's recent successes in labour organizing made him a force to deal with in Corner Brook. In the months leading up to the 1928 election, he visited every nook and cranny in the district. He visited homes, gave speeches, and

risked his own safety in travelling to some of the more re-
mote communities. He had studied the history of the Liberal Party and concluded, "The Liberal Party, as long as it
lives up to its own tradition, was soundly and constructively
a labour party in almost everything but name."

As the Liberal Party nomination date approached, he received a cable from Squires telling him that Squires himself
had decided to contest the Humber District. According to
Dr. Fred Rowe, a close friend of Smallwood, and one of
Smallwood's longest serving cabinet ministers, Joey was dev-
astated by the message. Rowe said:

> In a conversation with me, he said this was the worst
> blow he had ever received in his political life. But he
> swallowed his bitter disappointment, became Squires'
> campaign manager, and had the vicarious satisfaction
> of seeing Squires elected by an overwhelming majority
> in November 1928.[3]

Smallwood's efforts to unite Coaker and Squires had succeeded and the two came together in 1928 to defeat the Tories twenty-eight to eight seats. Squires appointed Joey to
the post of Justice of the Peace.

THE NEWFOUNDLAND DEPRESSION WAS LONGER!

The Great Depression struck North America in 1929, but
by then Newfoundland was already in a depression since
1918 at the end of WWI when the cod fishery collapsed. Author Richard Gwyn described the terrible hardship that ordinary Newfoundlanders encountered daily. He wrote:

> Men were unemployed, on the average one in three, and
> earned an average of $150 a year. Women were old at
> forty from relentless drudgery and from endless child-
> bearing. Children grew up under-clothed, under-fed and

[3] Frederick W. Rowe, *The Smallwood Era.*

91

ravaged by rickets and beri-beri. Tuberculosis scourged whole families and entire settlements. A 1930 government report noted that kids sometimes fainted in class from hunger. Since education was not compulsory, many of them never went to school at all.[4]

During hard times, many left Newfoundland to seek opportunities and to begin new lives on the mainland. Joey had also tried, but his faith in himself and in Newfoundland, as poverty stricken as it was, brought him back. After succeeding in organizing the two paper workers unions and the section men's union, he was drawn to the plight of the fishermen of the country. He attempted to fill the vacuum created by the decline of the Fishermen's Protective Union. By this time he was married with children. He moved his family to Bonavista where they lived for the next five years.

Smallwood's travels throughout Bonavista Bay organizing fishermen brought him into daily contact with the ordinary Newfoundlander in all parts of the colony. An experience at Tickle Cove left an impression on him for the rest of his life. In his autobiography he recalled:

Once I walked over the hills the five miles to Tickle Cove from Keels, in Bonavista Bay; and as I entered Tickle Cove, a resident full of curiosity, greeted me. After learning who I was and what I was up to (forming branches of Fishermen's Co-operative Union), he suggested that I must be hungry and in need of a meal. He took me to his house and got a meal going for me. He burned "blasty boughs' in the dilapidated kitchen stove to boil some water in an empty biscuit tin, and this he poured into another tin to make tea.

Meanwhile, he had put the square flat lid of the biscuit tin on the other damper of the stove, and on it a thin

---

[4] Richard Gwyn, *Smallwood the Unlikely Revolutionary.*

slab of fatback pork to be rendered. Then he laid a thick slab of dole bread in the rendered pork fat (this was in lieu of the margarine which he didn't have). And my meal was complete: the black, sugarless, milkless tea in a handleless cup with badly chipped drinking edge, the slab of grease soaked brown dole bread on a cracked plate; the whole eaten at a rickety table at which I sat on a flimsy empty wooden box that took the place of a chair. It was his best, and he gave it generously.

Newfoundland clearly was flat on its back, on the rocks, run ashore, bankrupt. With even my amateur dabbling in economics, I could see this, and I could see that the political parties were not dealing with the problem but were arguing about trifles.

Joey formed the Fisherman's Cooperative Union and signed up 8000 members with an annual fee of fifty cents. Even that small amount became impossible for most fishermen who began paying their fees with fish or vegetables. Joey had to abandon his Fishermen's Cooperative due to lack of funds to operate.

Years later, when Newfoundland faced the choice of going back to the politics of old or choosing union with Canada, Smallwood, personally, could have had it much easier and done well for himself by simply throwing in with the merchant cause, but instead he took on the battle for change at a time when the odds were against it.

THE RADIO SHOW THAT MADE JOEY FAMOUS

In 1937 Smallwood began a six-year career in radio as host of *The Barrelman,* a daily fifteen minute radio show that mesmerized Newfoundlanders in every nook and cranny of the island. The show was spawned by his column in the St. John's *Daily News* called *From the Barrelman,* after the masthead lookout on a ship. The success of the column was enough to persuade businessman F.M. O'Leary to sponsor the radio show which quickly became the most successful radio program in Newfoundland. The name Joseph R. Smallwood became a household name throughout the colony, and created a political platform for him that became a major asset when the opportunity presented itself in 1946 after a National Convention was announced.

People were required to pay a license fee to own a radio, and those who could not afford the fee would seek out a neighbour or relative who had one. Following the ringing of a ship's bell:

> '...the announcer would say: "F.M. O'Leary Limited pre-senting The Barrelman in a programme of making New-foundland better known to Newfoundlanders." *The Barrelman* told anecdotes and tales illustrating the ad-mirable attributes of Newfoundlanders through their history.[5]

Dr. Fred Rowe acknowledged Smallwood's days as Barrel-man as a most valuable contribution to his successful battle in bringing Confederation to Newfoundland. He explained:

> Smallwood spent part of every summer travelling around Newfoundland gathering information, and in the process making not only Newfoundland, but Joe Smallwood, better known to Newfoundlanders. Long before he retired from the project, he was probably the best-known living Newfoundlander. What no one fore-saw at the time was that Smallwood had a built-in audi-ence on which he could call if the appropriate occasion arrived.[6]

---

[5] Joseph R. Smallwood, *The Encyclopaedia of Newfoundland and Labrador*, 195, 196.

[6] Dr. Frederick Rowe, *The Smallwood Era*, 1985.

The basis for his first shows came from the volumes of material that he had researched for *The Book of Newfoundland* which he had published earlier. This material grew rapidly when listeners eagerly responded to his invitation to participate by sending in their own stories which he included in his program. His first show was broadcast over the government owned station, VONF in October 1937 and ran Monday to Saturday at 6:45 p.m., until 1943.

Author William Connors reflected on the impact Smallwood had on Newfoundlanders during his days in radio broadcasting in his book *The Best of the Barrelman*. He recalled:

There are those of us who still remember evenings in the years between 1937 and 1943 when we would wait for the sound of a ship's bell—a family sipping tea around the kitchen table, a gathering in the parlour, or a crowding of neighbours in an outport kitchen. Homework was briefly put aside. The rattling and sloshing of dishes ceased. Small children were hushed and shooed outside to play or at the very least stilled. At the clang of a bell struck six times, laughter, chatter, and debate would fall silent. For fifteen minutes, at 6:45 p.m., Monday to Saturday, Newfoundlanders listened to *The Barrelman* – a show 'dedicated to making Newfoundland better known to Newfoundlanders.'

Mike Critch, who covered the National Convention as a journalist, described *The Barrelman Radio Show* as much a part of life in Newfoundland in that era as going to church on Sundays. Critch said:

Everyone looked forward to it, and Joey's stories would be the talk of the town next day. Going into the National Convention his radio experience served him well. He was by far the best known of all the delegates throughout Newfoundland. Joe Smallwood was also a great orator, very persuasive, which was a big plus in the both the National Convention and the referendum battles.[7]

Mike Critch was right! Smallwood's years in journalism, public speaking, and fearlessly facing large and small audiences in Britain, the United States and at home had contributed to his becoming one of the colony's top communicators. As his show grew in popularity, he appealed to the national pride of his fellow countrymen. Joey would broadcast, "There are some people, you know, who don't think much of Newfoundlanders. Let us prove to them that Newfoundlanders have courage, brains, strength, great powers of endurance. Let us show them that Newfoundlanders are witty and smart."[8]

Mike Critch, recalling from among his memories of growing up in old St. John's, gave another example of Joey's pitches to the public. He said:

Joey would tell his radio audience, 'I am trying to show the world that Newfoundlanders are a smart people. I am trying to show that they always succeed, every time that they get a decent chance. Help me to prove this, by sending me cases you know about yourself.' The response was overwhelming and people sent their stories from just about every community in Newfoundland.

William Connors also noted how Joey helped instill a deep pride among Newfoundlanders. He explained:

Smallwood informed us and reminded us about: our magnificent and diverse geography; the successes, and

---

[7]Interview with Mike Critch June 2011. Critch, born and bred in St. John's, worked in public relations with the Americans at Fort Pepperrell, as journalist with the *Daily News*, and best known as the most familiar voice in radio news, when he worked as newsman with VOCM. He is the last surviving journalist who covered the National Convention.
[8]Ibid.

enduring potential of our economy; the chronicle of the great accomplishments, individual and collective in our history; and our ability to imagine, entertain and teach, through story in the tall tales of our folklore.[9]

Joey Raised $65,000 for 'Our Troops'

Through his radio show, Joey launched a fund raising effort which he called The Annual Fish-a-Man Appeal. Each fisherman was invited to donate a salt-dried cod to be sold to the highest bidder. All money raised went to the Newfoundland Patriotic Association which used it to purchase comforts for Newfoundland soldiers fighting overseas.

Leo Moakler, a printer who worked with Joey on his first *Books of Newfoundland* and *The Barrelman*, noted:

Schooners would come in to O'Leary's wharf. (West of the War Memorial) Out would troop the crew, each man carrying his choicest fish and into The Barrelman office to be greeted by an ebullient host. Conversation would fly thick and fast, with every man a story to tell the Barrelman. The fish would pile up in mounds in the office, its pungent though not unpleasant odour hanging around long after the fish had been carried away. The Fish-a man scheme netted $65,000 for the Newfoundland Patriotic Association.[10]

Moakler revealed another interesting ability of Smallwood's. He pointed out:

It never ceased to amaze me how he would get at that portable typewriter, and his two-fingered system, without stopping apparently to think, punch out his five-page double-spaced script. And when finished, with never an erasure or cross-out, fold the manuscript, slip

---

[9] William Connors, *The Barrelman* (1938-1940).
[10] James R. Thoms, Editor, *Call Me Joey* (Harry Cuff Publications).

it in his inside pocket and that evening read it over the air just as it came out of the typewriter.[11]

Aubrey McDonald, once a Dean of Broadcasters and most popular after dinner speaker in St. John's, knew Smallwood during his Barrelman days. He recalled Joey as a voracious reader and said, "He read anything and everything, often devouring two books a night. I remember him having nothing written for his (*Barrelman*) programme twenty minutes before air time, but he'd peck away furiously on his broken-down typewriter, and be on the air at the appointed time. Incredible."[12]

Mike Critch recalled that Smallwood went live on one program without having prepared anything in advance:

Why he broke with his practice of typing his daily show is long forgotten, but what is remembered is that he went on live and devoted his entire fifteen minutes telling the audience, he had nothing prepared, and why. His delivery was so interesting that people felt compelled to listen to his every word. His audience was not disappointed. Many people sent letters telling him how they enjoyed the 'non-show' show, and adding an anecdote or two for him to use in case he ever got caught up in the same situation again.[13]

Critch recalled that a memorable part of witnessing Joey in action in those early days was his remarkable memory. "During the National Convention, he was the expert on Confederation. History, facts and figures poured out of him like an encyclopedia, without even referring to notes," Critch said.

[11] Ibid, 20.
[12] Ibid.
[13] Fitzgerald interview with Mike Critch.

During the period from June 1938 to December 1940, Joey published a newspaper called *The Barrelman* which published his radio show material and sent copies free to every household in Newfoundland, a total of 44,000 copies per issue. That newspaper was renamed *The Newfoundlander,* and after he left, it declined in popularity.[14]

JOEY'S 1940 VISION OF NEWFOUNDLAND IN THE 1990S

In a *Barrelman* broadcast during October 1940, Joey devoted a program to presenting his ideas on what Newfoundland would be like in 1990. The program was based on prophecies made in his book *The New Newfoundland* published in 1931. These included forecasts, made at a time, when Newfoundland had only thirty-three miles of paved road. He predicted that:

> The Railway would be a thing of the past, having been replaced by country wide paved roads that would handle all transportation, both cargo and passenger. Newfoundland will be one of the great summer playgrounds of America, with as many as 50,000 tourists visiting the Island each year. New hotels and road-houses will have been built in various parts of the country. Many tourists will have built summer cottages and camps in Newfoundland. There will be a large university at St. John's. Education will be free and compulsory. Illiteracy will be abolished. There will be technological colleges. Newfoundland literature would be full of creativeness and significance.

As Premier, he did introduce free education, but it had to be dropped due to the government's inability to continue funding it. While he had also predicted that Labrador

---

[14] The newspaper was published by F. M. O'Leary Ltd., and carried the firm's advertising. They also sponsored his radio show.

would be a great mining country of world-wide importance, he also predicted it would have several successful paper mills in operation. As Premier he unsuccessfully attempted to establish a paper mill in Labrador. It is interesting to note that these forecasts had been made at a time when union with Canada was not part of his vision for Newfoundland.

JOEY BEFORE BECOMING A CONFEDERATE!

While working in radio, he also served as editor of *The Express*, a short-lived newspaper founded by Frank O'Leary and several friends in 1941 to draw attention to the shortcomings and failures of Commission of Government and to argue for a new political arrangement with England. In one editorial Smallwood put forward an idea to turn the Commission into a democratic form of government. He explained:

I believe that the people of Newfoundland should seriously study various systems of government within the Empire, and especially the relative merits of Crown Colony administration, which may be adopted, say for five years, in preparation for a resumption of full Dominion status.

The benefits of this to Newfoundland would be that with a partly elected legislature, we would retain direct association with Great Britain, not only during the war, but during the tremendous financial, economic and social upheavals of the post-war period; and also share in Great Britain's new policy as announced last week by Mr. Clement Atlee, in the House of Commons, which would include "no unemployed, plenty of food, no idle rich.

In my opinion, it is absolutely essential that we retain the financial backing of Great Britain, with assistance from the Colonial Development Fund, when available,

British administrative supervision, and her great health and social welfare program.

We in turn would use all our resources to help her win the War, and increase our mutual trade, and as far as possible, do our share by co-operation with Government and in promoting general prosperity in the country.[15]

Smallwood's financial situation had improved due to these new enterprises. He was earning $75 weekly which was more than a school principal and many other professionals were earning in that era. This success enabled him to purchase a second-hand Dodge car and a house on Le-Marchant Road, on the north side, east of the Boncloddy Street intersection in St. John's. Later, as Premier of Newfoundland, Smallwood often credited Frank O'Leary with giving him his first break in life which came with *The Barrelman* radio show.

SMALLWOOD'S POLITICAL SKILLS
EVIDENT MUCH EARLIER

Jim McGrath who knew Joey in his early newspaper and radio days in St. John's and later served as Minister of Health in the first years of the Smallwood administration saw Smallwood's potential long before 1949. McGrath recalled:

His formidable memory, his electric personality, and his vivid and sincere concern for the social and economic underdog were as real then as they are now. I, and others who knew him, never had a moment's doubt of his capacities and political potential. Where our vision failed was that none of us could see where he was to get his starting point, but the platform was there, waiting patiently in the mists of the future, and

---

[15] Jack Fitzgerald, *Battlefront Newfoundland*, 2010.

it was dramatically unveiled in the Confederation campaign.[16]

McGrath observed that Smallwood never lost his interest
in and sympathy for the underprivileged. His long-time colleague and close friend, Dr. Fred Rowe, stated in his book
The Smallwood Era, "With his superb oratorical skills and
matchless memory, Smallwood dominated the Convention."

[16] James R. Thoms, Editor, *Call Me Joey* (Harry Cuff Publications).

CHAPTER 6

Tempers Flare Fists Fly

"Two in particular who frequently faced each other in these emotional verbal combats were Joseph R. Smallwood and Major Peter Cashin. In addition to the contest of ideas, bursts of great oratory, exchanges of wit, and all the tricks of outstanding debaters, these two delegates actually wrestled on the floor in physical combat."

- Jack Fitzgerald

Delegates from all over Newfoundland and Labrador gathered in St. John's in September 1946 to participate in the National Convention which marked a turning point in Newfoundland history and led Newfoundland into the 20th century. The debates were heated and informative. Strong viewpoints began to form. An example of just how deeply held some opinions were took place during a Steering Committee meeting of the Convention. Two in particular who frequently faced each other in these emotional verbal combats were Joseph R. Smallwood (Joey) and Major Peter Cashin. In addition to the contest of ideas, bursts of great oratory, exchanges of wit, and all the tricks of outstanding debaters, these two delegates actually wrestled on the floor in physical combat.

This occurred in mid-October 1947 when John McEvoy, a prominent St. John's lawyer, was filling in as chairman of the Steering Committee. Peter Cashin was seated to his left and Smallwood on his right and the other members were seated around the table. A heated exchange between Cashin and Smallwood led to an enraged Cashin jumping to his feet with clenched fists and rushing around the chairman in order to level a punch at Smallwood. Joey reacted quickly enough to seize Cashin's wrists, just in time to avoid receiving a bloody nose. But the battle was not over yet.

Joey's rapid response threw Cashin off balance, causing him to fall to the floor. When his fists were deflected, the Major had clasped Joey and dragged him to the floor. There the two wrestled and rolled around as the advantage switched from one to the other until the historic political brawl was stopped by others present. When the two pugilists got to their feet, each stared in defiance at the other. Joey, in the controlled style he displayed so often while showing contempt for an opponent, said, "Cashin, I'll show you how scared I am of you," then calmly lit a cigarette, inhaled it and blew smoke into Cashin's face. The Major, furious by the insult, reacted by tossing another punch which Joey ducked and it connected with either Malcolm Hollett or Pierce Fudge.[1]

---

[1] Joseph R. Smallwood, *I Chose Canada*, 227.

While Convention delegates debated and tested each other as they worked their way towards meeting the mandate of the National Convention, Canada's External Affairs Department, through their representative in St. John's, Scott Macdonald, continued to closely monitor the Newfoundland political situation.

In the early weeks of the Convention when Smallwood was the only elected delegate to support Confederation, the High Commissioner described him in a secret memo as a good propagandist but not of sufficient stature to succeed in getting approval to send a delegation to Ottawa to discuss Confederation. As the Convention unfolded, it became apparent to officials in Ottawa that Smallwood had been underestimated.

The Convention moved into high gear and Scott MacDonald informed Ottawa that the general population did not want a return to the conditions that existed prior to 1933. He explained:

> While economic conditions are not conducive to the growth of sentiment in favour of Confederation, general political conditions are not unfavourable. A large section of the electorate is dubious about the wisdom of handing the country back to the control of the local politicians, whose regimes are still associated with the graft, favouritism and wide-spread misery that prevailed under them.[2]

The High Commissioner made it plain to Ottawa that Confederation would have a better chance of winning in a referendum in which the people voted directly than it would if left in the hands of a future legislature. In fact, it was just that widespread distrust of the merchant class, and their control of political life in Responsible Government days that made the referendum process so widely

---

[2]*Documents on Relation Between Canada and Newfoundland*, 296.

supported. Most people felt if the merchants succeeded in having Responsible Government returned, their commitment to consider Confederation or any other alternative would be ignored, as history has shown they did in the past. This time the referendum took that power away from the merchant and professional class and placed it in the hands of the people. The Newfoundland people also felt that a return to Commission of Government could not be justified after a war fought for political freedom and democracy. There was a growing belief that the time had come for Newfoundlanders to escape the bonds of permanent poverty and begin catch up with the rest of North America.

On the other hand, they believed that Confederation with favourable terms would rally both those who are concerned over Newfoundland's ability to stand alone, and genuinely desired an elected government, but feared the old-time abuse of power when the merchants had possessed absolute authority.

The first session of the newly elected Newfoundland National Convention got underway on Wednesday, September 11, 1946. Forty-five delegates had been elected and all were present. The Chairman for the convention was Justice C.J. Fox, KC. The meeting was held in the old House of Assembly chambers in the Colonial Building on Military Road in St. John's. Professor K.C. Wheare of Oxford University, a Rhodes Scholar, was appointed as a constitutional adviser to the Convention.

In addressing this first assembly, Governor Gordon MacDonald instructed the newly elected convention members on their responsibilities to the people. He said:

> You must consider and discuss amongst yourselves as elected representatives of the Newfoundland people, the changes that have taken place in the financial and economic situation of the Island since 1934, and bearing in mind the extent to which the high revenues of recent years have been due to wartime conditions, to

examine the position of the country, and to make recommendations to His Majesty as to possible forms of
future government to be put before the people at a national referendum.[3]

It was never a function of the National Convention alone
to decide on just what form that would be. Their duties lay
in presenting Britain with forms of government favoured by
the Newfoundland people.

BATTLE LINES DRAWN

The battle line drawn between Cashin and Smallwood was
obvious from the beginning. Smallwood was a proclaimed
Confederate while Cashin strongly championed Responsible Government. Not only were the two opponents divided
on the choice of Government Newfoundlanders should
make, but they were sharply divided on its legality. In response to Cashin's condemnation of the Convention as
being "fundamentally illegal," Smallwood described it as
"the most democratic process in all Newfoundland's history."

Cashin condemned the National Convention and National Referendum and charged that it could have avoided
surrendering independence in 1933. He claimed Newfoundland was dragged into the deal to give up Responsible
Government, and he accused Britain of failing to live up to
its commitment to remove Newfoundland's financial difficulties. Cashin argued:

They led us into a valley of poverty and misery, which
condemned seventy thousand of our people to the
whiplash of dole and caused us to experience a period
of national suffering never equalled in the entire life of
our country.[4]

---

[3] Ibid.
[4] PANL 10/A Box 1 File #5.

Cashin condemned the Amulree Report as the first step by Britain in a series of acts of political sabotage towards ridding itself of Newfoundland. He reminded delegates that in 1933, because of Newfoundland's financial difficulties, the colony turned to Great Britain for help. He said:

> We would never have been in financial difficulties at all but for the extraordinary sacrifices made by our, what they term '... backward people and corrupt politicians,' when they voluntarily sacrificed our national credit to the tune of $40 million as our contribution towards the winning of World War 1. It would therefore follow that in 1933 our normal debt would have only been $60 million and this after seventy-eight years of strenuous national existence. Would this indicate our inefficiency in handling our affairs? Does this show incapacity on the part of our public men as the Amulree Report recklessly states?[5]

It is interesting to note that had Newfoundland chosen Confederation before, both the cost of the Railway and financing the war effort would have been borne by the federal government of Canada. There would have been no bankruptcy and no loss of independence.

Cashin urged those elected to the National Convention to accept the fact of its "fundamental illegality." He alleged, "We were specifically and categorically promised the return of Responsible Government upon our becoming self-supporting, which state we reached according to the Dominion's Secretary himself in the year 1941."[6]

---

[5] Ibid.

[6] There had been an improvement in Newfoundland's economic situation due to the war, but economists predicted that this success would not carry on too long after the war. A surplus was being built up towards financing Newfoundland's infrastructure after the war to help improve the colony's economy. Part of the Convention's mandate was to assess the role the war had on Newfoundland's improved financial status.

On December 11, 1945, Prime Minister Atlee announced that the three-year series of reconstruction measures already underway in St. John's would be pushed forward as rapidly as possible. Cashin told the Convention he felt that Atlee had been influenced and abetted by the local Commissioners whose main concern was in saving their positions. He described the Convention and referendum as nothing more than a glorified stall, and asked:

Why not save ourselves and the country all this trouble and expense and wait until three years' time when Mr. Atlee has completed whatever schemes he has in mind for our country. And in the working out of which it is apparently his intention that no Newfoundlander shall have any act, hand or part.

At another point in his address to the Convention, Cashin tackled the credibility of Atlee's promise that the Newfoundland people could choose the form of government they wanted. He said:

As for the opinions or representations, we may present to the Secretary of State for the Dominions, if such do not suit, he can and probably will throw them in the waste paper basket. Our status, despite what may be said to the contrary, is simply that of a mock parliament–a discussion group–a study club.[7]

Cashin said that the Convention's responsibility begins and ends–under present circumstances, the responsibility for Newfoundland's future rests firstly, in the hands of the British Government and secondly, in the hands of our people themselves, provided they are permitted to vote on a plebiscite authorized by Mr. Atlee. The Convention was only a third party to the whole transaction.[8]

[7] PANL 10/A-Box 1 .
[8] Ibid, file #7.

Cashin believed that Britain was only trying to prolong the rule of Commission Government in Newfoundland. His concern in this regard, as history has proven, was not justified. Newfoundlanders by secret ballot chose Confederation over both Responsible Government and Commission of Government.

SMALLWOOD CHALLENGED CASHIN'S VIEWS

While Peter Cashin strongly held that the National Convention was illegal, Joe Smallwood described it as a truly democratic process. He told delegates:

> I want to say that in my view the whole idea, the whole conception of the recent national convention election, of this National Convention, of the National Referendum to follow, constitute in the aggregate, the most thorough democratic procedure in the entire political history of Newfoundland.

> I see in it nothing sinister. I see in it no attempt whatever to railroad this people or this convention. I see, for example, in Professor Wheare, (constitutional expert assigned to advise delegates) if he will excuse my use of his name, I see in his presence and in his appointment nothing whatsoever, as I heard it suggested in public on the air, that he was to be, he, or the person appointed in his place, was to be a Dominion's Office dictator to come to Newfoundland and dominate the convention so that the delegates elected would be merely puppets in his hand.

Smallwood's view on the merits of holding a National Convention followed by a Referendum was echoed a year later by Prime Minister Mackenzie King who said that for the first time in the history of the North American continent, a people has been presented with the task of themselves determining in a referendum the form of government under which they should live. He said that Newfoundlanders will consider more than one form of government and they are by nature an independent and self-reliant race.[9]

To refute Cashin's charge that the National Convention and the referendum had no legal basis, Smallwood referred to the five legal documents related to Newfoundland's surrender of independence in 1933.

In 1946, Newfoundlanders were not well-informed on the details of these documents. The general belief which was fostered by Major Peter Cashin, particularly in his radio show, was that once Newfoundland was self-supporting financially that Responsible Government would be returned. But that was only one of the required conditions specifically stated in the legal documents. Over the following months, Smallwood succeeded in making both conditions known in all areas of the colony.

He began by carefully pointing out that each of the five documents, without exception, stated two conditions upon which Responsible Government would be returned to the people of Newfoundland: (1) Newfoundland be financially self-supporting; and (2) Responsible Government will be returned at the request of the Newfoundland people. The agreement neglected to provide a legal mechanism for the Newfoundland people to make their choice.

Smallwood argued that despite the accusations of "malignancy and nefarious purpose" there was absolutely no evidence to support that the United Kingdom would refuse to submit the matter to the people of Newfoundland. He explained:

> Because, remember we are not the people of Newfoundland, and even our unanimous asking for the restoration of Responsible Government still does not make it the request of the Newfoundland people. That

---

[9]*Documents on Relations Between Canada and Newfoundland*, Vol. 1. King's remarks were made to the Newfoundland Delegation in Ottawa on June 24, 1947.

right of the Newfoundland people to request the restoration of Responsible Government has not been removed. It is still here in the National Referendum, the particular machinery which has been set up through which the people can express that wish or any wish. Through that, the people can in fact, if they wish, request the return of Responsible Government, and there is no evidence that the request of the Newfoundland people would be refused.

After hesitating enough for his point to sink in, Smallwood asked, "If the right of the Newfoundland people to request a return of Responsible Government stands and is still here, where is the lack of democracy in the whole situation? He added that in addition to guaranteeing the people's right to choose Responsible Government, "We have gone further, our right to request anything has been specifically recognized." Smallwood addressing the Convention explained:

At most we can say today is that Newfoundland is self-supporting and the first of the two conditions has been met–quite clearly the other of the two conditions has never been met. The Newfoundland people have never requested the return of Responsible Government to this moment.

Up to this moment where has Britain violated a contract established? They have not! Have they been asked that they do it? They have not. No violations so far. If tomorrow morning, or at 3:00 o'clock tomorrow afternoon, any member of the convention stood in his place and moved that we recommend to the Government of the United Kingdom or to the Secretary of State for the Dominions Office, the restoration of Responsible Government, and the motion is seconded and voted on and carried, if indeed, perhaps not tomorrow morning because it might be impossible by tomorrow to fulfil completely and honestly the terms of reference, but at whatever point a motion is adopted in this Convention by the majority, we request or rather advise the Government of Great Britain that the Convention considers that Responsible Government ought to be restored, in that case, sir, we have not an iota of evidence to lead us to assume that the request would be refused. We have no evidence whatever, despite accusations of malignancy, despite suggestions of nefarious purpose, we have not the slightest evidence that a request of this Convention to the Government of the United Kingdom for the restoration of Responsible Government would be refused by them in the sense that they would refuse to submit it to the people of Newfoundland.

Because remember, we are not the people of Newfoundland, and even our unanimous asking for the restoration of Responsible Government still does not make it the request of the Newfoundland people. Mr. Chairman that right of the Newfoundland people to request the restoration of Responsible Government has not been removed, it is still here in the National Referendum the particular machinery which has been set up through which the people can express that wish or any wish. No evidence–opinions, suggestions, but no evidence whatever that would stand for five minutes in the minds and eyes of any man of thought or intelligence.

Smallwood then tackled Cashin's claim that the Convention and referendum were undemocratic. He pointed out that the process they were following which involved an election, convention and referendum, was the most thoroughly democratic procedure ever put before the people of Newfoundland. Smallwood showed anger over Cashin's attack on the Convention as he continued his response:

This anger has been boiling up in me for weeks and months, and I will not let this afternoon pass without stating my honest view, that I resent this as a Newfoundlander. I resent the suggestion that this convention is rigged, that it is a bluff and a camouflage which involves all of us in the possibility of being a pack of fools, and an insult to the intelligence of every Newfoundland man and woman who cast a vote on the 21st of June, an insult to every man and woman who stood as a candidate. The suggestion that everything is a cod–a plot–a dark design, I resent it on the grounds that it is the most thoroughly democratic procedure in all our history.

Smallwood did have support for his position from several delegates who were not Confederates. Mr. R. Job, St. John's East, a merchant and later a member of the Responsible Government League, deplored Cashin's condemnation of the National Convention and referendum process and supported Smallwood's criticism of Cashin. He stressed the importance of the fishery and said Newfoundland should try to obtain guaranteed markets and tariff concessions from the United, States, Canada and the United Kingdom both on the basis of reciprocity and also in return for the use of Newfoundland's strategic defence position.

Gordon Higgins, also later a Responsible Government League member, supported Smallwood's argument and condemned Cashin's assertion that members of the Convention are "subservient delegates to a Commission-inspired Assembly."[10]

This was the first of the major confrontations between Major Peter Cashin and Joseph R. Smallwood to take place during the National Convention, the referendum and the First General Election in Newfoundland as a province of Canada.

---

[10]Ibid, 287, 288.

CONVENTION GETS DOWN TO BUSINESS

At the beginning of the National Convention Smallwood was on the finance committee that held a private meeting with Ira Wild, Newfoundland's Commissioner of Finance. The Committee learned that Wild was leaving Newfoundland within two weeks and successfully persuaded him to meet with them in a private session. Considering the Convention's mandate, as it related to the country's financial position, Wild was a valuable source of information.

Smallwood was well-prepared for the session. He asked Wild how much Newfoundland needed in order to operate annually and if the needed expenditure could be maintained. Wild replied that Newfoundland needed $23 million yearly to operate and had the ability to do so for three or four years. He noted that a slump in the economy was expected due to loss of export markets after the war. Wild said, "It's anyone's guess when this slump would hit. That figure did not include the amount that would be needed for relief [dole]."

Wild revealed a problem prevalent among fishermen and lumberman that needed special attention. He explained:

> The Government was already giving financial help to the infirm and those unable to work, but we are finding a large number of ex-fishermen and lumbermen between the ages of 55-60 who are not really fit to work. In the past we did not help them, but now we are prepared to do so. It is surprising the heavy incidence of illness among those 55 onwards."[11]

Other countries facing similar problems were developing social networks. Wild pointed out that social programs to cover these problems were in effect in Norway, Ireland, the United Kingdom, the United States, and Canada was studying a plan to aid fishermen and lumbermen. Yet, at no time during Responsible Government in Newfoundland was de-

---

[11] Ibid.

veloping a social network for those in need considered. The Commission of Government was not permitted to undertake any major social spending that would become a recurrent annual expense.

Building an infrastructure after the war was a priority for Newfoundland. Malcolm Hollett, an anti-Confederate, added that Government had a ten-year plan which would cost $100 million to carry out. Newfoundland would be required to use up its surplus first, and then borrow the balance needed. Given these considerations, Hollett asked Wild, "Are we self-supporting?"

Wild, said he believed "we were," but added that was a question for the Convention to explore and answer. He added, "Reconstruction can be delayed until we can see daylight regards to money. This would have achieved little for the average Newfoundland family." Smallwood asked Wild:

> If we have to devise a system of Government, it is not for five or ten years but for fifty or a hundred years. Can Newfoundland, starting five or ten years from now, produce that amount of money annually?[12]

The answer to that question became apparent by the end of the Convention after committees had been sent to London and Ottawa to see what each had to offer Newfoundland after Commission of Government.

NO NEED TO HAVE LOST INDEPENDENCE IN 1933!

Many Newfoundlanders were still critical of the Alderdice Government's decision to surrender Newfoundland's independence in 1933. Long before the National Convention was called, Peter Cashin, and others had been claiming publicly that Newfoundland did not have to follow the political route it pursued in 1933. He told delegates what he had told listeners to his *Voice of Liberty* radio program that the obvious

---

[12] PANL GN 10/A/Box 1/File 8.

and proper course for Newfoundland, under the circumstances was to follow some form of default and in support of this he quoted the writings of Professor A.S.W. Plumptre, University of Toronto, published in the *Canadian Journal of Economics and Political Science.* Cashin said:

> Mr. Plumptre states that on June 15, 1933, the British Government actually paid $10 million to the United States instead of $75,950,000 which her bond called for and this therefore amounted to default on the part of Great Britain herself. Referring to the Newfoundland situation, Mr. Plumptre says, 'It appears on the evidence of the Report (Amulree Report) that Newfoundland had an incontrovertible case for honourable default–a case which was even stronger in its economic aspect than that of Great Britain a few months earlier.' But Newfoundland was not allowed to take advantage of such a course because of the efforts of a combine consisting of the British Government, the Canadian Bankers and our own Prime Minister at that time. The report (Amulree) says that Newfoundland was led to ask for assistance from the United Kingdom. I contend that the word led is not accurate. It should rather read we were mercilessly dragged and driven into the pit prepared for us. And above all, in its significance this report completely ignores the fact that the Alderdice Government with whom they were dealing was acting in callous violation of its election pledges.[13]

Peter Cashin's prestige among responsible men—always low, according to External Affairs records—had been completely destroyed by his unfounded attack on the management of the Newfoundland Savings Bank whom he accused of transferring the Bank's reserves to the Crown Agents in London. Fearing the charges might cause a run on the

[13]Ibid.

bank, the Advisory Board had issued a public statement repudiating the charges which they characterized as "false and unwarranted."[14] However, this did not prevent many people from sharing his view regarding the surrendering of independence in 1933.

By 1946, Peter Cashin was not the only prominent person holding that viewpoint. F. Gordon Bradley, a former leader of the Liberal party who had served as Attorney General in the government of Sir Richard Squires, cast the only vote in the Newfoundland Legislature against repealing the legislation that set up the Commission of Government. Bradley was a law-graduate of Dalhousie University, a man of means and well-respected throughout Newfoundland.

While serving in Newfoundland, C. J. Burchill of Canada's External Affairs Department referred to Bradley in a memo to senior officials in Ottawa:

He was a likeable person, very extreme in his views—not a heavyweight in 1942 but of stature in 1946. Personally, I find myself in considerable agreement with him as I cannot believe it was essential that Newfoundland should have had to do away entirely with its Legislature and revert to a status as low, or perhaps even lower, than that of a Crown Colony.[15]

Following the establishment of the Commission of Government, Bradley accepted the position of magistrate at Grand Falls. He left that position and moved to Bonavista where he became a successful merchant. His public views were described in Newfoundland as "communistic" or "anticapitalistic," even though he was a capitalist himself.

An introductory note in the *Documents on Relations Between Canada and Newfoundland* pinpointed the ten words that

---

[14]*Documents on Relations Between Canada and Newfoundland*, 234 #16.
[15]*Documents on Relations Between Canada and Newfoundland*, Vol. 1, p12.

ultimately made Confederation for Newfoundland possible. Referring to the phrase contained in the promise to return Responsible Government to Newfoundland, the Canadian documents explained:

> That phrase, *"...on request from the people of Newfoundland would be restored,"* sounded so benign but remained at the bottom of a controversy that divided the Convention. The italicized words, seemingly inoffensive and to the point, went almost unnoticed in the debate and discussion which followed in Great Britain and in Newfoundland. Yet, when subjected to analytical scrutiny, it had a simple and clear meaning that not all delegates understood. It suggested that the people of Newfoundland might not want Responsible Government restored, at least in its old form.

> It is instructive, and perhaps ironic, to note that a provision which apparently intended to give greater assurance with regard to prompt restoration of Responsible Government, and nothing else, became in fact a condition which postponed that step and ultimately prevented it.

The British may have been remembering an earlier Newfoundland Government which allowed the merchant class to throttle the Legislature in 1865 and 1866, thus thwarting the Newfoundland people the only time, however naively, they had had the good sense to view Newfoundland's political future in the same terms as, in its wisdom, the British did.

LEGAL RESPONSE TO CASHIN

When Peter Cashin repeatedly, on radio, made a direct challenge to Hon. H.A. Winter, Commissioner of Justice for Newfoundland and later a court judge, to respond to his claim the Convention was unconstitutional, Winter replied with the following letter:

> In Newfoundland, the position is, for all practical purposes, the same as in England. It is true that we have, in a sense, a written constitution. It is contained in the Letters Patent. But these Letters are in no way comparable to the United States Constitution or the British North America Act. They do not say what must be or must not be contained in a Newfoundland statute. As Mr. Justice Fox and Mr. McEvoy have shown, the only ground upon which a Newfoundland statute can be questioned is that of its repugnance to some Imperial statute applicable to Newfoundland. This repugnance is always possible, but only, I think, in some very minor connection and on a point which all those in charge of the bill happen to overlook. And, of course, once the conflict is discovered, it can be removed by a simple amendment.
>
> Now, since nothing in the present Bill can, from its very nature, be repugnant to any Imperial law, it must follow that its validity, once it is formally enacted, is forever established. But to ask whether it is "constitutional" is again quite meaningless. It would be as sensible to ask whether a broomstick or a watermelon is constitutional. The only sensible question is whether it is effective or not.
>
> Major Cashin next says that the Convention is "illegal." Here his position is even worse. Since the Act establishing Convention will be valid it will itself be the law. Hence to say that it is illegal is tantamount to saying that the law is illegal. This may make sense to Mr. Cashin. But not, I am sure, to anyone else.
>
> For the above reasons, I am now in a position to accede to Mr. Cashin's request and to say emphatically and categorically as he has said to the contrary, that the Bill

121

establishing the National Convention is both constitutional and legal; or, if he prefers, that the National Convention itself will be both. I will go further and say that I cannot see how it could be otherwise.[16]

Sgd. H.A.Winter

THE NATIONAL CONVENTION ACT

The terms of the National Convention Act made it perfectly clear what the Convention was established to accomplish. It left no doubt that the Convention, in respect to choice of forms of government, was restricted only to making recommendations as to the possible forms. The Act stated:

It shall be the duty and function of the Convention to consider and discuss among themselves as elected representatives of the people of Newfoundland, the changes that have taken place in the financial and economic situation of the Island since 1934, and, bearing in mind the extent to which the high revenues of recent years have been due to wartime conditions, to examine the position of the country and to make recommendations to His Majesty's Government in the United Kingdom as to possible forms of future government to be put before the people at a national referendum.

---

[16]*Documents Relating to Canada and Newfoundland*, Vol. 2, p238.

CHAPTER 7

Confederation Moves Step Closer

"I am all for having this Convention send a delegation to the United States. I am all for it, if they will receive us and if they are prepared to talk business with us, and willing to have anyone go from this Convention to try. I am as much concerned as many for the standard of our people's lives. I know that our people have never had a square deal, and I know they are not getting a square deal now, I know they are being looted and plundered."

- Joseph R. Smallwood speaking in
the National Convention, 1946

Prime Minister McKenzie King was concerned over the reaction of the existing provinces to Newfoundland joining Canada. He timed the arrival of the Newfoundland Delegation to avoid conflicting with the delicate Dominion-Provincial relations which were being discussed in Ottawa. Canada was most cautious about any concessions to Newfoundland that might upset its Maritime provinces. R.A. Mckay, Secretary of the Special Committee, said that Canada was well-prepared for the discussions. By the time its special committee had completed its work, the Newfoundland file was the biggest file ever assembled by that department.

In 1946, Newfoundland was Canada's eighth largest customer, with annual sales having increased from about $10 million before the war to $40 million in 1946. Even considering the effect of wartime inflation, Canada was left with $25 million in annual trade with Newfoundland. The Canadians projected that Confederation would add $16-$20 million a year to its treasury, due to elimination of tariffs and trade barriers. Also important was the higher purchasing power in Newfoundland made possible by federal payments, made directly to individuals.[1]

Chairman Fox Died and NC Disrupted

After Cyril Fox, chairman of the National Convention, passed away on November 16, 1946, a replacement was appointed. The Commission of Government was called upon to allow the Convention to select its own chairman. On November 23, 1947, the Convention picked F. Gordon Bradley as its new chairman. To do this required an amendment to the National Convention Act in London. This action was needed in order to eliminate the requirement that stated the Convention chairman had to be a judge of the Supreme Court. On December 11th, Bradley chaired the convention that dealt with the debate on committee reports, Gander Airport, broadcasting and tourism.

[1] Ibid.

In the New Year, Smallwood was ready to make his next move in the continuing game of political chess. By February 1947, he had come up with a new plan that would get him the votes he needed to send a delegation to Ottawa.

SMALLWOOD FINDS AN UNLIKELY ALLY

Smallwood's highly developed political instincts served him well in moving his cause forward, and when he sensed political opportunity, he quickly availed of it. He had befriended the Hon. R.B. Job, a prominent Newfoundland merchant and much respected senior statesman among the delegates. Smallwood was well aware of Job's interest in turning to the United States for economic help. He knew that Job wanted to explore the possibilities of a special trade agreement with the United States that would benefit Newfoundland's salt fish industry, which had suffered due to lost markets resulting from the war. Job thought that Newfoundland could extract concessions from the Americans over the ninety-nine year leases for bases given to them during the war. Smallwood recognized an opportunity to make a mutually satisfactory deal with Job.

He approached him privately to encourage him to pursue his effort. Job felt more confidence when Smallwood reminded him that, as delegates, they had the obligation to gather facts on all reasonable alternatives for Newfoundland in a referendum. Job agreed. Neither delegate felt that the Convention, on its own initiative, could approach the United States. At this point, Smallwood asked Job a question for which he already knew the answer, "How can we get the information we need from the United States?" Job's answer was the chance Smallwood was seeking. He said the Convention would have to approach the Commission of Government.

Smallwood then suggested that a motion needed to be made in the Convention seeking Government approval to send a delegation to the United States. When Job asked Smallwood if he was willing to support such a motion, Joey

126

replied that he would even second it, if Job would support his efforts to send a delegation to Ottawa. "Why stop there," Joey asked. "While we are at it, let us also ask for a delegation to go to London. The people have a right to have all the facts put before them." Job agreed and Joey helped draw up the motion.

Despite Joey's belief that the idea would not work, he did not oppose an open discussion on the issue among Convention delegates. He reminded delegates of the solemn duty they had to search out and face the facts while pointing out that, "...it is because we did not do that, we lost Self-Government in 1934. We must face up to them now. Whatever we can get out of the United States, I am all for it." He continued:

> I am all for having this Convention send a delegation to the United States. I am all for it if they will receive us and if they are prepared to talk business with us, and willing to have anyone go from this Convention to try. I am as much concerned as any man for the standard of our people's lives. I know that our people have never had a square deal, and I know they are not getting a square deal now. I know they are being looted and plundered. My own family, who are working class people, my father and mother and my brothers, are being looted. I happen to have been a bit luckier than the rest because a rich uncle educated me, (after looting the people to get the money, and I happened to benefit from part of that looting!). But I am still of the blood and guts of the class I sprung from. If it becomes necessary to tell some of the truth, I am quite prepared to tell it, but I do want the facts to be faced. I don't want this Convention to be led down a blind alley, but let us try with our eyes open, knowing where we are likely to land before we begin.[2]

---

[2] PANL GN/10/A/1 File 10.

Confederation was now a step closer to reality. Smallwood biographer, Richard Gwynn observed:

In the spring of 1948, the cause of Confederation stood exactly where it had in 1869, dragged there by Smallwood's oratory, will power, and effrontery. If history were not to repeat itself, he would have to demonstrate talents for stamina, organization and attention to detail that no one had ever suspected in him. He rose to the challenge.[3]

Smallwood was by this time centre stage in the debate but a thorn in the side of the merchants who heaped scorn on him, but the harder they tried, the more popular he became. Dr. Peter Neary observed:

In short order, he had become the convention's lightning rod, a figure upon whom the Newfoundland conservative social and economic elite would heap their scorn, but whom they would not soon silence. The country at last had a leader in the making but one decidedly not to the taste of the comfortable upper class.[4]

APPROVAL FOR DELEGATIONS TO LONDON AND OTTAWA

As Smallwood anticipated, the Commission of Government turned down the request to send a delegation to the United States because it was a foreign country. The remaining parts of the piggy backed resolution to send two delegations: one to Ottawa, the other to London, was passed by the National Convention on Tuesday, February 4, 1947.

The next challenge for Smallwood was to get elected to the Ottawa delegation. The declared Confederate support-

---

[3] Richard Gwynn, *Smallwood, the Unlikely Revolutionary*.
[4] Peter Neary, *Newfoundland in the North Atlantic* (McGill Press, 1988), 290.

ers saw Smallwood as their most important asset in dealing not only with the general population but also in representing the Convention in Ottawa. They anticipated that the anti-Confederates would do all in their power to block Smallwood being elected to the delegation. Joey saw a way to overcome that hurdle. He recommended that his supporters, in a minority inside the National Convention, give him "plumper" votes. This meant instead of selecting six delegates, they would vote only for Smallwood. The Convention elected delegates for each delegation: one to London;the other to Ottawa. Smallwood's strategy was successful.

Those elected were as follows: (1) The London delegation included: Peter Cashin, Ches Crosbie, Bert Butt, Malcolm Hollett, Pierce Fudge and Bill Keough. (2) The Ottawa delegation included: Gordon Higgins, T. Ashbourne, Reverend L. Burry, Joe Smallwood, Hon. R. B. Job (later replaced by Crummy), and Charles Ballam. As Chairman of the Convention, F. Gordon Bradley was automatically included in both groups. Scott Macdonald was optimistic over the group elected to go to Ottawa. He informed Hon. Louis St. Laurent, Secretary of State:

> This is an excellent delegation, better than the delegation named to the United Kingdom. It is thoroughly representative; a nice balance between St. John's and the outports; and between various religious denominations and various economic classes. All delegates, except Job, are well disposed towards Canada, providing reasonable terms are offered. His opposition, in any case, would not be formidable because of his vulnerability by reason of his wealth and his position as a Water Street merchant.[5]

Macdonald told St. Laurent that the delegation chosen offered the best opportunity Canada has ever had to bring

---

[5] Ibid, 441.

Newfoundland into Confederation. He pointed out:

> Ashbourne was a graduate of Victoria College, the University of Toronto and served in the Canadian Army in WWI. Reverend Bursey, a graduate of Mount Allison University and is well disposed towards Confederation. Bradley, felt the best future for Newfoundland was in union with Canada. He is a fighter and the best speaker in Newfoundland. Joseph R. Smallwood never held public office, has considerable political experience, is aggressive, well-informed and the best organizer and propagandist in the country. With reasonable terms, these two could without others wage a powerful campaign for Confederation.

> Confederation was beaten in 1869 largely because under the credit system then prevailing, men dependent on the merchants for food, were compelled to exercise their franchise under a system of open voting.[6]

The Ottawa delegation had no power to negotiate terms. The Canadian Government had been requested by Newfoundland's Commission of Government to meet with the delegation to provide them with information on what Canada had to offer Newfoundland. At the same time a delegation was elected to visit London and determine what Britain had to offer to the different forms of Government being considered. On March 29, 1947, St. Laurent shared the Government's information regarding Newfoundland with all three opposition parties. He wanted the discussions to proceed as a Government effort rather than a Liberal party effort.

---

[6] Ibid.

THE SCHEDULING OF
DELEGATE TRIPS WORRIED JOEY

The second phase of the National Convention was focussed on the forms of government to be included on the referendum ballot. The National Convention had insisted on the condition that the Ottawa delegation not be allowed to go to Ottawa until the London delegation had returned from the United Kingdom.[7] Anti-Confederates were convinced that if Britain came through with financial assistance to an independent Newfoundland, or to continue support to the Commission of Government for another five years, there would be no need for an Ottawa delegation. Smallwood had similar thoughts, and made a futile attempt to involve Ottawa.

In a secret letter to Louis St. Laurent on March 21, 1947, Smallwood reminded the Minister of the summary of the political situation in Newfoundland he had given to the Minister during his 1946 Ottawa visit. Smallwood stated:

I take the liberty of writing you to repeat what I said then. You may remember that I said that of all the forms of government, Commission of Government was the most popular. The reason for this was that Commission of Government was regarded by most of the people as representing a helping hand from the United Kingdom in case of need. For this reason also the people dreaded the thought of a return of Responsible Government with Dominion status, for this would represent launching out upon the uncertainties of independent national existence. Confederation interested a growing number of people, as witness the fact, amongst other facts, that I had been elected in one constituency on that platform, with the largest majority in the election.

---

[7] Not all supporters of a return to Responsible Government wished that it be permanent. A large part of the movement saw its return as a stepping stone to Confederation or Economic Unions with the United States.

Since then Responsible Government has faded even more, and Commission of Government has lost fairly heavily. Confederation has made very important gains in the public estimate, and is growing rapidly.[8]

Smallwood wanted to make the Minister aware of how easily the chance for Confederation could be lost if London showed a willingness to provide financial assistance. He said:

> It is very important that this delegation come back to Newfoundland with a clear-cut official statement by the British Government of exactly what they are prepared to do for Newfoundland. If the British Government is not willing to do anything for Newfoundland, it will destroy utterly any pro-Commission strength here. The danger is that the British Government will state that they would not welcome an indefinite continuation of Commission of Government but would be prepared to countenance it for a limited period of say five years. This would be fatal. If they state any maximum that maximum is bound to become an idee fixe (fixed idea) in the Newfoundland people. They will seize upon it, for it would have all the mesmerizing effect of a slogan: 'We'll keep Commission of Government for five years and then see what we'll do after.'

This idea would save people all necessity for further thinking. Commission of Government would win by a substantial majority over all other forms.

Smallwood told St. Laurent that a continuation of Commission of Government, even for a fixed period, would be disastrous. He reasoned that it would be unfair to Newfoundland for the British Government to even suggest a continuation of Commission of Government. The Confederate spokesman stated, "The fairest thing they could do would be to say frankly that even under a continued

---

[8] *Document Newfoundland and Canadian*, Vol. 2 part 1. 414,415.

Commission of Government, they could not give us any financial help."

Smallwood's intention in writing St. Laurent was that External Affairs would inform Britain of the real political atmosphere and expectations in Newfoundland. He explained:

If the British Government say that they cannot help us, even under Commission of Government, then it is very doubtful whether the National Convention would feel justified in recommending that Commission Government be submitted to the people in the forthcoming national referendum. In that case, there would be only two forms on the ballot–Responsible Government and Confederation.[9]

St. Laurent was not the only one Smallwood and Bradley approached on this issue. They had brought this concern to the attention of Scott Macdonald around the same time. At that time, Macdonald explained Canada's position:

I made it quite clear to them, however, that the Canadian Government takes the position that relations with the United Kingdom and the future form of Government in Newfoundland are entirely matters for the people of Newfoundland to decide and that I could not undertake to transmit any such request to the Government at Ottawa.[10]

Regardless of the Canadian Government's hands off policy on the issue, Macdonald expressed his personal opinion to Lester B. Pearson which confirmed Smallwood's assessment:

If the Government of the United Kingdom extends financial aid to Newfoundland, there would be no point in considering further the question of encouraging the

---

[9] Ibid.
[10] Ibid, 416.

country to enter the Dominion or even of permitting the question of federation to appear on the ballot.[11]

CASHIN'S LONDON REPORT DISCREDITED

The Responsible Government supporters among the delegation to London returned to Newfoundland disappointed with the outcome of the visit. Peter Cashin alleged that Britain was involved in a conspiracy to sell Newfoundland to Canada. In contrast to the London delegation's cool treatment, he suggested that the delegation to Ottawa would be given a warm welcome.

Despite the uncooperative attitude of the British, Cashin claimed that the delegation succeeded in extracting some beneficial concessions. Included among these were:

• A commitment to cancel the $400,000 (pound Stirling) loan made during WWI.
• A promise to convert the Stirling debt from three percent stock to two and a half percent.
• A promise to use the sinking fund for the purpose of reducing the value of the debt.
• A commitment to assume part of the deficit at Gander.

In a secret letter from Scott Macdonald in St. John's to Lester Pearson in Ottawa on May 20, 1947, Macdonald contradicted Cashin's account of the London meeting. He wrote:

The Governor assures me that not one of these claims is, in fact, valid. All of these matters mentioned have been under discussion with the Commission of Government and there is no reason to think that the representations of the delegation, or of any member of it, had any influence on the British Governor's decision.[12]

---

[11] Ibid, 416, #3.
[12] PANL G10 A/1

Years later, Joe Smallwood described Cashin as the most capable personal campaigner among the anti-Confederates, but unpredictable. He elaborated:

Major Peter Cashin, though nominally of the Responsible Government League, was really a soloist who just didn't like choirs and orchestras, and he always made the League nervous when he was around. Yet, he had more followers in the country than the whole League put together.[13]

Smallwood also noted that Cashin was not beyond plagiarizing. In the late 1920s, as a member of the Newfoundland Legislature, he delivered a speech which was inspiring and well received but was actually plagiarized from William Jennings Bryan's "Cross of Gold" speech made in 1896. Part of that speech read," You shall not press down upon the brow of labour this crown of thorns; you shall not crucify mankind upon a cross of gold."

Cashin did have the ability to touch the emotions of Newfoundlanders. In 1948, he gave his version of the "Cross of Gold Speech" in an inspirational address to the National Convention during debate on the motion to send delegates to London and Ottawa. Cashin told Newfoundlanders:

The people amongst us who love freedom–who love the traditions of this fine land–who cherish our traditions, must prepare themselves to defend those things if they would preserve them. At this very moment the lines of battle are drawn up, and walking amongst us are those whose burning ambition it is to see this country passed into the hands of strangers–to haul down the flag of our fathers and replace it with an alien one, to make the "Ode to Newfoundland" a forgotten thing on the lips of our children and to extinguish the torch which our

[13] Joseph R. Smallwood, *I Chose Canada*, 292.

liberty-loving ancestors cherished for nearly a hundred years. All these things they will try to do under a banner to which they have nailed a dollar sign. But I tell them they will not succeed. Once before in our history our country had to meet such an attack. Once before there were those who sought to destroy her identity and sabotage her liberty, but a far poorer country and a less enlightened people gave them their answer. Shall we of today blessed inhabitants of one of the most solvent countries in the world fail where our fathers triumphed? I feel that I have the endorsement of all right-thinking Newfoundlanders with me when I say that we shall not fail.

BRITISH SYMPATHETIC TO NEWFOUNDLAND

Smallwood saw the position of the anti-Confederates in seeking financial assistance from the United Kingdom as reflecting a lack of knowledge of British history on their part. Historically, he argued, British policy has been to recognize that a self-supporting government did not need financial assistance. Indeed, this was the policy behind Newfoundland's loss of independence in 1933. Now, in 1947, when one of the stipulated conditions in the return of Responsible Government was that the colony be self-supporting, the London delegation was looking for financial support. Smallwood observed:

All this was made abundantly clear to the delegation, and it did not speak well for their knowledge of British history, and the history of Britain's relationships with the colonies and dominions that the response surprised and disappointed them.

Scott Macdonald was not at all surprised by the reception received by the London delegation. He felt Britain was in poor financial shape after the war and referred to, "...its heavy burden of taxation, the immense sacrifices made in the war and the necessity of re-establishing its own economy."

The war had left Britain in such dire economic straits that they were unable to continue to support Newfoundland. However, they favoured Newfoundland joining Canada as being in the best interests of Newfoundland. Canadian interest in union with Newfoundland began after Smallwood's 1946 visit to Ottawa. While both sides tried to influence Newfoundlander's choice, the final decision was entirely in the hands of the Newfoundland voter. One writer compared the situation to that of the federal government and provinces of Canada trying to influence the outcome of the referendum for Quebec independence. They could only go so far, but the final decision was entirely left in the hands of the Quebec voter.

GOING TO OTTAWA

While the anti-Confederates tried to make the most out of their London meeting, the Ottawa delegation were getting ready for their meetings in Ottawa. They had used the time while waiting for the scheduled meetings to prepare themselves for the challenges ahead of them.

The trip to Ottawa had to be made by train because of Bradley's fear of flying. The delegation arrived in Canada's capitol on June 24, 1948, in the middle of one of the hottest summers in years. The meetings dragged out for three months, much longer than anyone had expected, due to Ottawa's committee members being involved in meetings with Canada's provincial representatives to discuss the new tax rental agreement.[14]

---

[14] In 1941 all provinces entered into tax agreements with the Federal Government which gave Ottawa the right to levy and collect direct taxes, including income taxes. The agreements covered the period from 1941 to 1946. In return, to make up for the loss of income, Ottawa compensated the provinces with payments called *tax rental payments*. At the same time Canada was meeting with the Newfoundland Delegation from the National Convention, Ottawa was holding federal-provincial meetings to work out a new *tax-rental* agreement. Due to these meetings, Ottawa was careful not to offer Newfoundland any more or less than it would give to the other nine provinces.

Although Bradley was Chairman of the delegation, most of the work fell on the shoulders of Joey. Bradley found the sweltering heat of Ottawa difficult to function in and was content to let Joey do the work. The Canadians had set up eleven joint committees with Smallwood being the only Newfoundland delegate to serve on all Committees. He had enriched his knowledge of Newfoundland public affairs by doing the same at the National Convention. There he served on four committees and attended the meetings of the other six.

The Canadians were still dealing with the question of whether to give the delegation the actual terms of Confederation or a general statement of what it could offer Newfoundland.

CHAPTER 8

The Man Who Made A Difference

"I felt intuitively that if I could convince the people that
a majority of the Convention members were absolutely refusing
to allow Canada to be asked for the terms and conditions of
Confederation, that if the majority refused to allow Confederation as a possible, or at least conceivable, form of government
to be raised, then the people would become indignant. They
would suspect the motives of the majority, and they would become
curious to know what those terms might be. My every instinct
told me to fling the issue boldly into the Convention and thus
perhaps win the majority. I needed to make Confederation an
issue that would not lie down in the minds of the people."

- Joseph R. Smallwood

On June 21, 1946, after the delegate election, Smallwood realized there was a serious problem among the electorate. The turnout for the election had been low, and the emerging leader of the country was convinced that a means to inspire them and to generate political enthusiasm for the referendum had to be found. He considered that Newfoundlanders were at a critical turning point in their history. The Convention-referendum process was a chance for real input that could have a positive impact on their future; a chance to break from the past and to control their own destiny for the first time in almost 500 years. The importance of the opportunity being presented to Newfoundlanders had not yet registered in the public mind.

At this stage in the battle for Confederation, Joe Smallwood was the only openly declared delegate supporting Confederation. There were others who were hiding their loyalties and were not yet ready to make a public commitment. One of those was F. Gordon Bradley, one of the most prominent and respected delegates participating in the Convention. An indication of the extent to which Smallwood's role in the Confederation battle rapidly grew can be found in the following assessment of a possible leader for the pro-Confederation movement recorded in External Affairs records. The Canadian High Commissioner to Newfoundland, Scott Macdonald, recorded in a memo to Ottawa on October 17, 1946, the following comments:

> Mr. Smallwood, while a good propagandist, is not a very substantial man and a motion sponsored by him asking the Government of the United Kingdom to request the Canadian Government to receive a delegation to discuss the question of union would not command wide support. The best prospect of success would be to have such a motion put forward by the Honourable Gordon Bradley, K.C., member for Bonavista East, the leader of the Liberal Party in the last House

of Assembly, who is generally well disposed toward Confederation but has taken no public stand on the question.[1]

Meanwhile, Joe Smallwood had prepared himself for this battle to a far greater extent than anyone realized. He considered the circumstances that brought Newfoundland to the current political situation. His thoughts went back to 1933 when individuals were overwhelmed by what was happening to their country. Smallwood remembered feeling that:

Newfoundlanders needed a political holiday or armistice. We got it, we got thirteen years of it, but with it we also got what Gordon Bradley had forecasted, 'The death of public sentiment.' Herein lay the source of the lack of enthusiasm for political involvement in 1946.

Newfoundlanders got their holiday from democracy in 1933. Political parties were gone, the politicians had disappeared, and there were no elections, no democracy. The precious independent country, lamented by so many, had actually deteriorated into a dictatorship of six. The people had the right to send their young men off to war to shed blood in defence of freedom, and they generously shared the little wealth they did possess with King and country, but their own country was no longer theirs. Now that they were poised and ready to claim and take control of their country, they were in danger of once again slipping back into the hands of their old political masters.

Smallwood pondered this problem of how to reverse the disappearance of public sentiment and arouse widespread public enthusiasm sufficient for the general population to seize that political power for themselves. The answer to his dilemma came on October 20, 1946, when two Newfound-

[1]*Documents on Relations Between Canada and Newfoundland*, Vol. 2 part 1, p296.

land radio stations began broadcasting the Convention. It was an immediate sensation, yet, not immediately appreciated as such.

Smallwood recognized that people in every part of the country were tuning into their battery-powered radios to hear their future being debated. He commented, "Nothing of this magnitude in communications had ever taken place." In addition to the radio coverage being given to the Convention, the daily newspapers were giving it prime coverage. Joey, in addressing the Convention regarding the broadcasts, explained:

I had tried to visualize what was happening throughout the Island. I was trying to picture in my mind hundreds of families around the Island in hundreds of settlements sitting in their homes listening to the broadcasting of the events of the Convention of that day. That has gone on now for a week and two days, and it has been good stuff, it has been suggested, and to a very small extent, I admit, that it is information programming, but it has to do with public affairs and that is to the good. It seems to me that what is needed in this country is a great revival of interest, public interest in public affairs and I do not mean politics, God forbid.[2]

SURVEYING CONFEDERATE STRENGTH

Early in the Convention, Smallwood realized that for Confederation to have any chance he would have to go over the heads of delegates and appeal to the general population. In the days leading up to the opening of the National Convention, Joey methodically sought out the opinions of other delegates. He kept note of his efforts, carefully sorting out the different allegiances encountered until he knew the strength of the pro-Confederates and the chances of having a motion passed to send a delegation to Ottawa to explore

---

[2] PANL GNA 10/A/1

Canada's views on union with Newfoundland. This information he kept to himself, not even sharing it with F. Gordon
Bradley. Out of the forty-five delegates at the Convention,
Joey knew his motion would be doomed. He could depend
on only sixteen absolute votes. This included several who
would vote for Smallwood's motion but were not prepared
to take a public stance on Confederation until they heard
more debate. Smallwood recorded in his autobiography:

> There it was. In a Convention of forty-five members, I did-
> n't have a chance: I would be voted down, and Confed-
> eration would die there on the floor. It would die, that is,
> if it were left entirely to a vote of the forty-five. But per-
> haps not; not if I could get it out of the hands of the forty-
> five and into the hands of the Newfoundland people.

Edgar Hickman, a Responsible Government delegate for
St. John's East, had two reasons for opposing Smallwood's
motion. All the committee reports from the first phase of
the Convention had not been dealt with, especially the Financial Committee's report, and the delay would discourage the pro-Confederates from strongly attacking the
reports. His second motive was that if the anti-Confederates
did not have enough votes to stop the Confederate move,
then his allies had time to lobby to get anti-Confederates
elected to the Ottawa delegation. At this stage in the Convention, there were uncommitted delegates who wanted to
gather information on all the alternate forms of government available to them before making a decision.[3]

Joey recognized the possibility that his motion might
never get passed. This was a fact that influenced his future
strategy in the Convention. He recalled:

> I felt intuitively that if I could convince the people that
> a majority of the Convention members were absolutely

---

[3]*Documents related to Newfoundland and Labrador*, Vol. 2, part 1.

refusing to allow Canada to be asked for the terms and conditions of Confederation, that if the majority refused to allow Confederation as a possible, or at least conceivable, form of government to be raised, then the people would become indignant. They would suspect the motives of the majority, and they would become curious to know what those terms might be. My every instinct told me to fling the issue boldly into the Convention and thus perhaps win the majority. I needed to make Confederation an issue that would not lie down in the minds of the people.

Smallwood Consulted A Constitutional Expert

Before the debate got underway Smallwood asked Chairman Fox and Professor Wheare, constitutional adviser to the Convention, for their opinions on the National Convention's authority to appoint a delegation to seek terms from the Canadian authorities. Both gentlemen agreed that the Convention had such an authority. Smallwood reasoned that while the Convention was examining Newfoundland's financial position, a simultaneous effort could be underway to find out the terms and conditions that Canada was willing to offer Newfoundland.

On October 28th, he made a controversial move that sparked criticism. He introduced a motion to advise the Commission of Government of the Convention's desire to send a delegation to Ottawa to determine Ottawa's attitude, and the terms and conditions which Ottawa would offer this country. The delegates listened attentively, but they were not his target. Smallwood's real audience were the thousands of people across the country tuned into their radios. The radio audience heard him tell the delegates, "The whole history of Newfoundland is an unbroken story of struggle. The struggle is more uneven now than ever before, and the people view the future with more dread than they did a century ago." At another point in his speech he stated:

> In the North American family, Newfoundland bears the reputation of having the lowest standards of life, of being the least progressive and advanced of the whole family. We love this land. It has a charm that warms our hearts, go where we will; a charm, a magic, a mystical tug on our emotion that never dies. With all her faults, we love her. But a metamorphosis steals over us the moment we cross the border that separates us from other lands. As we leave Newfoundland, our minds undergo a transformation; we expect, and we take for granted, a higher, a more modern, way of life such as it would have seemed ridiculous or even avaricious to expect at home.[4]

He emphasized that he was not asking that the delegation be given the power to conclude any agreement. Smallwood pointed out, "Newfoundlanders needed to be informed of all possible facts having bearing upon the forms of government that might be submitted in a National Referendum." This was a theme he repeated often during the Convention.[5]

He argued that we did have the choice to maintain independent national status but the cost would be to reduce the already poor standard of living even more. In addition, it would be necessary to lower the level of government services. He told the Convention:

> But, if such a decision is made, it must be made by the 60,000 families who would have to do the sacrificing, not the 5,000 families who are confident of getting along pretty well in any case. We have, I say, a perfect right to decide that we will turn away from North Amer-

---

[4] Ibid, 256.
[5] *Documents on Relations Between Canada and Newfoundland*, Canadian External Affairs 1984, part 1-P 308.

ican standards of public services, and condemn ourselves as a people and government deliberately to long
years of struggle to maintain even the little that we
have.[6]

After five days of debate, Smallwood's motion was defeated by a vote of twenty-five to eighteen. At the time, Don
Jamieson was doing a nightly report on VOCM of the day's
proceedings at the National Convention. That night, with
his usual flair, he opened his report with the authoritative
statement, "Confederation was born and died in the National Convention today." Joe Smallwood did not think so.
He had expected a battle and he was up to continuing it.

NOT ALL NEGATIVE REACTION

Gordon Higgins, St. John's East, K.C. (King`s Counsel),
although an anti-Confederate, supported the motion. He
felt that Confederation with Canada was a fact that must be
dealt with by the Convention and the terms must be acquired from Canada sooner or later. Albert Penney of Carbonear, who opposed Confederation, put forward an
amendment to defer Smallwood's motion until later in the
Convention.

Peter Cashin, supported by Malcolm Hollett, argued that
the Convention had no authority to send a delegation to Ottawa. Their argument was based on a reference made by His
Excellency the Governor during the opening of the National
Convention in which he gave the impression that the Convention had no authority to indulge in "roving commissions."

On the third day of debate, October 30th, Kenneth Brown,
an uncommitted delegate from Bonavista, had suffered a
heart attack and collapsed while supporting the Penney
amendment. He was rushed to the General Hospital for
emergency treatment.

---

[6] Joseph R. Smallwood, *I Chose Canada*, 258.

Canada's High Commissioner to Newfoundland, Scott Macdonald, and many of those delegates who favoured Confederation, but were not yet ready to publicly commit themselves, were critical of Smallwood's effort. Macdonald explained:

Smallwood's indiscreet action has dealt a heavy blow to the cause of Confederation here. The motion was deplorably ill-timed, being put forward before reports had been received from various committees' studies of the economic and financial position of the country. It was tactlessly presented, for instead of merely setting forth desirability of securing information on what conditions Canada might be prepared to offer, he made an impassioned plea for Confederation, in the course of which he painted a very dark picture of Newfoundlanders and their position.[7]

There was one prominent bureaucrat with External Affairs who saw the political wisdom in Smallwood's actions. That person was A. E. Connors, Canada's Acting High Commissioner in St. John's, who told Ottawa that Smallwood's motion was a smart move that took the wind out of his opposition. Connors noted:

The whole debate has somewhat gotten out of hand and the pro-Confederates and the anti-Confederates are becoming more clearly defined. No delegate has yet dared oppose the motion in principle but by supporting the amendment concerning the deferment of the motion, these delegates hope to side-track the issue. The motion showed that most all delegates were interested in knowing the terms of Confederation. It was not defeated, just deferred. It revealed some prominent names in favour of union.[8]

[7] *Documents on Relations Between Canada and Newfoundland 1940-1949,* Vol 1.
[8] Ibid.

Smallwood expected the criticism that followed from among observers but was quite pleased with the result of his efforts. He never wavered in his commitment that the New-foundland people had the right to know the attitude of the Canadian Government on the important question of Con-federation before the Convention made its recommenda-tions as to the forms of government to choose from in the referendum vote, or before they decided their destinies at the polls.

His performance, in the long run, turned out to be a plus for the Confederate movement in Newfoundland. It forced pro-Confederate delegates, including F. Gordon Bradley, to take a public stand. It also strengthened the cause of Con-federation among those across the country listening in on radio.

Although his motion was defeated, as Smallwood had ex-pected, he was able to dominate the Convention debate for five consecutive days debating Confederation, all of which were broadcast in full and heard on radios throughout the country. His plan to ignite interest in Confederation among the people had begun and many more feathers were yet to be ruffled.

As Francis Bacon once said, "If there be fuel prepared, it is hard to tell whence the spark shall come that shall set it on fire."

The Convention adjourned after Kenneth Browne had collapsed, and it resumed on November 4th. This was only the beginning of the long battle to bring Newfoundland into the Canadian fold. Radio was to play a major role in that battle.

Dr. Peter Neary, in his book *Newfoundland in the North Atlantic World*, referred to the effectiveness of radio broadcast-ing of the Convention sessions. He observed:

These broadcasts more than anything else drew the at-tention of the Newfoundland public to what was now happening. They also helped create a new generation of Newfoundland political stars, the chief of whom would be Smallwood, a polished performer on the airwaves. In his quarterly report of the 20th of November 1946, W.F. Galgay, the General Manager of the Broadcasting Corporation, noted that its National Convention broadcasts had been the organization's most important work in the period under review. If anything, this understated the importance of what the corporation had done. Not surprisingly, the reports produced by the Convention's committees mixed frustration with hopes and dreams. But in the long run, they may also have had the effect of awakening Newfoundlanders generally to some harsh realities, of giving local politics a badly needed focus, and of providing the prospective leaders of the country with a working agenda.[9]

BEHIND CLOSED DOORS IN OTTAWA

Less than ten days before Smallwood's first motion to send a delegation to Ottawa, the federal cabinet was seriously considering what position to take on the Confederation issue in Newfoundland. They asked for and received a briefing from Scott Macdonald who outlined some of the advantages and disadvantages of union with Newfoundland. The High Commissioner's memo read:

The accession of Newfoundland could increase the Canadian population by 312, 889 people and enlarge the Dominion by 192,000 square miles, an area larger than Finland or Sweden and nearly four times the size of the Maritime Provinces, possessing very considerable mineral and forest resources as well as easy access to the finest fishing grounds in the world. It would solve, permanently, all questions of post-war military and civil aviation rights which are at present terminable after March 31, 1949, on twelve-month notice. It would make

---

[9] Peter Neary, *Newfoundland in the North Atlantic*, 1988.

possible a common jurisdiction over North Atlantic Fisheries. It would, in a sense, give Canada a frontage on the Atlantic and "a window towards Europe," and prevent the Dominion being shut off from the Atlantic as it is, to a considerable extent, from the Pacific. It would add materially to the extent and variety of Canada's resources and enhance her prestige and place in the world.

It should not be overlooked, in considering the advantages of Newfoundland to Canada, that those advantages are a good deal more substantial than in 1895 when the subject was last considered. Newfoundland is larger now by 110,000 square miles of territory commonly regarded at that time, in Canada at least, as forming part of the Canadian Labrador but since awarded to Newfoundland by the decision of the Judicial Committee of the Privy Council.

Moreover, the country is richer by the investment of at least $100 million by Canada and at least $300 million by the United States primarily for defence but much of which was spent on roads, wharfs, telephone lines, warehouses and similar buildings, radio ranges, airfields, the training of Newfoundlanders in various technical jobs etc., and has redounded to the general development of the country.[10]

Accepting Newfoundland into union with Canada presented some obstacles for Canada. Macdonald outlined some of the costs Ottawa needed to accept in order to bring Newfoundland into the Canadian fold. He pointed out:

On any terms that would be acceptable to Newfoundland, the Island would undoubtedly receive from the

---

[10] *Documents on Relations Between Canada and Newfoundland*, Vol 2, Part 1 , 297.

Federal Treasury for many years, a good many millions of dollars per annum more than it would produce in revenue. One important reason for this is that New-foundland, as a Province, would not be able to raise any substantial amounts, as the existing Provinces do, by taxes on gasoline and motor vehicles. Another reason is that virtually the whole cost of administration falls on the central government of the island, there being no general system of local taxation, and only a few munic-ipalities, all of which, except St. John's, have been estab-lished only within the last three years. Newfoundland would thus require a special grant from the Dominion to enable it to carry on as a Province. The crux of the problem of Confederation is to find a formula under which such a grant could be made without appearing to give Newfoundland more favourable terms than the existing Provinces enjoy or which they could make the basis of demands on the federal treasury.

The presence of the US bases on the Island in St. John's, Stephenville and Argentia, on territory on which the leases have still ninety-five years to run, would constitute a limita-tion on Canadian sovereignty. Even if the United States would be prepared to hand over the bases to Canada, which is extremely unlikely, the investment involved amounting to more than $300 million is clearly too large a sum to pay for a free hand in Newfoundland, and Canada could not, in any case, take over the physical task for which the naval base at Argentia was constructed since it would require a power-ful navy disposing of capital ships.[11]

Other negative affects to Newfoundland not joining Canada included:

Newfoundland might even, because it sells so much to countries allied with sterling, be led to attach itself to

---

[11] Ibid, 298.

the sterling bloc and terminate the special position accorded to Canadian financial institutions. If its finances strained it could end up selling Labrador not to Canada, but the United States. Even though all this would not be aimed specifically against Canada, they would react more heavily against Canada then against any other country. If Canada sought to pressure London and Washington to restrict such moves, the obstructive action would arouse hostility in Newfoundland and permanently embitter relations with Canada.

We cannot, indeed, rule out altogether the possibility of a more far-reaching development–political union with the United States. Such a contingency, though unlikely at the moment, could easily take on great importance if the United States Government, influenced by strategic developments, should desire a free hand in Newfoundland and Labrador.[12]

The High Commission noted that failure to encourage Newfoundland to join Canada could pressure Newfoundland in moving towards becoming an independent country. If that were to happen, Newfoundland would be competing against Canada for sale of fish in the United States, Cuba, West Indies, Brazil, Spain, Portugal, Italy, Greece, and others. He argued that such a move could also result in a decrease in Canada's export trade to Newfoundland, as well as the suspension of Canada's permission for its fishing vessels to store fish and salt in bond while operating on the Banks. In addition, Newfoundland might raise the royalties on iron and other minerals to buttress falling revenues. Canada's defence rights in Newfoundland could also be affected.

The quest for diversification would be stimulated involving further development of local manufacturing which already includes paint, nails, rope, tobacco, biscuits, beer and

---

[12] Ibid, 299.

soft drinks, oilskins, clothing, etc., cutting down our market and adding to the vested interests that would be opposed to closer relations with Canada.

The conclusion drawn by the High Commissioner was that it would be in Canada's best interest to encourage Newfoundland's entry into Confederation. However, the condition attached to that recommendation was that union would not result in an annual cost to the Federal Treasury which would be too great a price for the advantages the union would bring, including Canada rounding out its territory on the Atlantic seaboard.

CANADA NEEDED TO DECIDE
IF IT WANTED NEWFOUNDLAND

In response to a request by External Affairs for his opinion on this issue, the High Commissioner to Newfoundland replied that it would be preferable if negotiations on terms and conditions of union were to be carried out with a duly Constituted Government. He added that in the absence of such a Government, the United Kingdom could give approval to a delegation from the National Convention to carry out the negotiations. However, such a delegation would have no authority to enter into a formal agreement with the Government of Canada on terms of union. Macdonald informed External Affairs that such a delegation could carry out more than a purely exploratory mission. He elaborated:

> It could discuss terms of union and provide the Canadian authorities with full information on the economic and financial position of Newfoundland and could undertake to recommend to the Convention an offer of terms if the Government of Canada should decide, on hearing its representations, to make such an offer. It becomes desirable therefore, that the Canadian Government consider carefully whether or not it desires to encourage Newfoundland to join the Dominion as the

Tenth Province, and, if so, how far it is prepared to go in bringing it about.[13]

Prime Minister McKenzie King, speaking in the House of Commons in March 1948, recognized the limited powers given to the National Convention. He said, "The National Convention was only empowered to make recommendations regarding the questions to be included on the referendum ballot, decision on the matter remaining with the United Kingdom government."

DO NOT USE THE WORD "NEWFIE"

On October 30, 1946, after Smallwood had forced fellow pro-Confederates into the open and aroused interest among the population, the Canadian Cabinet decided that, if approached by Newfoundland, it would welcome a delegation from the National Convention to discuss terms for Confederation. Senior bureaucrats, motivated by Macdonald's recommendation, had already begun preparations for the possibility. A cabinet committee of King's most influential ministers was appointed to oversee the operation and to advise the Federal Government. Deputy Prime Minister Louis St. Laurent was appointed its chairman.

In preparation for the arrival of the Newfoundland delegation, Canadian civil servants were coached in the correct pronunciation of the word 'Newfoundland.' Charles J. Burchill, who had been reappointed Canadian High Commissioner to Newfoundland, a position he held in the early 1940s, told Ottawa that the rule is simply to give the syllables the same emphasis as in the word 'understand.' They were warned against calling any resident of the island a 'Newfie.'[14]

---

[13] Ibid, 297.

[14] *Documents on Relations Between Canada and Newfoundland. Department External Affairs,* 1984.

Mike Critich, the only surviving reporter from the National Convention, is shown here at the Delta Hotel celebrating his 90th birthday. He is chatting with journalist and broadcaster Gerry Phelan. In the background is author Jack Fitzgerald. (Mike Critch photo)

A large crowd outside the CLB Armoury in St. John's where Joey Smallwood was speaking. Smallwood was attacked at his first rally here. Among his team of bodyguards was Jack Ford, who, three years before as a prisoner of war, survived the atomic bombing of Nagasaki. (PANL)

Hon. F. Gordon Bradley. Scott Macdonald, Canadian High Commissioner to Newfoundland, said in a memo to External Affairs that Smallwood and Bradley acting on their own were capable of winning the Referendum. (PANL)

Jack Ford, who had survived as a Japanese POW at Nagasaki and there when the atomic bomb was dropped in 1945, a year later served as a body guard for Joe Smallwood at a Confederation Rally held at the CLB Armory on Harvey Road in St. John's. (Submitted Photo)

Joseph R. Smallwood addressing the National Convention at Colonial Building. He dominated the Convention for 34 days in presenting the proposed
terms of union. The entire presentation was broadcast across Newfoundland. (PANL)

Joseph R. Smallwood campaigning for Confederation in 1948. (PANL)

Premier Joseph R. Smallwood and author Jack Fitzgerald taken at Small-wood's Newfoundland Publishing offices on Smallwood's Lane off Portugal Cove Road. Photo was taken just before leaving for Smallwood's last public speaking engagement, which was held at Lawn, before he suffered a stroke in 1984. That trip was made by Smallwood, Tom Barron and Jack Fitzgerald. (Tom Barron Photo)

A riot at Colonial Building in 1932. (PANL)

Brazil Street in St. John's during the Commission of Government Days. The man and horse are from Torbay. They visited the city every Saturday delivering 'splits' to corner stores. Splits were used in coal stoves to get a fire going. The two stores behind the wagon are: Bob Glasco's Meat Market and Williams Shoe store which was replaced later by Jack Kidney's shoe store. (Rick Harris)

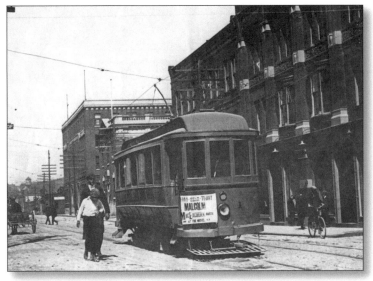

Water Street East during the days when Smallwood attended Bishop Feild College in St. John's. (City of St. John's Archives, PANL)

Smallwood was elected to represent the district of Bonavista Central at the National Convention. (Evening Telegram)

CHAPTER 9

Political Movements Emerge

"As the National Convention progressed and the differences in political positions between Smallwood and Ches Crosbie widened, they maintained a mutual respect for each other's political views. The two held many secret meetings late at night at Smallwood's Duckworth Street office and apartment in the east end of St. John's. At one point, Joey even tutored Crosbie on public speaking, using a broadcasting studio after its nightly sign-off at 11:00 pm."

- Jack Fitzgerald

As the Convention progressed, it became obvious that Newfoundlanders were divided on their choice for a future form
of government. Smallwood was gaining support for union
with Canada and Major Peter Cashin was a strong voice in
favour of returning to Responsible Government. Despite this,
other forces were at work behind the scenes that developed
organized political movements to contest the referendum.
Early in 1947, the League for Responsible Government was
formed to promote the choice of a return to Responsible
Government in the national referendum. A great deal of
planning and organizational work had been carried out before the League was officially announced. The League originated at a secret meeting called by F.M. O'Leary. It included
some of the city's prominent merchants and was held in the
home of Edgar Hickman in St. John's.

Far from the lofty patriotic ideals of fighting to preserve
Newfoundland's independence, the motivating forces that
sparked this political movement were the special interests of
those attending. These were prominent merchants meeting
to take stock of the current political situation and the consequences it would have on them. The one thing upon which
they all agreed was that the continuation of the Commission
of Government or the choice of Confederation both threatened the high profits they were reaping.

The merchants were particularly concerned by the intentions of Governor Gordon McDonald to alter Newfoundland's financial system including the imposition of direct
taxation in place of indirect taxation as Government's main
income source. Scott Macdonald, Canada's Acting High
Commissioner in Newfoundland, in a confidential letter to
the Secretary of State for External Affairs on December 23,
1946, noted in reference to a Commission of Government
study being carried out, "There can be little doubt that the
findings of the Commission will be detrimental to the merchant class. In the event of Confederation, it is obvious that
the whole economic system of the country would be altered."[1]

---

[1]*Documents on Relations Between Canada and Newfoundland*, Vol. 2 part 1, 366-7.

The Hickman meeting concluded that the best way to protect their interests was to form a political movement. The group recognized the need to adopt a cautious approach in organizing this new political party. They were well aware of the anti-merchant class sentiment among the country's fishermen which was why they took time to widen the party's base of support before announcing it. Another factor they recognized was the ordinary Newfoundlander's patriotic loyalty to his country. This fact was the basis for their decision to seek public support by appealing to that loyalty. To help broaden the new movement's political base, they sought support from the labour movement, religious groups and other private citizens.

Included among the founders of the League were: F.M. O'Leary, the Bowring's, the Ayre's and the Bairds. The League also had as its members: Charles F. Hunt, K.C.; Gordon Higgins, K.C.; C.E. Jeffery, editor of the *Evening Telegram* and A.B. Perlin, editor of the *Daily News*. Ches Crosbie, the most popular of the merchants, was prominent in the movement but asked that his membership not be made public.

SMALLWOOD COACHED CROSBIE IN SPEAKING

While Joe Smallwood was a confirmed Confederate going into the National Convention, he did not anticipate that he would emerge three years later as Premier of Newfoundland. The Confederate cause was in its infancy and his primary concern was to get Union with Canada on the ballot paper in the national referendum. Although he was critical of the merchants' influence on Newfoundland history, he admired Ches Crosbie and was willing to support him for the Premier's position if he joined and led the Confederation movement.

In fact, after getting his own campaign plans formulated, he made a special trip from Gander to visit Ches Crosbie in St. John's to persuade him to seek election to the Convention. Joey attended the first in a series of private meetings

Ches Crosbie held at his home on Rennies Mill Road. Crosbie was well-liked, deeply respected and very popular, but a terrible public speaker. Smallwood arranged secretly to use a broadcasting studio after it went off the air at 11:00 p.m. each night to tutor Crosbie in speech-making. He helped him with word pronunciation and wrote speeches, which Crosbie delivered on tape, then he coached Crosbie as the speeches were replayed. In recalling that period, Joey said:

> I was convinced that Crosbie wanted to be Premier and throughout a large part of the life of the convention I did everything in my power to persuade him to support my motion for terms with Canada. I said, 'You don't have to be a Confederate, Ches, to be willing to get the terms, and even after we get the terms, you don't have to support them if you don't like them.'[2]

Later, when the two were clearly political opponents, Ches Crosbie sometimes, late at night, slipped secretly into Smallwood's Duckworth Street office and apartment to talk politics. The building was owned by Crosbie's cousin Dick Chaulker.

MERCHANTS FEARED SMALLWOOD'S EFFORTS

Most candidates elected to the National Convention were publicly uncommitted on particular constitutional remedies. The exceptions were Smallwood, Bonavista Centre, an outspoken advocate of Confederation who polled 89% of the vote in his constituency, and favoured an open debate on other alternatives, and Peter Cashin who supported a return to Responsible Government but felt the National Convention was illegal. The majority of those elected were pro-Responsible Government but some shared Smallwood's advocacy for an open debate on the forms of government open to the people.

---

[2] Joseph R. Smallwood, *I Chose Canada*, 250.

Throughout the term of the National Convention, Smallwood consistently stressed the importance of delegates getting all the facts before making recommendations. Many among the RGL opposed this idea, and there were claims that they intended to recommend only one choice, Responsible Government.

Smallwood acknowledged the important role delegates needed to play in meeting its mandate, but reminded delegates that a bigger choice had to be made by the people of Newfoundland. He said:

> I feel the people are even more entitled to get this information than we are. They need it more than we do. If things went right as they ought to go, before this convention makes its recommendation, the people of Newfoundland will be able to sit down and write just what it is we are going to recommend; hearing the evidence we hear, they will be able to come to the same conclusions we come to.[3]

For almost ten months Joe Smallwood had been conducting a one-man public campaign in favour of Confederation. By the end of 1946, his efforts were causing deep concern among the merchant class. The new Responsible Government League had put together a political program which they hoped would appeal to voters and counter the almost daily press coverage Smallwood was receiving.

High Commissioner Scott Macdonald had socialized with the backroom leaders of the League and was convinced that they represented the business and professional interests of the colony and were not opposed to continuation of Commission of Government as long as the United Kingdom continued to provide financial aid. He informed External Affairs in Ottawa, "They are a fairly strong group but the predominance of Water Street will be sufficient to damn them in the eyes of the fishermen."[4]

---

[3] PANL GN10/A/1

[4] *Documents on Relations between Canada and Newfoundland 1940-1949*, Vol.1, 381.

The League had formed local groups around the country by May 1947 and was holding caucus meetings for Convention delegates to provide information on the procedures and workings of the Convention. To undermine any favourable publicity, which they expected might be generated by the Convention's delegation to Ottawa in June and July, the League booked advanced advertising time on local radio.

There was a general consensus among the founders of the League that Newfoundland could not carry on satisfactorily alone once normal conditions were re-established. Scott Macdonald in a despatch to External Affairs related that Charles Hunt, a prominent lawyer and founding member of the League, represented a different opinion shared by some members of the group. He summarized Hunt's comments:

> Hunt felt that no man can tell whether or not Newfoundland in the years to come will continue to enjoy the present measure of prosperity or something approaching it, and that in any case, the low, or as he called it, the simple standard of living prevailing in the outports offered at least equal opportunities for happiness with the more exacting conditions that are part of the life of an industrial community.[5]

The point missed by many in the Responsible Government movement was that the people of the outports, like many on the Avalon Peninsula, were already weary of the heavy price they paid in the past for the colony's independence, and they now wanted to bring an end to the perennial poverty which was their heritage. They had become open to considering other forms of independence that offered better opportunities in the future for themselves and their families.

---

[5] Ibid, 381.

A. L. Connors of External Affairs in a memo to Ottawa said that he felt it was unlikely that any members of the League intended to actively participate in public affairs but predicted that the group would unite with Major Cashin's group which they did. Cashin became spokesman for the Responsible Government delegates in the Convention and was included in their shadow cabinet.

Another prominent member of the League, Professor Allan Fraser, confided to Scott Macdonald that he found it embarrassing that the principal exponent of Responsible Government in the National Convention was Major Peter Cashin. Fraser said that most of the League was opposed to turning the country over to the old time politicians and said, "It would be a businessman's government."

Fraser was typical of a third faction comprising the Responsible Government League, those who wanted Confederation but felt a return to Responsible Government was necessary first.

Although the League was not intended to be a political party according to Professor Fraser, its choice for Prime Minister would be Ches Crosbie. He explained that Newfoundlanders would favour a man of means because there would be no temptation to feather his own nest.

Ches Crosbie was the most popular and well-liked of all the merchants. He, as well as his brothers George, Jack and Bill were considered as decent compassionate men who treated their employees with respect and kindness.

In an anecdote typical of Ches Crosbie, Mike Critch, then a journalist covering the National Convention, recalled the 1940s story of two Crosbie employees working on the wharves in a pelting rainstorm. Critch said:

> The two left the job site and were standing in a laneway to get some shelter from the rain so they could have a smoke. Crosbie eyed them from an office window and shouted, 'What are you doing?' The reply was, "Sorry sir, we just wanted to have a smoke."

Crosbie beckoned them to come inside. They thought for sure their jobs were gone! When they came face to face with their employer, Crosbie's words brought the two instant relief when he, joked, 'How can you keep a cigarette burning in that rain? Stay inside until you are finished then get on with your work.' That's the kind of man he was, and the ordinary man loved him for it. That is why when he sought election to the National Convention, he topped the polls in St. John's and he had some very competitive opponents.[6]

CONFEDERATE ASSOCIATION

The organization of the Confederate Association came almost a year after the Responsible Government League was formed. It began at a meeting held in the ballroom of the Newfoundland Hotel in St. John's on March 26, 1948. The movement was organized by Smallwood who made sure that F. Gordon Bradley was elected President and himself elected as campaign manager. In recalling the meeting twenty-five years later, Smallwood was not sure whether Bradley made it to town for the meeting or not.[7]

Smallwood chose a small group of bright capable people to assist him as campaign manager. The most valuable of these was Greg Power, who accepted Smallwood's invitation to become assistant campaign manager; Phil Forsey, a school principal; Irving Fogwill; and Harold Horwood with strong connections in the labour movement. According to Smallwood, Horwood was not dependable and "dropped in and out when the spirit moved him." While Horwood succeeded in getting himself elected as House of Assembly

[6] Jack Fitzgerald interviews with Mike Critch, the only surviving reporter of the National Convention, in November and December 2011.

[7] Bradley was among the most respected and prominent of all the delegates elected to the National Convention. He was a lawyer and had served in the cabinet of Sir Richard Squires. Canadian observers were predicting privately that he would become Premier if Newfoundlanders voted for Union with Canada.

Member for Labrador in the province's first election, Small-wood did not choose him for a cabinet position. Horwood did not seek re-election and became one of Smallwood's strongest critics in the 1950s.

JOEY A DICTATOR?

In his 1973 biography, Joey said his opponents often called him a dictator which he said was not true, but that label would have been appropriate for him in the campaign for Confederation. He felt it was necessary for him to play that role for Confederation in order to win the referendum. Smallwood explained, "The cause needed nothing so much as the thinking and work of a strategist and tactician, a co-ordinator, a band leader, an orchestra conductor; but a conductor with more than the usual authority over the orchestra."

That was because the organization was not as large as the public thought, and it could not succeed in gaining support if its members were not delivering the same and consistent message all over the province. As a result, Smallwood wrote and controlled all campaign speeches and succeeded in maintaining unity in the Association. The others under-stood and accepted this strategy. The only exception to Smallwood's speech writing was Sir Leonard Outerbridge, but he agreed to allow the campaign manager to read the speech before it was delivered.[8]

The Confederate Association moved rapidly to bring its message to the general public. This was done by way of a radio broadcast on April 5, 1948, with Smallwood introduc-ing the speaker President F. Gordon Bradley. Some ob-servers were disappointed that Bradley did not use his well-known devastating logic to attack the Economic Union with the United States idea.

He did, however, attack the delegates in Convention for their attempt to keep Confederation off the ballot and

---

[8] Joseph R. Smallwood, *I Chose Canada*.

claimed success for the Confederates petition to London which was signed by 50,000 Newfoundlanders.[9] The large petition was followed soon after with the first issue of the Association's newspaper, the *Confederate*. Sixty-thousand copies were distributed in all areas of the country.[10] Smallwood later said that 90% of the material published in the Confederate was written by himself and Greg Power. The cartoons were done by Jack Boothe of the *Toronto Globe and Mail*, whom Smallwood had become a friend of while visiting Toronto in 1946.

His first campaign headquarters was set up at 158 Water Street in a room behind Bartlett's Barber Shop. The movement had no money to start with and to get the necessary funds, Phil Forsey mortgaged his home. Joey persuaded Muriel Templeman to work for him during the campaign. She lived on Gower Street, and had served as a secretary to Newfoundland Prime Minister Walter Monroe. She served in that position until Smallwood resigned as Premier of Newfoundland in 1972.[11]

CROSBIE'S HIDDEN AGENDA

Smallwood's confidence in the Confederate cause was shaken when Ches Crosbie introduced a new political party into the first Referendum campaign. "The Economic Union With the United States Party," as it was awkwardly called, had no chance of success and was little more than a political strategy to draw support from the Confederate movement to the Responsible Government Party.

Few people knowledgeable in Newfoundland history or American affairs attached any credibility to the new party, but most recognized it could mislead the public and split

---

[9] *Documents on Relations between Canada and Newfoundland*, Vol.2. part 1 p 853

[10] Ibid, 853.

[11] The 1972 election was a controversial tied election that, when the dust settled, ended with a Progressive Conservative win and Frank Moores becoming the first PC Premier of Newfoundland.

the Confederation vote. It was just such a potential that worried Smallwood.

Author Harold Horwood described the new political movement as "a smokescreen." He elaborated:

> The idea had been good for many an election campaign in the past and it proved to be the bait that almost persuaded Newfoundlanders to swallow the Responsible Government hook. It is difficult, in retrospect, that its most eloquent advocates could have been anything other than hypocrites, but, in fact, most of them were slick young men in their twenties, totally ignorant of political history, and they thought they had a brilliant new idea.[12] [13]

The Canadian External Affairs Department through the offices of their High Commissioner in Newfoundland was actively involved in gathering political intelligence on public figures in Newfoundland who were likely to take part in the process to return control of government back to the people of Newfoundland. Ches Crosbie was among those targeted by their information gathering efforts.

Ches Crosbie had topped the poles in the district of St. John's West and was elected as a delegate to the Convention. Although he entered the National Convention as an uncommitted delegate, External Affair files indicate he had a hidden agenda. This point was revealed in a secret memo among Department files and published in 1984. It noted that "Crosbie favoured Responsible Government or Commission of Government, if financially subsidized by Britain, as long as he and his cronies could run it."

---

[12] Harold Horwood, *Joey*, 1989, 116.

[13] Newfoundland had succeeded in negotiating a trade agreement with the United States in 1890, but the combined pressure exerted by Canada, United Kingdom and American fishing interests scuttled the deal. Newfoundland was just not big enough a trading partner with the US to succeed on its own with such a trade agreement.

The 'Catch 22' in the Economic Union strategy was that it required its supporters to vote for the return of Responsible Government first. This split the RGP because many prominent members of the Party were promising to negotiate for Confederation if they were successful.

Canada's External Affairs Department was convinced that had Responsible Government succeeded, history would repeat itself and neither Confederation nor Economic Union would have been sought. Smallwood was certain that if the merchants gained control again through Responsible Government, it would be the end of the Confederation cause. It was that knowledge which inspired Smallwood and his followers in the aggressive campaign they launched.

CANADA'S REACTION

Not only did the Economic Union Party cause concern among Newfoundland pro-Confederates, but Ottawa officials, committed to non-interference in the referendum process, were forced to take extra precautions to protect their position.

Lester B. Pearson, External Affairs and later Prime Minister of Canada, informed Scott Macdonald, in Newfoundland, that the emergence of the Economic Union Party was a serious threat to the Confederation Movement. Pearson advised Macdonald that he should not provide Smallwood's forces with any special materials to enable them to better confront the issue.

In a "Secret and Personal" memo on April 5, 1948, to Macdonald, Pearson reminded him of Canada's commitment "not to interfere" in the election. He wrote:

> The issue, after all, is not immediately union with Canada or union with the United States, but rather union with Canada or restoration of Responsible Government. The Canadian Government has committed itself to complete abstention from influencing the election in any way. Care should therefore be taken to

provide the confederation group with only such material as would be available to anyone requesting it.[14]

LEGALITY OF ECONOMIC UNION QUESTIONED

The Economic Union leaders intended to use the American Bases in Newfoundland as leverage in obtaining trade concessions. Sir Albert Walsh, in an address to the Rotary Club, no doubt caused them some concern when he pointed out that the bases agreement could not be used in any such negotiations.

Foremost in his argument was that the lease deal was made during wartime when Newfoundland was not in a position to defend itself. The deal, agreed to by the Commission of Government, was part of the defence plan for the whole Western Hemisphere. According to Walsh, it was actually:

A large contribution to our own security at a time when the outcome of the war was most uncertain and we were not in a position to undertake our own defence. A proposal that, by unilateral action, this agreement to be reviewed is unusual. It entirely overlooks the wider international questions of inviolability of agreements and assumes willingness on the part of the other party. Moreover, it overlooks the implications of results upon most favoured nation clauses of trade and tariff agreements, conventions and treaties and would introduce a new factor in international arrangements, arising from a change from reciprocal agreements in trade matters.[15]

AMERICAN DIPLOMAT CRITICAL OF NEWFOUNDLANDERS

The Americans were hardly enthusiastic towards the idea. At least that was the impression given to Canadian diplomats

---

[14] *Documents on Relations between Canada and Newfoundland*, Vol. 2 Pt 1. p550.

[15] Dr. Peter Neary, *Newfoundland in the North Atlantic World and* Jack Fitzgerald, *Battlefront Newfoundland*.

by the American Consul General in St. John's, George K. Donald, after learning of R.B. Job's move to have the Convention investigate the possibility of an economic association with the United States in regards to our fishery.[16]

He told Scott Macdonald he felt that, at this stage in the Convention, it appeared that Newfoundlanders felt the world owed them a living. Certainly, the feeling that the strategic advantage Newfoundland gave the United States in WWII was a valuable tool in such negotiations was believed by many delegates, regardless of what form of government they favoured as choices in the Referendum. Recognizing the weakness of this argument, Dr. Raymond Gushue, a Convention delegate, successfully persuaded the fisheries' committee not to send a delegation to Washington.

By the time the referendum took place, the Responsible Government Party was actually a coalition of four groups. These included :

Crosbie's new Economic Union Party which campaigned for a return to Responsible Government first before negotiating Economic Union with the United States.

The Cashin group, Return to Responsible Government as it existed in 1933.

A group (including Dr. Allan Fraser) which wanted a return to Responsible Government as a stepping stone to Confederation.

The F.M. O'Leary group formed at Edgar Hickman's house which simply favored a return of Responsible Government.

In reality, when taking into account that a section of those who voted for Responsible Government were actually Confederates, the pro-Confederate support was much stronger than indicated in the referendum of July 22, 1948.

---

[16] Job's motion preceded Crosbie's launching of the Economic Union with the US Party.

CONFEDERATES WEAK AT FIRST

As hard as Smallwood worked, the Confederate Party did not have the resources to launch an effective countrywide campaign for the first referendum. Smallwood turned to using smart political strategy to offset this weakness. He deliberately set out to organize public meetings only in communities where huge turnouts would be guaranteed. By doing this, he avoided public confrontations and created a bandwagon effect. He also used radio and newspapers to promote his cause.

The anti-Confederates did the opposite which undermined their campaign. Don Jamieson and Geoff Stirling boldly organized an anti-Confederate rally in the Smallwood stronghold of Bay Roberts and were "lucky enough to get out with their skins." The same political blunder was made by Ches Crosbie and Phil Lewis in Grand Bank where pro-Confederate supporters tried to stop them from getting off the wharf. Peter Cashin was shocked to get a cold shoulder in Grand Bank and Bert Butt took the Responsible Government Campaign to Twillingate and had to hide under the church hall.

Author and Professor Peter Neary in his assessment of Smallwood's political success in the battle for Confederation said, "Smallwood was blessed with one of the finest assets of the successful politician; incompetent and myopic opponents who lacked both realistic expectations and political savvy."

Harold Horwood went even farther when he said that the Economic Union leaders were either hypocrites or else they had no knowledge of Newfoundland history, particularly the Bond-Blaine Treaty. Otherwise, they would have known Newfoundland could not match what Canada or Great Britain had to offer the United States in a trade agreement.

A stronger force against any trade agreement with Newfoundland and the United States was the Americans themselves. The American north-east coast fishermen had already started lobbying Congress in opposition to any idea of making such a deal with Newfoundland.

For Crosbie, however, the proposal had the prospect of taking votes away from Smallwood's Confederates in favour of the Responsible Government Party. Smallwood was justifiably alarmed. As Canada investigated and assessed the value of Newfoundland joining in union with it, the prospects of a closer relationship between Newfoundland and the United States was of major concern. The War had just ended and western security was as much on the minds of Canadians as it was in the United States. It boiled down to the fact that if the opportunity of Confederation passed, then an independent Newfoundland could move towards the US, forcing Canada into becoming completely dependent on the Americans for the defence of its Newfoundland border. Such a prospect posed a great threat to Canadian sovereignty.

THE SEEDS FOR ECONOMIC UNION

The idea for special trade agreements with the United States as an alternative for Newfoundlanders was not an original idea. It was as old as the 19th century Bond-Blaine Treaty and was repeated when politically expedient on several occasions thereafter. Perhaps, Newfoundland politicians drew from the much grander plan hatched by the Americans in 1945. At that time, the United States invited the United Nations to discuss the establishing of an international trade organization that would cover a wide area including banking matters, trade practices and tariffs.[17]

In fact, the idea had already advanced in Newfoundland to the point where not only the Commission of Government, but the Board of Trade, Fisheries Board, and the two Newfoundland paper companies were studying the concept. The Commission of Government pointed out to the others that in dealing with other countries and Dominions, Newfoundland, in return, would have to make concessions and give up some advantages also.

---

[17] PANL-GN-10/A Box 1- File 8.

R.B. Job put a twist to the American idea by suggesting
that the colony should negotiate concessions directly from
the Americans based on the grant of land for bases to the
Americans during the recent war. The Newfoundland Commissioner of Finance, Ira Wild, told Job that Newfoundland
would not be able to have direct negotiations with the
Americans, who were insisting on bargaining tariff for tariff.
When Smallwood asked Wild if the proposed organization
had any chance of succeeding, he replied, "The Massachu-
setts's fishing interests were already getting on the warpath."
That, however, did not deter Job from pursuing the idea
later in the convention.

CHAPTER 10

A Knock Down Drag 'em Out Contest!

"If ye don't trust the people, the people won't trust ye!"

- A Church Congregation condemning
anti-Confederates' denial of Confederation
choice appearing on the Referendum Ballot

Attitudes towards Labrador, prior to 1949, in both Canada and Newfoundland were very different from what they are today. The official recognition that Labrador belonged to Newfoundland had been made less than twenty years before the National Convention. Quebecers still questioned the decision and most Newfoundlanders still viewed Labrador more as a territory rather than a part of Newfoundland. The challenges of developing or even estimating the value of Labrador resources in pre-Confederation Newfoundland was a nearly impossible task.

The location of its vast resources remained mostly unknown because no effort had been made to survey and identify them. Few people showed any interest in developing Labrador because of the almost insurmountable problem of getting the resources discovered there to world markets. Labrador had no railway, no roads and no year-long open ports. Newfoundland did not have the financial resources to tackle the job on its own, and its political and financial sectors showed no interest in doing so. It is not surprising under such circumstances that serious consideration had been given on several occasions to selling Labrador.

In 1924, Walter Monroe was elected Prime Minister of Newfoundland after presenting himself to the electorate as a man of business rather than a politician. He promised to put the ship of state back on an even keel.[1] Monroe triggered controversy over the ownership of Labrador when he offered to sell it to Quebec for $15 million. It wasn't the amount that bothered the Quebecois, but the fact that Newfoundland was asserting its ownership of the territory.

The dispute went all the way to the Privy Council for a decision. That decision, which awarded Labrador to Newfoundland, was announced on March 1, 1927. This was a cause for celebration in Newfoundland, but the problem

---

[1] Joseph R. Smallwood, *The Encyclopaedia of Newfoundland and Labrador Vol.1*.

of poverty that hounded Newfoundland until after it became a province prevented it from independently developing Labrador. Smallwood later said:

> The Quebec officials who had rejected this offer were afterwards subjected to rough criticism at the hands of some of their constituents; in Newfoundland, since then, Mr. Monroe has come in for considerable criticism for having been willing to part with Labrador for so paltry a sum. The proffered bargain was likened by Newfoundlanders to the ancient story of Esau selling his birth-right for a 'mess of pottage.'[2]

Again, in the late 1920s, when Newfoundland's financial condition was worsening, many people favoured selling Labrador to wipe out the country's national debt. The price suggested was $110 million which, in addition to paying off the debt, could have helped finance development of the fisheries, highway construction and technological education. In 1931, Smallwood wrote:

> We are in the unfortunate position of not knowing, and having no means at hand of telling, the value of our great dependency. The territory has never been subjected to a survey. It has never been economically measured. A few surveys of particular spots have been made, it is true; but these are only important in so far as they are a hint of what is really in Labrador. These spasmodic surveys only confirm the words of an American observer who visited Labrador as long ago as 1905, Dr. J.S. Johnson then editor of *The Business Man*'s Magazine, who accompanied a Canadian Government Solar Eclipse expedition to North West River that year.

---

[2] Joseph R. Smallwood, *The New Newfoundland* (New York: The MacMillan Comapny,1931) 127.

Wrote Dr. Johnson:

'When the truth about Labrador is known, the silence of centuries will be broken by the pick and hammer and spade of the prospector, the throb of the lumber mill, the pulp and paper mill and the factory.'[3]

Quebec's discontent over the Privy Council decision of 1927 surfaced in the Parliament of Canada during 1943 when Mr. Roy, a Quebec Member of Parliament asked Prime Minister MacKenzie King if his government was intending on negotiating with the British Government to have Labrador returned to Canadian ownership in return for the vast amount of merchandise supplied by Canada to Britain during the war.

In replying to the MP, the Prime Minister recognized Newfoundland's sovereignty over Labrador. He said:

I am inclined to believe the citizens of Newfoundland rather resent the idea that Labrador belongs to the British Government; they regard Labrador as belonging to Newfoundland. Should it come to a question of our Dominion seeking at any time to secure Labrador, I am sure the people of Newfoundland would expect that the negotiations in the first instance would be with their government rather than with the British Government.[4]

Malcolm Macdonald, High Commissioner of Great Britain, when made aware of the references to Labrador in the Canadian Parliament, said he did not feel the matter was of much significance. He felt the move resulted from public awareness of the airfield development going on in Labrador which he noted revived old stories of "...extensive deposits of iron or large reserves of water power." He stated:

---

[3] Ibid.

[4] *Documents on Relations Between Canada and Newfoundland*, Vol. 2 part 1.

There is, I know, a certain amount of discussion going on in the Department of External Affairs about the postwar position of Newfoundland as a whole, and I understand that the original draft put up to the Prime Minister for a reply to Mr. Roy's question was much more detailed and hinted at the possibility of Canada considering the incorporation of Newfoundland in Confederation. I do not think that Canada might absorb Labrador alone, though there is no doubt that the Canadians are anxious to make the most of the concessions which they have acquired at Goose Bay and facilities.[5]

The idea to hang the for sale sign on Labrador came up twice during the days of Responsible Government, and a third time in 1946, when Joe Smallwood made such a suggestion in his historic "Smallwood Letters," published in the *Daily News*.

In 1946, Smallwood saw Labrador as a bargaining chip in negotiations with Canada. In the Smallwood Letters, he pointed out that Newfoundland once considered selling Labrador for $15 million, but, "today we have other ideas about Labrador's value–bigger ideas based on more knowledge of values." He wrote:

Today we feel that whoever buys Labrador for $200 million would be getting a bargain. But, as we ourselves do not have the capital to develop Labrador–our government can't spend $70 or $80 million to put a railway through part of it, for instance–we should, I think, be willing to sell it for $200 million.[6]

He distinguished between selling Labrador for $200 million and his suggestion of selling it as part of a larger more significant deal with great benefits to Newfoundland. These

[5] Ibid, 67.
[6]"The Eleven Smallwood Letters," *Daily News*, March 1946.

benefits, according to Smallwood, were that Newfoundland could raise enough money annually to meet its financial obligations as a province, and Canada would be expected to be more generous in its terms of union with Newfoundland.

Smallwood felt that the transaction would result in increased job opportunities for Newfoundlanders in building the Labrador railway, roads, infrastructure and the development of its resources. Added to these advantages, part of the deal with Canada would be that Newfoundland would retain its fishing rights along the coast of Labrador.

If such a deal was made, Newfoundland would be surrendering all its rights to taxation forever to the Canadian Government. He suggested that Canada would be required to pay Newfoundland annual instalments of $4 million for fifty years.

J. S. Macdonald, Canada's High Commissioner to Newfoundland, told Smallwood he felt it was peculiar that, "...if Newfoundland should wish to enter the Dominion, the Dominion should be expected to buy Labrador from Newfoundland as well and to pay a fancy figure for it."

Joey defended his proposal. He explained that it was reasonable because it was the means by which Canada could provide Newfoundland with enough money annually to provide provincial services. He told Macdonald that a similar transaction had been involved in Saskatchewan's entry into Confederation. In that deal Saskatchewan sold Canada a considerable area of its lands which Canada paid for through annual instalments.

Smallwood's willingness to use Labrador as a bargaining chip was short-lived and he dropped the issue. After becoming Newfoundland's first Premier, Smallwood often claimed that the biggest failure of the Commission of Government was in not carrying out a mineral survey of Newfoundland and Labrador. He said that had they carried out such a project his administration would have been seven years ahead in its efforts to develop the province's resources.[7]

---

[7] Jack Fitzgerald's conversation with Smallwood in 1984.

187

While the Newfoundland delegation was in Ottawa, its efforts were being undermined at home by Responsible Government supporters. An editorial in the *Relations,* a monthly publication in Quebec, reported that Canada was preparing to survey the border between Quebec and Newfoundland. The editorial was repeated in the *Daily News* and broadcast by the *Newfoundland Broadcasting Company.* Opponents of Confederation used the material to suggest that the delegation was bargaining away Labrador.

All members of the Ottawa delegation were upset by these reports and Smallwood, a Confederate, and Gordon Higgins, a Responsible Government League member, approached the Chairman of the Canadian negotiating team with the request that he make a public statement renouncing the claim and point out that the Labrador boundary was not at all part of the negotiations.

The Chairman acknowledged that such a survey was planned to locate on the ground the boundary between Quebec and Newfoundland as defined in the Privy Council decision of 1929. He explained that if Newfoundland joined Canada, the survey would be paid for by the Federal Government. However, if Newfoundland remained independent, Quebec and Newfoundland would pay the costs.

In response to the delegates' request, the Chairman cautioned that if there was any public announcement referring to the status of Labrador, it would only aggravate the situation. He explained, "The Canadian Government accepted, without reservation, the existing situation with respect to Labrador and the sole purpose of the survey under consideration was to locate the boundary on the ground."[8] In fact, Ottawa wanted to "let sleeping dogs lie," otherwise Duplesiss would interfere with the negotiations and spark discontent among the Maritime provinces, as well as Quebec.

---

[8] *Document on Relations Between Canada and Newfoundland,* Vol. 1 p642.

An Attempt to Scuttle Negotiations

For the Newfoundland delegation, it was a long, hot summer in Ottawa. Back home, the anti-Confederate group was sweating it out in St. John's over the best way to discredit the delegation's high propaganda effect.

The weekly broadcasts by the Responsible Government League were not having a great public impact. The first speaker in the series was Charles Hunt, among the most influential persons in Newfoundland. However, according to J.C. Button of External Affairs who monitored the broadcasts, "Hunt introduced nothing new and the general consensus was that it [the broadcast] was disappointing." The Convention had been adjourned when the delegation left, and the Responsible Government League was anxiously awaiting its return to reconvene.

The group was concerned over any advantages that might flow in favour of the Confederates as a result of the long time spent in Ottawa. At first, they tried to short-circuit the delegation by sending a telegraph to Bradley demanding its immediate return. Bradley replied that their work was not yet completed and the delegation would not be returning until it had completed the work it was mandated to carry out.

Not satisfied by the Chairman's answer, the group encouraged other members to join with them in signing a telegraph to the Prime Minister of Canada repudiating the Newfoundland delegation. In addition, they sent a threatening telegraph to Bradley who responded by accusing them of national treachery. Frustrated by their unsuccessful efforts, they came up with a strategy to undermine the delegation by demanding Bradley's resignation as Chairman of the Convention when it resumed.

On October 10, 1947, the anti-Confederates got their opportunity to implement the first part of their plan. On that date, the report of the Ottawa delegation was tabled at the Steering Committee meeting by a motion from Joe Smallwood and seconded by Ches Crosbie.

Cashin, Responsible Government's spokesperson in the Convention, jumped to his feet with a motion that the Convention resolve itself into a Committee of the whole to continue leftover work from the report of the Finance Committee. His plan was to stall the Ottawa delegation's report until he had a chance to collect information of what Canada had offered. If his motion had gone through, the house would have adjourned and the members' daily pay would have stopped. Cashin's motion was defeated.

SPLIT IN ANTI-CONFEDERATE FORCES

By this time, the anti-Confederate group was spilt on strategy. Bert Butt, a prominent member of the group, was chosen to initiate the move to force Bradley out and have him replaced with someone more sympathetic to Responsible Government.

Smallwood and Bradley had already anticipated such a move and entered the chambers ready to counter the Responsible Government League's plan with a move that caused instant pandemonium. Smallwood had prepared a mutually agreed upon resignation speech for Bradley to deliver. When Butt rose to make his motion, Bradley, still chairman, interrupted him saying, "I have something I wish to say." Scott Macdonald described what happened next in his confidential memo to Ottawa:

> He [Bradley] made a very effective speech, expressing in forceful but dignified language his outraged feeling at the conduct of certain members of the Convention and stressed the devastating effect of their bitterly partisan attitude on public confidence in representative institutions in Newfoundland. He completed his remarks saying, '...this convention is now without a chairman,' then stepped down from the Speaker's Chair and left the chambers.[9]

---

[9]*Documents on Relations Between Newfoundland and Canada*, Vol. 2, Part 2, p1515.

Bradley's departure left the chamber in an uproar. Delegates Job, Reverend Burry and others left their chairs in disgust and stormed out of the chambers. Macdonald reported that the majority of delegates shared Bradley's disgust and if he had sought re-election to the chair, he would have easily won. John C. McEvoy, a graduate of Dalhousie Law School, was appointed to replace Bradley by the Governor. Political observers expected him to be much stricter on the rules of debate than his predecessor.

CONFEDERATES A MINORITY

With the new chairman in place, the National Convention reconvened on Thursday, November 20th and Smallwood's responsibility was to present the proposed terms for union to the Convention. He fully realized that there was little chance of Confederation succeeding on the floor of the Convention so he remained committed to his strategy to go over their heads and appeal to the people. He still held a couple of aces: (1) The daily radio broadcast of the Convention which was so popular; (2) The people, right across the country, were following the broadcasts with intense interest.

Smallwood, once again, moved front and centre in the debate and dominated the radio broadcasts, this time for twenty-four consecutive days, all the while feeding the voters with detailed information on the advantages of Confederation over the other choices. It was a Public Relations coup for the Confederates. He recalled:

I had the time of my life explaining and expounding Confederation. The Convention sat in Committee of the Whole, a procedure that leaves a great deal of freedom of debate. I explained every point and attempted to answer every question and every debating speech made against Confederation or any point related to it. I never enjoyed anything more in my life than those twenty-four days of explaining and championing Con-federation.[10]

Mike Critch, who was in the press gallery covering the Na-tional Convention, was amazed at Smallwood's remarkable display of memory and his outstanding speaking and debat-ing skills. Critch was present during the twenty-four days that Joey dominated the debate. He remembered the expe-rience as one of the most impressive displays of a remark-able memory and alertness to detail that he had ever witnessed in his long career as a reporter. He recalled:

When the records of the negotiations arrived from Ot-tawa, there weren't enough copies for everyone. There were two sets of books, black ones and grey ones. The black books told about how the Canadian system worked, and the grey books contained the Terms of Union offered by Canada. While the delegates were waiting on the delivery of more, the debate on the terms offered went ahead. It became Joey's task to present the full report of the Ottawa delegation to the Convention. It took nearly a month to do the job. Smallwood gave up his own two large books to a fellow delegate and then went on to deliver his own presentation from memory. He also fielded a barrage of questions without having to refer to the written documents. I remember occa-sions when delegates raised questions and Joey would answer without hesitation. Then there were the dele-gates who would suggest that the documents did not cover certain issues and Joey, without consulting any sort of reference, would rely on memory to refer them to the exact page in the documents where they would find an answer. All the while, this impressive display was being heard by radio listeners right across the country. There is no doubt he made a great impression on radio

---

[10] Joseph R. Smallwood, *I Chose Canada*, 275, 276.

listeners. Any reporter who covered Joey Smallwood at
any time was impressed with his remarkable memory.[11]

The debate concluded on Thursday, January 15, 1948.
Considering all the time Joey had spent on his feet advanc-
ing and explaining the Confederate cause during live radio
broadcasts, he had racked up thirty-four days of countrywide coverage in the National Convention compared to just
four days by his opponents. Looking back twenty-years later,
he remarked, "They must have been sleeping."

Actually, the anti-Confederates were concerned over what
was unfolding before their eyes but could not agree on a
political move that would stop it without having it backfire
on them. They considered the consequences of allowing
him to continue, or squashing him by cutting off debate.
They feared the second choice most because it might bring
about a rush to public condemnation of both them and
their cause.

Mike Critch pointed out that Joey added to their indeci-
sion by starting the rumour that he was fatigued and near
exhaustion. The opposite of which was true. But the
thought of him collapsing and thereby ending his presentation appeared to be better than stomping on him. This
turned out to be another strategic blunder in the long list
of blunders committed by the anti-Confederates.

The debate was not without its humour and drama. When
Al Penney, Carbonear delegate, addressed the Chairman
and after noting the loudness of Smallwood's voice, asked,
"Is there a way to stop Mr. Smallwood from splitting my
eardrums?"

Joey quickly responded, "Perhaps I have a loud voice but
that is something I can't help. It is part of me. I cannot be
blamed for my loud voice any more than Mr. Penney can
be blamed for his nose!" Unfortunately, Penney did have a
large nose, and the comment stirred up loud laughter.

---

[11] Jack Fitzgerald interview with Mike Critch October 2011.

Among those listening to the debate on radio at home was a delegate, known for his intellect and his heavy drinking, who failed to attend that day's session. He put in a call to the Colonial Building, identified himself and insisted on having the Chairman, John McEvoy, come to the telephone. Feeling it was a matter of urgency, McEvoy took the call and was alarmed to hear a familiar voice tell him, "I'm coming down there to shoot that traitor Smallwood." In minutes, the Chief of Police was informed and a police guard was stationed around the building. Smallwood continued without interruption.

Captain Charles Bailey, a delegate from Trinity South, a veteran and spirited sailor who had sailed the seven seas, commanded the attention of delegates mainly because of his 'folksy' style of speaking. He delivered a rambling, disjointed, statistical type speech but in an authoritative manner and concluded, "Well, Mr. Chairman, there you have it! The people can't say I haven't warned them." After a short pause, greeted by silence, likely because delegates were trying to make sense of what they had just heard, he added a sentence that resulted in a burst of uproarious laughter and hand clapping. He said, "All I can say now is them that gets their arses burned needn't complain if they have to sit on the blisters."

MAIN ARGUMENT OF ANTI-CONFEDERATES

The anti-Confederates repeatedly promoted their main argument against choosing Confederation without first returning to Responsible Government. Journalist Mike Critch recalled that the anti-Confederates hammered away with the argument that Britain, in 1933, had promised Newfoundland that it would restore Responsible Government when the country was again self-supporting. They argued that Newfoundland was now self-supporting and Britain had the legal obligation to restore Responsible Government. It was simple and uncomplicated but a strong case. Critch said that Joey always responded with the Confederate case which was quite effective as far as the radio audiences were concerned.

However, Smallwood reminded delegates and the people of Newfoundland that as convincing as the RGL case sounded, "...it was quite untrue." Smallwood elaborated:

Britain had never said that it would restore Responsible Government to Newfoundland when the country became self-supporting again. What Britain had promised was that Responsible Government would be restored, when Newfoundland became self-supporting again, *on request of the Newfoundland people.* It was short-sighted, to say the least, to omit that second vital condition. It was not enough for the Newfoundland people to request it, for the country itself had to be self-supporting. It was not enough for the county to be self-supporting, for Responsible Government had to be requested by the Newfoundland people. You couldn't have one without the other, but the ardent advocates of Responsible Government chose on every occasion to ignore that vital and thoroughly fair and democratic condition imposed by the British Government.[12]

THE CONVENTION VOTES

Following the debate, the Convention voted on which forms of Government to recommend to Britain for inclusion on the referendum ballot. Higgins, whose style of speaking was compared to that of a law professor delivering a lecture, put forward a motion to include two choices:

Responsible Government as it existed prior to 1934, and Commission of Government. Before this motion was voted on, Bradley put forward an amendment that the Higgins motion would not preclude the Convention recommending other forms of government. Both the

---

[12] PANL GN/10/1A

Higgins motion and Bradley's amendment were unanimously passed.

When the Convention Chairman called for a standing vote on the delegates' choice of Responsible Government or Commission of Government, the Commission of Government failed to get a vote. The standing vote had resulted in twenty-eight for Responsible Government and zero for Commission of Government. Ten delegates abstained and there were seven absented delegates.[13]

Smallwood had supported the Commission of Government in its first two years but, by its seventh year, became an outspoken critic and described it as a Newfoundland tragedy. During a meeting of the Newfoundland National Association in 1941 at the CLB Armoury in St. John's, he said:

The tragedy for Newfoundland consists in having had her representative institutions wrested from her, in having been kept for the past seven years under the paralyzing domination of the British Dominion Offices, with its resultant stagnation of economic enterprise, alarming increase of social poverty and swelling discontent.

Smallwood elaborated on his opinion of the great failure of Commission of Government. He said:

I think that the great unsolved problem of Newfoundland is the economic problem: that of surveying, measuring and developing our natural resources, and/or reorganizing our existing industries. The difference is that now I know that if that problem is to be solved at

---

[13]*Documents on Relations Between Newfoundland and Canada*, Vol. 2. Part 1. p783

all it will be solved only by a Newfoundland Government elected by the Newfoundland people both of whom would have so much to gain as to furnish the incentive of real action.

Smallwood's belief in the prime importance of launching a country-wide survey of Newfoundland's natural resources remained consistent in the years following 1941. As the first Premier of the Province of Newfoundland he included it among his first initiatives towards economic development.

ANTI-CONFEDERATES BLOCK CONFEDERATE SUPPORT

When the motion to add the choice of Confederation to the National Convention's recommendation was made, it was defeated by a vote of twenty-nine to sixteen. Although Confederation had made a considerable showing, the anti-Confederates did not include it on the Convention's recommendation to London. Yet, Commission of Government with zero support was included.

Had the anti-Confederates succeeded in blocking Confederation from the ballot, it would have marked the third time that the merchants had stolen the chance for Confederation from the people. Their actions sparked public cries around the country that "a dictatorship of twenty-nine" had denied the rights of the people of Newfoundland.

There was a general belief that Smallwood had won the debate. Smallwood had followed through on his repeated commitment that the people of Newfoundland had the right to know the facts about the alternate forms of government being considered. Although the Responsible Government League fought hard to keep Confederation from discussion in the National Convention, Smallwood had supported the motions to send delegations to London to explore Responsible Government and to Washington to discuss Economic Union.

When the critical time arrived in the Convention to recommend the forms of government to be included on the
referendum ballot, the anti-Confederates put forward a motion to include Responsible Government and Commission
of Government. Smallwood and his supporters made it
unanimous. His conduct was in keeping with the Confederates policy of sharing information related to all alternative
forms of government with the Newfoundland people and
allowing them to make the final choice.

This was a principle not shared among the anti-Confederates and had cast them in a bad light. Most observers held
that all three forms of Government explored and debated
in the Convention had large numbers of supporters among
the population, and it was an injustice to exclude the choice
of Confederation on the ballot.

The legality of the restriction of choices appears to have
been anticipated and dealt with as early as September 17,
1946, when Nish Jackman, delegate from Bell Island, asked
the Chairman of the National Convention if any form of
government apart from that of Commission of Government
and Responsible Government could be submitted to the
people in the referendum. The Chairman gave a clear response explaining that such a restriction would limit the
choice of the people and would be contrary to the terms of
the Convention Act by which the delegates were governed.[14]

SMALLWOOD SHOWS CONTEMPT
FOR ANTI-CONFEDERATES

Smallwood introduced the motion to include "Confederation with Canada upon the basis submitted to the National
Convention on November 6, 1947, by the Prime Minister of
Canada." In doing so, he complimented, "...the wise states-
manship of the United Kingdom Government in providing
for a referendum in which the people could freely choose
the form of government under which they desire to live."

[14] Ibid, 286.

Smallwood held most of the RGL members in contempt and made no effort to conceal it. In concluding his remarks, he told them they could hate Confederation if they liked but appealed to them to support his motion and let the people decide.[15]

Gordon Higgins' introduction of the divorce issue during the last minutes of the debate was viewed by some observers as a deliberately planned attempt to stir up sectarian feeling among voters. Higgins said that Confederation would increase opportunities for divorce and lead to a position that the Roman Catholic people of Newfoundland could not accept.

Smallwood told several colleagues that Higgins' action was unfortunate for the Confederate cause because people did not understand the complicated situation and, "...it would consequently be difficult to prevent propaganda based on exaggeration and deliberate misrepresentation."

In regards to the defeat of his motion to add Confederation to the ballot, Smallwood said:

> I never felt so sure of winning as I did the day we were defeated in the National Convention. I had never accepted the Convention itself as being representative of the will and sentiment of the people. I had learned too much about the sentiment of the people while living at Gander. But I knew that it was going to be a fierce fight.[16]

Lord Christopher Addison, British Secretary of State for the Dominions, described it as "...intolerable that a group of political aspirants, acting on bitter party lines, should be successful in a manoeuvre which would prevent the matter being submitted to the people of Newfoundland."

---

[15] Ibid, 784.

[16] Joseph R. Smallwood, *I Chose Canada*, 279.

Macdonald, the Canadian High Commissioner in St. John's, in a private memorandum to the Canadian Secretary of State on January 28, 1948, observed:

If the United Kingdom Government is worried about putting Confederation on the ballot because it got only sixteen votes out of forty-five, it should be even more worried about putting retention of Commission of Government on the ballot since it has no support in the Convention at all.[17]

One of the first telegraphed protests against the exclusion of Confederation came from a Protestant minister and signed by the members of his congregation. The telegraph stated, "If ye will not trust the people, the people will not trust ye."[18] The National Convention terminated on January 30, 1948.

The end result of the Convention was a disappointment to Smallwood but certainly no surprise. He wasted little time in launching a nationwide petition, signed by 50,000 voters, to Britain demanding that the choice for Confederation be included on the ballot.

PUBLIC OUTRAGE

There was genuine countrywide anger over the actions of the anti-Confederates. Some who were not Confederates felt the move was unjust and signed the petition. Recalling the reaction later, Smallwood said:

The result was electrifying. The telegrams poured into my flat on Duckworth Street East in a rising flood for days. Some only contained one or two names, some a dozen, some a hundred; a few contained several hundreds of names. I rigged up a table in my living room to

[17]*Documents on Relations between Canada and Newfoundland*, Vol.2, pt.1, p789

[18] Harold Horwood, *Joey*.

accommodate volunteers who came every day and night in relays to make faithful copies of the telegrams, with every name, for the forthcoming campaign. Every few hours I gave out a press statement about the progress of the "crusade," and this fanned the fire, of course.[19]

Instead of sending the actual signed petitions to London, the Governor kept them at Government House and instead sent a detailed report to London regarding the petition and related information. In less than a week, London was considering the petition and diplomatic circles in Ottawa and Washington were made aware of it. It was a key factor in Britain's final decision.[20]

THE ISSUE THAT DIVIDED THE COUNTRY

The legality of negotiating Terms of Union with Canada without first returning Responsible Government to Newfoundland divided; the National Convention and the public. There were a sizeable number of voters and delegates who preferred Confederation but believed that negotiations should not be held until Responsible Government had first been restored. Others held that if the old political masters regained control of the country through Responsible Government, then Confederation would become a dead issue, as it had on two earlier occasions.

Joe Smallwood was among the latter group and he asserted the legality of the referendum as well as his conviction that the will of the people on this issue would be more democratically expressed in a referendum. He explained:

A general election would inevitably involve large numbers of irrelevant issues, personalities, and non-sequiturs, but a simple secret-ballot referendum confined to direct issues would be a far fairer and more realistic

---

[19] Joseph R. Smallwood, *I Chose Canada*, 283
[20] Raymond Blake, *Canadians at Last*.

referral of the matter to the people. As for the terms, there was no finality in those in any case, an elected Responsible Government might obtain better terms, but it would do so after the alternative had been accepted.[21]

J. B. McEvoy, who later succeeded Bradley as Convention Chairman, held a similar view. He argued that the terms that might be offered by Canada would not be greatly different whether Newfoundland waited to have an elected Government to negotiate with the Canadian Government or not.

PRESS REACTION ACROSS CANADA

Most of the press coverage in Canadian newspapers condemned the Convention decision and some saw it as indicative of the historic merchant dominance of Newfoundland. *The Edmonton Journal* suggested "...the whole issue of union with Canada is rapidly becoming a class issue between the business interests in St. John's, and the fishermen and lumbermen in the little coastal settlements."

The *Toronto Star* reported, "The influential merchant class in St. John's are opposed to union," and an editorial expressed doubt "Confederation would carry at present in the face of the organized opposition which would develop." The same position was taken by the *Sydney Post Record* and *Vancouver News Herald* which reported, "Ottawa circles expected the National Convention to turn down Confederation. This body was composed chiefly of businessmen. They are represented as feeling that it would not be desirable to start paying Canadian taxes and to compete with industries in their lines in Canada."

The general trend of editorials across Canada was that the issue of union with Newfoundland was an issue for the Newfoundland people themselves to decide without interference from the outside.[22]

[21] PANL GN/10/1A

[22] *Documents on Relations Between Canada and Newfoundland*, Vol. 2 pt.1 p836.

McKenzie King expressed as much in Parliament when he said, "The question as to their future form of government is, of course, one for the people of Newfoundland alone to decide. Neither the government nor the people of Canada would wish to influence in any way the decision."

CROSBIE'S PETITION

In an attempt to offset the momentum being created by Smallwood's massive petition, Crosbie had introduced a new factor into the political uncertainty. He argued that if Britain was going to put Confederation on the ballot paper, then it should also recognize an Economic Union Party's petition and include it on the ballot as well. In response to this, the United States Consul General told Canada's High Commissioner in Newfoundland, "It [petition favoring Economic Union] would be embarrassing to his government." The Americans were already working through the League of Nations in an effort to develop international trade agreements, but not of the restricted nature being advocated by Crosbie. The American diplomat observed, "The [Crosbie] proposal will not stand careful examination." Strategically, however, it had the potential of bringing out a strong pro-American feeling which the Responsible Government League felt would damage the Confederate campaign.

The Canadian Government when made aware of the situation stood fast on its position not to intervene in the matter, despite some historians claims that Canada was party to a conspiracy to force Confederation upon Newfoundlanders.[23]

BEHIND ENGLAND'S CHOICE TO INCLUDE CONFEDERATION ON BALLOT

England reluctantly included Confederation on the referendum ballot because of their concern that it would result in the election of Commission of Government and set

---

[23] *Documents related to Canada and Newfoundland*, p817

Confederation back for three to five years. Their overriding consideration was the democratic voice of the Newfoundland people—reflected in the referendum, the sixteen districts that elected pro-Confederate delegates and the massive 50,000 signature petition supporting Confederation. Canada's High Commissioner in London explained in a dispatch to Ottawa:

> They (British) think there is a good prospect of COG being endorsed on such a referendum, and there is a better chance of Confederation receiving a really decisive majority vote in say three or five years' time than it is likely to get this year, though they recognize the pro-Confederate leaders are confident they could get a clear majority even in the three way referendum this year. They argue that it will take some time for what they regard as the generous terms of the Canadian offer really to impress the people of Newfoundland and that this impression is likely to grow stronger and deeper as Newfoundland finds its marketing difficulties increase and its budget surplus shrink.[24]

Not only were anti-Confederates angry over the inclusion of Confederation on the referendum ballot, but private Canadian memos show that Canada felt, "Confederation was entering the fight under a considerable handicap." The Canadian High Commissioner J.S. Macdonald in Newfoundland informed Canada's Secretary of State , "Confederation is dealt with in the most unfavourable terms."

The Canadians had hoped that the wording on the ballot would include a qualifying term making it clear that the choice would be based on the terms put forward by the Prime Minister of Canada in 1947 and made known to all Newfoundlanders through the radio broadcast of the National Convention. They believed that the Newfoundland

---

[24]*Documents on Relations between Canada and Newfoundland*, Vol.2, pt 1.

people were well informed on these terms and able to make their own choice.[25] When Gordon Bradley was informed of Britain's failure to include the petition's recommended wording, he came close to quitting and returning to his home in Bonavista.

In Britain, Prime Minister Atlee, after supporting the inclusion of Confederation because "…it was the democratic thing to do," observed that the ballot decided upon gave,"… maximum advantage to the Commission of Government."[26] It was widely believed that the majority of Newfoundlanders recalled only too well the days of Responsible Government before 1934 and would prefer the choice of another five years of Commission of Government. The prospect of this happening was a disappointment to the British.

Although decades later, anti-Confederates accused Britain of manipulating the ballot by adding to the choice of Responsible Government the words, "…as it existed in 1934," that wording was not Britain's idea. The National Convention had passed the motion recommending that choice be on the ballot and Britain complied with its request. The wording of the motion passed in the Newfoundland National Convention was, "Responsible Government as it existed prior to 1934."[27]

Neither the Canadians, the British, nor the Commission of Government members held much confidence in the mostly "illiterate" Newfoundland people being able to choose the best of its options for financial stability.[28] At this point, all sides had underestimated Joe Smallwood.

---

[25] This was the wording put forward in the country wide petition circulated by Smallwood and Bradley.

[26] *Documents on Relations Between Canada and Newfoundland*, Vol. 2 pt. 1 pgs 838,839

[27] Ibid, 840.

[28] Ibid.

CHAPTER 11

The Ballot Debate Shifts to London

"After 450 years of history, it was the little man in the fishing boat, on the farm, or working in the factories, the stores, on the waterfront, etc. who seized control of his country's destiny by exercising his choice, for his future, with the marking of a simple "X" on a ballot paper. That simple "X" ended 450 years of servitude to a system beyond his control."

- Jack Fitzgerald

Smallwood brought the battle for Confederation to the brink, and then had to endure the long tortuous wait for a decision from London. A friend of Smallwood's, Richard (Dick) O'Brien of the *Newfoundland Broadcasting Corporation*, was sent to Government House to get Britain's answer from the Governor, which had been received the same day. Joey waited in the hallway at the radio studio. He was anxious to know the decision before it was broadcast and O'Brien had agreed to give him a sign when he arrived back in the building. Recalling that moment in history, Joey said:

> As Dick arrived, he gave me a broad wink that sent my spirits soaring. The announcement said that the British Government did not think that it would be right to deny the Newfoundland people the opportunity to pronounce on the question of Confederation. We had won! Glory hallelujah![1]

The merchant block supporting Responsible Government had split after the first referendum with the fish merchants coming out in support of Smallwood. Among those was Clyde Lake, owner of Newfoundland's largest salt fish exporting firm, who also contributed financially to the Confederates and Herbert Brooks of Harvey & Company. Also included were some St. John's merchants who recognized the potential for business due to the instant flow of money into the pockets of Newfoundlanders through Canada's Social programs.

The merchants powerful unfluence over most of the Avalon Peninsula had to do with the extent to which they controlled the work force. The merchants owned 130 firms and another seventy-nine manufacturing and related industries which, combined, employed over 8000 people. In pre-Confederation Newfoundland, with few unions, workers had to be cautious about their political choices. This was even more important in the battle for Confederation.

---

[1] Ibid.

The British had been studying Newfoundland's future political prospects since early in the war and believed, "There was no long-run solution of Newfoundland's problems outside Confederation." However, they were aware of Confederation's unpopularity among Newfoundland merchants and expected that the motion to add Confederation to the referendum ballot would be defeated. They even came close to forecasting its defeat with their prediction of a twenty-six to fourteen vote in opposition to it. Yet, the anticipated outcome was still a disappointment to them.

Sir Eric Machtig, of Britain's Commonwealth Relations Office, informed Canada's Secretary of State, "The United Kingdom was in favor of Confederation but concerned that by putting it on the ballot [under the circumstances] Britain might be charged with pushing it, and they wanted to avoid such a position."

He added that the British had no doubt that Commission of Government would be far better than Responsible Government for Newfoundland "...over, say, the next four or five year period." Senior British Bureaucrats were advising the British Prime Minister to include Confederation on the ballot rather than ignore the large segment of the people who favored it. They recommended that Canada should be consulted first because there would be no sense in including this choice if Canada was against it.[2]

The British officially sought Canada's opinion on the matter. In a memo to Canadian External Affairs from London, Canada was informed that the British view was "...it would not be right to deprive the people of Newfoundland of an opportunity of considering the issue at the referendum," and they asked for Canada's position on the matter. Lester Pearson responded with the following secret message to Canada's High Commissioner in London on February 5, 1948. The message read:

---

[2]*Documents on Relations Between Canada and Newfoundland. External Affairs*, Vol.2 part 1, p781.

At the meeting of the Cabinet on February 5th, it was agreed that the Canadian High Commissioner in the United Kingdom be instructed to inform the U.K. authorities that the Canadian government considered that the form of the referendum to be submitted to the people of Newfoundland was a matter solely for decision by the U.K. government; no reference should be made as to any views of the Canadian government as to whether or not confederation should be included and no request for such views should be anticipated.[3]

Prime Minister Atlee thought it would be "unjust and reprehensible" to exclude the Confederation option simply because a majority within the Convention made up of the supporters of Responsible and Commission of Government had voted it down. The National Convention's mandate was limited to gathering information and submitting recommendations on the forms of government to be included and not to deprive the general population of making the final choice by excluding any of the popular choices. The constitutional choice for options to put forward in a referendum rested with the British Government. It acknowledged that Confederation had gathered significant support in the colony and believed it would be unjust not to include it.

The dilemma facing Britain was whether to exercise its constitutional right and add Confederation to the ballot, or omit it in accordance with the Convention vote, knowing that a large segment of the Newfoundland people favored it. By including it, they risked creating the perception that they were forcing it upon Newfoundland.

The British Make a Final Decision

After much consultation and debate, Britain decided to add Confederation to the ballot. In doing so, they felt it would likely set the Confederation cause back for years. On

---

[3] Ibid, 811.

March 2, 1948, P.J. Noel-Baker, Secretary of State for Commonwealth Relations of Great Britain, London, communicated the decision to the Governor of Newfoundland. The message defended the decision:

> The terms offered by the Canadian Government represent, however, the result of long discussion with a body of Newfoundlanders who were elected to the Convention, and the issues involved appear to have been sufficiently clarified to enable the people of Newfoundland to express an opinion as to whether Confederation with Canada would commend itself to them. In these circumstances, and having regard to the number of members of the Convention who supported the inclusion of Confederation with Canada in the ballot paper, His Majesty's Government have come to the conclusion that it would not be right that the people of Newfoundland should be deprived of an opportunity of considering the issue at the referendum and they have, therefore, decided that Confederation with Canada should be included as a third choice on the referendum paper.[4]

The Confederates' request that the wording of the ballot state "Confederation as proposed by the Prime Minister in 1947" was not totally accepted by Britain. The ballot would only use the word 'Confederation.' After learning of this, Gordon Bradley seriously considered resigning.[5] He feared that if the Responsible Government League gained power, it would scuttle the chances for Confederation by appointing partisan delegates to negotiate the terms. The 1947 delegation to Ottawa had been elected by the National Convention and all factions were represented.

---

[4] Ibid, 840.

[5] Bradley had resigned earlier as Chairman of the National Convention. At this time he was threatening to resign as President of the Confederate Association.

In a letter to the *Daily News*, Sir Leonard Outerbridge responded to charges that by adding Confederation to the
ballot, the UK had broken its pledge to Newfoundland. He
emphasized that the final choice of the form of Government was the right of the Newfoundland people and if they
chose Responsible Government, the UK would restore it.
The referendum vote was set for June 3, 1948.

WORLD COURT JUDGE ATTACKED
ECONOMIC UNION PARTY

The Economic Union Party had the rug pulled out from
under it three weeks before the first referendum date by
Judge Manly Hudson, internationally respected American,
serving as Judge of the World Court who was also Professor
of International Law at Harvard University. Judge Hudson
caused a sensation in the election campaign when he said
there was no prospect of economic union or even free trade
between the United States and Newfoundland. John
McEvoy met and interviewed Manly in the United States as
part of his research into the chances of Newfoundland negotiating economic union with the Americans.

The McEvoy report was published in the *Evening Telegram*
on May 8, 1948, and a summary of it was sent to Lester B.
Pearson by Scot Macdonald. That dispatch noted:

> Judge Hudson's memorandum and supporting docu-
> mentation practically swept the ground from under Mr.
> Chesley A. Crosbie's movement to stampede the elec-
> torate with the promise of free trade with the United
> States and demonstrate, as conclusively as anything short
> of a statement from the United States Government itself
> could do, that the promise was a vain and an empty one.
> Seldom if ever in the political history of Newfoundland,
> has an irresponsible promise boomer-anged with such
> effect on the fortunes of the party that put it forward.[6]

---

[6] Ibid, 864.

Judge Hudson pointed out that the relationship between the Americans, British and Canadian Governments was so intimate and important to the U.S. that Washington would not do anything that the other two countries objected to doing. This was the same condition which had sunk the Bond-Blaine Treaty between the U.S. and Newfoundland in 1890. The Judge also said, "It seems to me most improbable that the United States would make any concessions to Newfoundland which would not also be applicable to the Maritime provinces of the Dominion of Canada." The revelation resulted in Crosbie changing his message in the second referendum from one of advocating Economic Union to simply negotiating trade treaties with the Americans.

By this time, the Economic Union Party and the Responsible Government League had merged their resources in a final effort to stop Smallwood. There was also a tendency to consider speakers from each of the parties as speaking for the one. The two supposedly separate parties had already pooled their facilities for publishing pamphlets and other related campaign matters.

When the ballots were counted, no party had obtained a majority vote, but the Confederates had made an impressive show. The third place Commission of Government choice was dropped from the next ballot which was set for July 22, 1948. Smallwood was confident that the Confederates would pick up most of the Commission of Government vote and win the second ballot. However, some prominent Confederates, including Smallwood, were disappointed in the effort put into the campaign by Gordon Bradley. Some even maneuvered to take over the Confederate movement. That story is told in detail in a later chapter.

There were 176,297 names on Newfoundland's voters list. Eighty-five percent, more than 154,000 votes were cast in the first referendum. Many voters not on the list had to be sworn in. This marked a big improvement over the turnout for the election of delegates to the National Convention in June 1946.

The results in the first referendum were:

Responsible Government	69,400	44.551%
Confederation	64,066	41.127%
Commission of Government	22,311	14.322%

OTTAWA'S REACTION TO REFERENDUM

Canadian observers did not expect Responsible Government to do so well in the referendum. There were some in Ottawa and London who, because of the wording on the ballot, believed the final result would be a win for Commission of Government for an additional five years.

Prime Minister Mackenzie King attributed Responsible Government's first place showing to two main factors. The first of these, he said, was religion. King felt the influence of the Roman Catholic Church boosted the Responsible Government cause in many districts. However, he wrote in his diary, "I know of no evidence that the Church exerted any sort of untoward moral pressure on its members with respect to the referendum."

King's second factor was the promise that Responsible Government would endeavour to negotiate Economic Union with the United States. He noted, "This caused many voters to view Responsible Government as a means to an end rather than an end itself."[7]

Following the second referendum, Sir Edward Emerson, Newfoundland's Justice Minister, told Canada's High Commissioner that he felt relieved the vote did not divide the country on religious lines. He said, "The floating vote [mainly Commission of Government Supporters] did not fall any more along religious lines than it had on June 3. In fact, people voted irrespective of religious convictions."

---

[7] Ibid, 889.

SMALLWOOD TAKES CAUSE TO VOTERS

In preparation for the referendum campaign, Smallwood had engaged a business manager to handle the Confederate finances. The business manager went across Canada soliciting contributions to the cause. Main targets in this effort were Canadian business people who could benefit from Newfoundland's union with Canada. This financial campaign was a failure because Canadians believed that the Confederation campaign had ended with its defeat in the National Convention. Smallwood's ability to raise funds for the Confederate cause improved as the campaign progressed. The failure to raise funds in Canada did not deter Smallwood from setting out on an aggressive political campaign.

Smallwood ran the Confederate election campaign but not alone. He recalled, "I had the loyal help of a tiny group: Gregory Power, Philip Forsey, Harold Horwood, Irving Fogwill, and a few others. He launched the *Confederate* newspaper using funds which Phil Forsey raised by taking out a mortgage on his home with the Bank of Nova Scotia. Greg Power became his closest confidant. Smallwood recalled:

> I persuaded Gregory Power to leave his family at Dunville and come to St. John's to join me. He was as eager to come as I was to have him; and from the moment he arrived, we were inseparable and saw eye to eye at every point of battle. Phil Forsey was teaching at Prince of Wales College and could get in only after school and at night.

Although Harold Horwood claimed to be one of the top four in the Confederate movement, Joey said that Horwood's interest "...fluctuated, and he would drop in as the spirit moved him." Historians have described the *Confederate* newspaper as being far superior to the *Independent* published by the Responsible Government League.

As mentioned earlier, Smallwood began with headquarters at 158 Water Street, behind Bartlett's Barbershop, using a limited area suitable for office space. He enticed Muriel Templeman, who had served as secretary to Walter Monroe, an early Newfoundland Prime Minister, out of retirement to become his secretary. She remained with him until his defeat in 1972.

When the Confederates rented the CLB Armory on Harvey Road in St. John's for a giant rally, it angered some anti-Confederates. Among those was Peter Outerbridge, who was criticized himself after writing the following letter to the *Evening Telegram* which was published on July 5, 1948. It read:

> The Church Lads Brigade Armory on Harvey Road contains a Shrine to the Sacred Memory of the members who fell in the First World War fighting for King and Country and for Newfoundland. As a brother of one of those members, as a son of a former Colonel of the CLB and as a former member of that organization, I publicly protest against the announcement contained in your advertising columns on Saturday last, stating that the CLB Armory has been hired out as the St. John's Headquarters of the party for the Confederates.

Mr. W.H. Hayward of Rennies Mill Road penned the following comment which appeared two days later in the *Evening Telegram*: "As a member of the Church Lads Brigade for seven years, and a war veteran, I cannot understand the protest of Mr. P. Outerbridge as expressed in Monday's *Telegram* against the hiring of the CLB Armory to a political association." Over the following days several more letters on the issue were published. Major Earl W. Best of the CLB felt obligated to enter the fray and he wrote:

> The decision and the responsibility for this policy rests on me alone. Obviously, there can be no ground whatsoever for identifying the Brigade or anyone connected with it with the views or aims of the renters. The Armory

217

is available on equal terms to any responsible person or persons during its use.

MOB ATTACKS SMALLWOOD

Emotions were running high going into the second referendum when Smallwood scheduled a giant rally at the CLB Armory for July 5, 1948.[8] St. John's was a hotbed for the anti-Confederate movement, and there was reason to believe that Smallwood would be assaulted. Just a month earlier a gang of thugs had entered the offices of VOCM on Parade Street where they awaited Smallwood's exit from a broadcasting studio. Veteran journalist Mike Critch recalled that radio management became aware of the gang's presence and intentions and called in the police. Smallwood was safely escorted from the building and taken to his headquarters by supporters.

As a result of the growing hostility towards Smallwood in the city, an increased security team was organized and present inside and outside the CLB hall on the night of July 5th. About 1600 Smallwood supporters were inside the hall and nearly 1000, mostly followers of Peter Cashin, were outside. Irving Fogwill, a local labour leader, had plenty of experience in dealing with mobs. He put together the unit which included: Herb Wells, Bill Case, Ted Garland, Rudy Williams and Doug Kelsey. Bill Case had recruited Jack Ford, the Newfoundland war veteran of Japanese prison camps and the atomic bombing of Nagasaki.

While the speakers were stirring up enthusiasm among the crowd inside, those outside were shouting and trying to drown out the outdoor loudspeakers which were carrying the audio to the streets.

At the conclusion of Smallwood's speech, he was given a standing ovation with thunderous clapping and shouting.

---

[8] The information for the attack at the CLB comes from a variety of sources including: Smallwood, Harold Horwood, Herb Wells, Ted Garland, Mike Critch and Jack Ford. Also *Evening Telegram* July 5-8, 1948.

The first sign of trouble came during a speech by Leslie R. Curtis when a truck plastered with Economic Union Campaign posters moved slowly past the CLB blowing its horn and with its speakers on full volume to drown out the Confederate speeches. Children in the truck were tossing political posters into the crowd.

Herb Wells had been checking the crowd inside and outside and became alarmed at the changing mood of the outdoor mob. He made his way up the hall and warned Harold Horwood, "That crowd outside is looking for blood." Although Joey was informed, he remained confident and undeterred and he decided to leave the building by the front door anyway.

Jack Ford recalled that he was at the front door of the hall, and there was a feeling that something was going to happen. He said:

> I noticed that as Joey made his way towards the door to leave that a big tough-looking fellow named Coady from the Southside was forcing his way towards him. There were others with him and I sensed they were looking for trouble. That's when I and another bodyguard quickly separated Joey from the crowd and got him out the door. The mob outside was getting more aggressive. As Joey left the building a boisterous group led by two instigators moved in and separated Smallwood from us at the foot of the front steps to the building. Joey was knocked down and his glasses were broken. From there, they forced him a short distance east along Harvey Road. We [several bodyguards] caught up with them and there was a free-for-all. We seized Joey and brought him to a nearby car which had a rumble seat in it. It was driven by Kevin McCarthy.
>
> I was a bodyguard only for that night and I don't recall the name of the other bodyguard with me. I do remember two others guarding Joey at that time, Bill May of

Livingstone Street, [father of Dr. Art May, later President of MUN] and Jim Pike from the west coast. We got Joey into the rumble seat and the mob tried to overturn the car. We told McCarthy to get away. He moved the car slowly, forcing an opening in the crowd, and the trouble-makers tossed rocks at it as it escaped down Harvey Road. Kevin dropped Joey off at the Hotel Newfoundland.[9]

Harold Horwood remembered in his book *Joey*:

The next time I saw Joey, he pulled out a small six-gun given him by a supporter. I think it must have been de-signed to fire .22 caliber shells. 'It's not loaded,' he said, 'but I bet it would make those toughs back off if they came for me.'

'You know,' I joked; 'we really need a martyr to crown our cause.'

'You can be the martyr if you want,' he retorted. 'It's not going to be me if I can help it.'

He had among his other qualities what seemed to be lim-itless physical courage. Threats, instead of intimidating him, charged him with the will to fight.

Journalist Mike Critch recalled, "That was quite a sensa-tional time. Smallwood did not go home that night. That was twice within a month Joey had been attacked. Nobody was surprised when bodyguards began accompanying him on his campaign."[10]

Speaking at Memorial University in 1971, Smallwood, in recalling the battle for Confederation as "...a really rough one," told a filled auditorium:

---

[9] Interview with Jack Ford by author in February 2011.
[10] Interview with Mike Critch by author in December 2011.

I had to have a bodyguard, a bodyguard of men, who would meet me at the door of my house and fall in beside me–I've only seen it in gangster pictures; that's the only time I ever saw it–they'd fall in on both sides; and when I'd come out of my house, they'd fall in behind me, three men, one on each side and one behind me, to the car, across the sidewalk, aboard the car. They would sit on both sides of me in the car, and one in front, and the driver would start up, get down to Confederate headquarters, and the same thing in reverse. Wherever we went, we had bodyguards, and in spite of the bodyguards, I did get beaten up a few times. This was quite a hot campaign.[11]

A newspaper letter published in response and signed by L. J. Sullivan, Portugal Cove Road, St. John's, compared the incident to the actions of Hitler's Storm Troopers. He wrote, "While they might have been the accepted behavior for Hitler's Storm Troopers, they have no place in any democratic country."

Sullivan questioned how the Economic Union Party was controlling its pamphlet distribution. He wrote, "It is not known where Economic Union pamphlets are going. Is any Tom, Dick or Harry free to load up a truck with party pamphlets and set out to break up a confederate meeting and assault its leader?"

In a letter to the *Evening Telegram*, July 8, 1948, a Mrs. C.M. Peters of St. John's noted that she was at the CLB meeting where the attack occurred. She blamed the Economic Union Party for the trouble and suggested:

The authorities should see to it that as free people we are at liberty to advocate the form of Government we think best for our people, and that occurrences of this

---

[11] Smallwood-Pickersgill Conversation, MUN-Canadian Historical Association Annual Meeting, May 31, 1971.

sort do not happen again. We are told we have freedom of speech. I, for one, doubt that after Monday night's happenings. This is not helping their cause any. No one in this city can charge the Confederates with causing disturbances at either the Responsible Government meetings or the Economic Union meetings.

Mrs. Peters referred to the first referendum outcome as evidence that Newfoundland was divided with Confederate support in the outports and Responsible Government confined to the Avalon Peninsula.

Ches Crosbie's Economic Union Party published an advertisement in the *Daily News* a couple of days after the incident disclaiming responsibility for the rowdies and the attack on Smallwood.

CONFEDERATE MAGIC IN CARBONEAR

A novel approach to campaigning took place during one of Smallwood's first outport rallies at Freshwater near Carbonear. The hall was filled to capacity and in addition to Smallwood there were several speakers including Tommy Sergeant, an Englishman, living and working in St. John's as a teacher. When Sergeant's turn came to speak, it marked the only time in the election that any speaker upstaged Joey Smallwood, and Joey was quite happy with the outcome.

Sergeant began by claiming he was not a great speaker and not in a position to explain the great benefits that will flow to Newfoundland with Confederation, "but if anyone could pass me a full page from a newspaper, I would be happy to demonstrate what they are."

After some fussing around among the audience, someone stepped forward and passed Sergeant a newspaper page. Silence fell over the hall, as people wondered what the hell he was doing. The speaker pulled a lighter from his pocket and lit a bottom corner of the page which burst upwards in flame. Tommy then clapped his hands to put out the fire.

As the audience watched intently, he rubbed the burnt ashes in his hands and then with a flourish produced, and held up so all could see, a ten dollar bill! "That's all, ladies and gentlemen. It's really quite easy to do, and you should all be able to do it. If you can do this, you don't need Confederation. If you can't then I can tell you that Confederation is the next best thing."

SMALL MAJORITY PREDICTED

The Newfoundland Governor and the Commissioner of Justice, secretly, were predicting that there was no chance of a big majority vote for Confederation. They estimated no more than a 3000 vote majority for union with Canada. In anticipation of this possibility, the British considered what they would accept as a majority. Canada's High Commissioner in London relayed the UK's position to Ottawa. He stated:

> Britain's position on what would constitute a majority was that any majority for Confederation, however small, as binding and that, if the decision were solely for them, they would arrange for Confederation, even though the majority were as small as one. But they recognize that, Confederation being two-sided, the ultimate word must be with Canada and if Canada decides that a majority is too small to justify acceptance of Newfoundland into Confederation, they could not but acquiesce in that decision.[12]

AMERICAN INTERFERENCE

Smallwood wasted no time after the first referendum. He had become aware that some officers of the American Military in Newfoundland had openly campaigned in favor of Responsible Government. He faced the issued head on by exposing the effort publicly and accusing the Americans of

---

[12] Ibid, 918,919.

interference in a Newfoundland political matter. The headline in the *Confederate* on June 16, 1948, read "Hands off Americans." The article stated:

> We direct the attention of the Newfoundland and United States authorities to the fact that some American personnel on the bases intervened unwarrantably and inexcusably in the recent National Referendum. They intervened by throwing their weight on the side of one of the forms of government on the ballot paper–namely, Responsible Government. They intervened by speaking against Confederation. They intervened by suggesting openly, or covertly, that under Confederation the U.S. bases in Newfoundland would close down, with consequent loss of their jobs by Newfoundland civilians.

Was this impertinent intervention into the domestic political affairs of the Newfoundland people by the U.S. personnel made with the knowledge and consent of the U.S. Government, the U.S. Consul General, and the Commanding General of the bases? Are we to expect a repetition of this grave breach in the forthcoming campaign?

Joey argued that the situation had the potential of influencing thousands of voters. The Americans were embarrassed by this revelation and took measures to assure it was not repeated in the second vote.

OUTCOME OF SECOND REFERENDUM

The outcome of the referendum failed to catch any of the three governments involved by surprise. The United Kingdom, Canada and Newfoundland were expecting a narrow margin of about 3000 votes for Confederation. It took a week before the final vote was counted and the count varied from that released the day after the vote. This, no doubt, is the factor behind the variation recorded by writers since 1949 which claimed figures between 5000 to 6000 votes, and as low as "the razor-thin margin of 1%." The first decade after the vote, some records refer to 51% Confederation and 49% Responsible Government. The actual outcome was:

Confederation	78,323	52.335%
Responsible Government	71,334	47.664%

Smallwood's Confederates won 70% of the total votes cast outside the Avalon Peninsula. On the Avalon Peninsula, Responsible Government won 67% of the vote.

The Confederates had increased their vote in every district where they had led Responsible Government on the first ballot and closed the gap in the other districts. In the Responsible Government stronghold of St. John's, the Confederates went from 24% of the vote in June to 31.07% in the July vote. King felt that the Confederate movement led by Smallwood made a remarkable showing despite not having the public support of many of the country's prominent people.[13]

The referendum had divided Newfoundland geographically between the Avalon Peninsula and the outports. Some voters even suggested that Canada accept Newfoundland minus the Avalon Peninsula.

Professor Mackay told Ottawa officials that the RGL leaders were shaken by the outcome and almost in a state of collapse. A week after the referendum, both Canadian and British officials had trouble contacting many of these men who were gone salmon fishing, "...among the St. John's businessmen and professionals salmon fishing was considered something of a 'rite' to which the historic occasion took second place." Over the days that followed some prominent merchants and professionals decided that it was time to unite and bring people together rather than divide the country. Some deserted the Responsible Government League and became Confederates.

---

[13]*Documents on Relations Between Canada and Newfoundland*, Vol 2. Part 1, p951

MACKENZIE KING CONSIDERED
NOT ACCEPTING THE VOTE

The victory was almost scuttled by the Canadian Cabinet the day before the vote took place. On that day, at a cabinet meeting in Ottawa, the Prime Minister, supported by some in cabinet, felt that in view of the outcome they were anticipating, that Canada's position would be that Newfoundland proceed with a third vote but this time to elect a Responsible Government to negotiate union. [The final count was more than double what Canada expected].

Louis St. Laurent, very soon to become Prime Minister, strongly disagreed. He argued that if that position was taken, it would be a slap in the face to the majority who voted for Confederation and would mean that all the effort put into the negotiations with Newfoundland would be wasted. Subsequent events changed the direction of the Prime Minister's thinking.

Newfoundland's Governor felt that if Canada failed to accept the outcome of the referendum, it would cause a major split in Newfoundland. He warned:

> Not to proceed with Confederation at the present time is not only to decline to accept the decision of the majority of the Newfoundland people, but also, broadly speaking, to support the Responsible Government people on the Avalon Peninsula against those favouring Confederation on the other side.

However, word of the federal hesitation reached St. John's and John McEvoy called an urgent meeting at his house on Patrick Street. The list of those who attended included: Smallwood; Bradley; Ches Pippy; Monroe; Brooks; Harvey & Co.; Justice Brian Dunfield; John Clouston; Clyde Lake, the colony's largest fish merchant; Dr. Moore; Dr. Roberts and his son, also a doctor. The centre of their discussion was the legal background to the unfolding political event.

Some of the points made at the meeting and communicated to Canadian officials were as follows:

The majority rule is the normal procedure in democratic governments and the UK had specified in the conditions for the referendum, distinctly that the majority be accepted.

The Canadian Government could have disputed this after the first referendum but did not.

Some prominent people, some in attendance, had come out publicly in support of Confederation with the belief that the majority rule would apply. Canada had inferred this. If Canada changed the conditions at this time it would be a breach of faith with the people of Newfoundland.

If Canada breached that faith, he (McEvoy) and others would be finished with the Confederation movement.

Newfoundlanders would feel rebuffed. Compared such a move to the betrayal of 1933.

There was a possibility that a Responsible Government election would return an anti- Confederate party that would scuttle Confederation.

There was 70% support for Confederation off the Avalon Peninsula.

Governor MacDonald argued that the phrase used in references to what an acceptable majority would be, "clearly and beyond all possibility of misunderstanding," was written when the Canadian Government had no way of knowing how many choices would be on the ballot. Unlike the first vote with a three-way contest and the need to rule out a simple plurality vote, the second election was a two-way fight. He concluded, "The phrase may perhaps be considered to have lost its validity."[14]

---

[14]The above information is drawn from conversations held by R.A. MacKay with the Governor and Commissioners Herbert Pottle and Albert Walsh, July 26, 1948, and included in *McKay's report to the Prime Minister*, External Affairs Documents, 981.

"Important Moment for the People"
In recalling the vote that led to Confederation in 1949, Smallwood borrowed a quote from Winston Churchill:

> At the bottom of the tributes paid to democracy is the little man, walking in the little booth, with a little pencil, making a little cross on a little bit of paper, no amount of rhetoric or voluminous discussion can possibly diminish the overwhelming importance of the point.[15]

After 400 years of history, it was the little man in the fishing boat, on the farm, or working in the factories, the stores, on the waterfront, etc. who seized control of his country's destiny by exercising his choice for his future, with the marking of a simple "X" on a ballot paper. That simple "X" ended 450 years of servitude to a system beyond his control.

Emotions Ran High in 1948
During the July 22, 1948, referendum, Smallwood's headquarters in St. John's was often a beehive of activity. When one voter turned up several times in one week looking for Smallwood, who was out of town campaigning, Greg Power asked him why he wanted Smallwood.

"We want him to come down to visit our community," answered the powerful-looking visitor.

Power politely explained, "Mr. Smallwood is trying to visit every community possible but I doubt if he is going to be able to cover all of them. Is there anything special you have in mind if I can arrange a visit?"

"We certainly do. We want to hang the bastard." responded the visitor as he walked out slamming the door behind him.[16]

---

[15]Joseph R. Smallwood, *I Chose Canada*, 285.
[16]A conversation between the author and Greg Power at Smallwood's Liberal Reform offices in 1973.

Results of Referendum July 22, 1948–
Official results, Chief Electoral Officer, August 26, 1948

Electoral District	Registered	Confederation	Responsible Government
St. Barbe	3755	2353	633*
White Bay	5663	4171	1331*
Green Baby	4650	2392	960*
Grand Falls	11458	6228	4802*
Twillingate	5513	2524	830*
Fogo	5652	2438	1499*
Bonavista North	6743	3466	1187*
Bonavista South	7137	2730	2530*
Trinity North	6983	3153	1691*
Trinity South	5915	2593	1709*
Carbonear, Bayde Verde	6843	2705	2427*
Harbour Grace	4173	1206	1995
Port de Grave	4603	1565	1626
Harbour Main-Bell Island	9168	1431	6784
St. John's West	19586	6193	12513
St. John's East	16313	4895	10784
Ferryland	3791	612	3353*
Placentia and St. Mary's	5699	920	4081
Placentia West	5488	2067	1704*
Burin	5683	4079	722*
Fortune Bay and Hermitage	6267	3675	840*
St. George's-Port au Port	6769	3817	2911*
Humber	10745	7133	3245*
Labrador	2886	2681	766*
Total	176297	78323	71334

*Confederate win

Margin of Victory for Confederates–6989 votes
By percentage–Confederates–52.34%
Responsible Government–47.66%

DISTRICT WINS:
Confederates-18
Responsible Government–7

MILITARY READY

The British cabinet had overestimated the anti-Confederate emotions among supporters of the Responsible Government Party and they held concerns about an outbreak of violence occurring in St. John's after the final referendum on July 22, 1948.[17] Their assessment of the election was that the vote would be close and might result in civil disorder. In a memo to the Cabinet, Philip Noel Baker, Secretary of State for Dominion Affairs, reported:

> As a precautionary measure, and after discussion with the Prime Minister, I have thought it right to ask the First Lord of the Admiralty whether he can arrange for a warship to be available in Western Atlantic waters at the time of the referendum and able to move in to St. John's at short notice on call. I hope very much in fact there will be no disturbances; but we must be prepared to maintain order as long as we are in charge of the island.[18]

---

[17] Documents *on Relations Between Canada and Newfoundland,* Vol. 2 pt. 1.

[18] Phillip McCann, *Confederation Revisited New Light on British Policy,* 1983.

Counting ballots in the 2nd Referendum at a St. John's polling stadium. (PANL)

A voter casting his ballot while a constable of the Royal Newfoundland Constabulary stands by. (PANL)

This cartoon was used in Smallwood's pro-Confederate newspaper. (PANL)

Prime Minister Mackenzie King and Joseph R. Smallwood, at the National Liberal Leadership Convention in 1948. (PANL)

Smallwood organized a country-wide petition which collected over fifty-thousand signatures supporting the inclusion of the choice for Confederation on the Referendum ballot. Clara Russell, Smallwood's daughter, is seated third from left. (PANL)

Joseph R. Smallwood working for the Confederation cause late at night in his bedroom on Duckworth Street. His wife Clara stayed up to keep him supplied with tea. (PANL)

The Responsible Government van with sound system campaigning on Bonaventure Avenue in the July 22, 1948, referendum was driven by Jack Fitzgerald Sr., father of the author. (PANL)

Joe Smallwood and Jack Pickersgill surrounded by a crowd while campaigning in a federal general election. (PANL)

Lloyd's of London refused to insure this Duckworth Street house during the referendum Battle because Joey Smallwood lived there. The house stood next to where the restaurant Zachary's stands today. (Jack Fitzgerald)

CHAPTER 12

It Took More Than Pickersgill
To Convince Mackenzie King

"After listening to Pickersgill's argument that the majority vote was valid, King remained undecided. His concern was how the Newfoundland public would react to Canada accepting the final vote. The possibility of demonstrations and violence could affect the maritime vote in the pending federal election. To clarify this, he had Professor R.A. Mackay go to Newfoundland to carry out an assessment of public reaction to the outcome."

- Jack Fitzgerald

When Jack Pickersgill learned of the vote in Newfoundland, he requested Gordon Robertson [Clerk to Cabinet] to calculate the votes received by the Liberal party in every election since 1921. Robertson determined that the Liberals had exceeded 50% of the vote only on one occasion, which was in 1940. Pickersgill later recalled:

When Mackenzie King called me that morning and asked my opinion of the vote, I was able to tell him how favourably the vote of Confederation compared with the support he had received in successive elections which he had regarded as clear expressions of the will of the Canadian people. Whether my opinion had any influence on the Prime Minister I had no means of knowing, but the Cabinet decided on 27 July, that the majority was substantial enough to justify proceeding with negotiations.[1]

Pickersgill's information was not the clincher, even though many believe it was the case. King had other concerns over how Canada should proceed after the referendum vote. He debated whether to proceed with union or to await the election of Responsible Government and then deal with it.[2] Although the final vote was double what he had expected, he worried that accepting it might spark an outbreak of rioting in Newfoundland and cause him political problems. After listening to Pickersgill's argument that the majority vote was valid, King remained undecided. His concern was how the Newfoundland public would react to Canada accepting the final vote. The possibility of demonstrations and violence could affect the maritime vote in the pending federal election. To clarify this, he had Professor R.A. Mackay go to Newfoundland to carry out an assessment of public reaction to the outcome.

---

[1] J. W. Pickersgill, *My Years With Louis St. Laurent*, pgs 79-80.
[2] St. Laurent disagreed with King on this point.

Mackay sought the opinions of many people who had supported the return of Responsible Government. Some of those he met with included: Gordon Higgins, R.B. Job, Dr. Allan Fraser, Wick Collins, Vice-President of the Responsible Government League; John Cheeseman and Malcolm Hollett.

Of special interest to Mackay was that the RGL had decided to challenge the July 22nd vote. He reported, "I doubt if it indicates complete unity among all who voted for Responsible Government. The League is only one wing of the group supporting the return of Responsible Government."

He advised the Prime Minister that many Responsible Government supporters were actually Confederates who felt union should be negotiated with a restored Responsible Government. Of particular interest to Mackenzie King was Mackay's reference that "...none of the more prominent people in the Responsible Government League camp wish to associate with the League's present actions to try and overturn the vote."

Mackay noted that Frank M.O'Leary, who tendered his resignation as president of the RGL on August 13, 1948, had stated:

Any further action at this time, by the RGL, would not be in the best interests of the League or the country. I understand that it is the intention of the League to continue to oppose the decision of the people. I view with alarm any measures which may result in keeping our people divided. I cannot in honesty, play any further part in its activities.

Ches Crosbie shared O'Leary's sentiments. Lewis Ayre, president of the NL Board of Trade said, "There will be little room for dissension among us, and anyone attempting to divide the country for political or selfish reasons will be guilty of a great injustice to his fellow Newfoundlanders." Gordon Higgins, a prominent St. John's lawyer and member of the 1947 federal delegation to Ottawa, accepted the verdict and was ready to work within union. He subsequently ran as a Conservative in the 1949 federal election.

The Mackay report included references from two St. John's newspapers. The *Daily News*, he wrote, reported that Confederation was inevitable and that the newspaper would no longer be in opposition to it. *The Evening Telegram* stated, "This is not a time for rank partisanship."

Mackay concluded that with the plebiscite over, the majority of responsible and well-known figures in the Responsible Government Party were satisfied to accept the outcome. He pointed out that there was still some in the RGL who were determined to use every means at their disposal to oppose Confederation despite its majority win. Mackay calmed King's concerns of any outbreak of demonstrations in St. John's in the event of Canada accepting the outcome of the election. Anti-Confederate leaders told him that while some may question the legality of the referendum, no violence was expected.

After considering legal and constitutional opinions, political history, Pickersgill's advice and finally Mackay's report, King was ready to make a firm decision. On July 30, 1948, he announced that the referendum in favour of Confederation was "...clear and beyond all possibility of misunderstanding."

He added that the decision was made by the Newfoundland people without any pressure from Canada. Earlier Britain sought Canada's opinion on the issue of whether or not to include 'Confederation' on the ballot. It was told it was a matter entirely between Newfoundland and the United Kingdom. Mackenzie King wrote in his diary later that day:

I have never dreamt that my name would probably be linked through years to come with the bringing into Confederation of what will be the 10th province and quite clearly the last. Having relation to my grandfather's part in laying the foundation of responsible government, it is interesting that it should be left to me as practically the last of the completed tasks before giving up the leadership of the Party. To have been the one as Prime Minister to announce the entry within a few months' time, of Newfoundland into Confederation. Might even be listed as one of the Fathers of the larger Confederation.

FINAL TERMS NEGOTIATED

Once Canada accepted the referendum outcome, preparations for negotiations of the terms of union moved into full gear. The Newfoundland Commission of Government appointed the following people to form Newfoundland's delegation to Ottawa: Sir Albert Walsh, Chairman; Joseph R. Smallwood; F. Gordon Bradley; John McEvoy; Phil Gruchy; Chesley Crosbie; and Gordon Winter. Canadian officials were impressed with the composition of the delegation and felt it represented Newfoundland's interests very well.

External Affairs had described both Gordon Winter and Ches Crosbie as anti-Confederates and Crosbie as the most effective opponent of Confederation. While Crosbie had reserved the right to oppose the final terms if he felt they were unfair to Newfoundland, Mr. Winter did not attach any condition to his appointment to the delegation.

The 1948 Canadian Delegation, in preparing for negotiations with Newfoundland on the terms of union, discovered an error made in the 1947 Ottawa negotiations which threatened to bring an end to the Confederation cause. External Affairs and Finance were not always in agreement with one another during the negotiations. The snag came when Mitchell Sharp discovered that the Canadians had overestimated the potential for tax income from Newfoundland during the first years of Confederation. He recalled that Canada was embarrassed by the discovery and worried that the Newfoundland delegation would think that Canada was playing a game.

Despite this, Sharpe convinced his delegation to remain firm on the issue because it would mean an annual $10 million Newfoundland deficit, and might instill resentment among the nine Canadian provinces.

R.A. Mackay, External Affairs, told Pearson that Newfoundland would not sign the agreement unless better financial terms were offered. Smallwood warned that the Confederation cause was about to end unless the Canadians changed their position.

A strategic argument, developed and repeatedly used by Smallwood, saved the day. It was his insistence and repetitious assertions that Newfoundland had to be treated as a special case, and needed additional financial help in the first years after union that brought about a solution to the deadlock.

This argument, presented to the Canadian delegation by Mackay, was that Newfoundland would be starting off as a province with a poor tax base, and it would require time to catch up in the taxation field with the Maritime provinces. He argued that the cost of maintaining services for a small population scattered over a long coastline would impose a heavy burden on the new government which was not used to direct taxation.

Unlike the existing Canadian provinces, Newfoundland, after 100 years of Responsible Government, had no municipal government system to share the costs of providing government services with the provincial government. It would need time to build such a structure. Also noted was that, unlike other Canadian provinces, Newfoundland had practically no automobiles and gas to immediately turn to as a source of tax revenue.[3] Implementing a taxation system to meet the demands of the new province would be challenging.

Sharp feared that improving the conditions might cause resentment particularly among the maritime provinces. In

---

[3] *Documents on Relations Between Newfoundland and Canada*, Vol 2 part 1.

1948, the level of taxes per capita in Newfoundland was thirteen dollars compared with fifty dollars in New Brunswick, forty-nine dollars in Nova Scotia and twenty-nine dollars in Prince Edward Island. Canada's Minister of Fisheries, Milton Gregg, was included in Canada's delegation to ensure that Canada did not offer terms that might anger the Maritime provinces.

At this stage, Lester B. Pearson wanted to keep negotiations on track. He wrote St. Laurent:

> I still feel that the national interest requires that Newfoundland should be brought into the federation if at all possible and that the present may be our opportunity to do so. I think, therefore, that we should be prepared to improve our financial position to the extent necessary on the assumption that the Newfoundland delegation do not make impossible demands, and if this can be done without raising difficulties with the existing provinces.[4]

Mackay successfully used Joey's argument to convince Lester Pearson and other negotiators of the merit of the Newfoundland case. The final negotiations allowed Newfoundland to keep its sterling deposits and revenues due which left it with a surplus of $46.6 million. Under Term 24 of the terms of union, one third of this amount had to remain on deposit with the Federal Government for the first eight years of union to cover current account expenditures. The other two-thirds were left to use to develop the province's resources and the improvement of public services.

The total federal grant was increased from $26.25 million to $42.75 million over a twelve year period. The Newfoundland delegation did push for an additional $2.75 million which was turned down. The delegation recognized that Ottawa had made a considerable improvement on the offer of 1947 and decided not to press the issue any further.[5]

[4] Raymond B. Blake, *Canadians at Last*, 2.
[5] Ibid.

Before the negotiations ended, St. Laurent had replaced King as Prime Minister and agreed to Smallwood's argument for Term 29 to strengthen the Canadian offer. This guaranteed that Newfoundland's financial position would be reviewed eight years after Confederation.[6] Canada also exempted Newfoundlanders from all income and corporation taxes for the first three months of union.

DELEGATES UNHAPPY WITH TERMS

All of the Newfoundland delegates felt that the terms offered did not provide for Newfoundland's financial security. Ches Crosbie, however, felt strongly enough to quit the delegation and walk away from the deal. He refused to sign the terms, claiming that the financial position of Newfoundland was far from secure.[7]

"It was courting chaos," he said, "to use accumulated surplus to cover the budgetary deficit, even for the short term." Crosbie pointed out that the secondary industries would be very vulnerable after Confederation, "...it is impossible to adapt the Canadian economy to this country overnight without causing chaos and distress in many places, particularly when for centuries we have had our own economy peculiar to this country." He felt high unemployment would follow. Crosbie explained:

In view of this, I could not and would not take the responsibility of committing the people of Newfoundland,

---

[6] Term 29 led Newfoundland into a major conflict with Ottawa in 1959. Before it ended, in Newfoundland's favour, it split the Progressive Conservative Party in Newfoundland, saw the creation of the Newfoundland Democratic Party, led by those who left the PC party, and had an influence on the defeat of Prime Minister John Diefenbaker. Smallwood as Premier of Newfoundland during the "Term 29" debate, campaigned across Canada, against Diefenbaker.

[7] After accepting Governor MacDonald's invitation to become a member of the Newfoundland delegation to Ottawa, Crosbie informed his supporters that he had accepted the position with the condition that he could quit the delegation if he disagreed with the terms. However, the Newfoundland Governor disagreed with this statement and explained that Crosbie's condition was to be allowed to disagree with the terms.

without their consent, to such financial suicide. If the tax load is not increased the services we now have will have to be greatly reduced. This in my opinion would be disastrous.[8]

The other Newfoundland delegates felt that the terms were not carved in stone and that Ottawa would prove responsive later if the province encountered financial difficulty. T.G.W. Ashbourne, National Convention delegate and Confederation supporter, reacted to the criticism of the terms of union saying:

If 12 million people could live happily in Canada enjoying Progressive Government, good living conditions and a greater degree of security than was possible in an isolated community like Newfoundland, 12,300,000 people could do the same.[9]

After three months of discussions, the terms were finalized on December 11, 1948. Recalling the campaign by anti-Confederates to stop Confederation, Smallwood said:

Two days after we arrived in Ottawa, the Responsible Government League held a big rally in the CLB Armoury to put the finishing touches on a petition to the House of Commons in London. The meeting adopted a resolution denying the right of our delegation to Commit Newfoundland to Confederation without the holding of a plebiscite. Further to bedevil the picture, Premier Maurice Duplessis of Quebec expressed publicly his belief that the Quebec Government could sue for adjustment of the boundary separating Quebec and Newfoundland. Duplesiss announced, too, that he was opposed to Newfoundland's entry into the Confederation.[10]

---

[8]*Documents Relating to Canada and Newfoundland*, Vol. 2, pt. 1
[9]Ibid.
[10]Joseph R. Smallwood, *I Chose Canada*, 316.

"Crosbie aggressive and uncouth"

With the terms of union agreed upon, Scott Macdonald was concerned that the Confederation proposals could spark criticism of Canada in St. John's and have a bad effect on general relations between the two countries. These fears were unwarranted, and he was pleased with the general response he encountered. In a memo to Lester Pearson in January 1948, Macdonald reported:

> Though the financial effect of Confederation will be serious to many of the people we see most frequently, there has only been a single incident where any remark reflecting unpleasantly on Canada had to be objected to. The offender, Mr. Chesley Crosbie, an aggressive and rather uncouth individual prominent in local manufacturing enterprises, has since invited us to the wedding of his daughter. Our New year's reception was more largely attended than any outside Government House and one of the good humored toasts, "Canada Ever, Confederation Never," while it certainly didn't show much feeling in favour of union, at least indicated a degree of friendliness that has been absent from earlier campaigns.[11]

Opportunity Knocks

With the political system and power now rapidly shifting away from the St. John's establishment, many prominent in the Responsible Government Party began mending fences and moving to situate themselves into positions of influence. Similar intrigue was taking place within the Confederate movement but behind closed doors.

McEvoy, with close friends in the Commission of Government, managed to get himself appointed to the Ottawa delegation to negotiate the terms of union with Ottawa.

Ches Crosbie made it known to Mackay that he was disposed towards accepting the outcome of the vote and

---

[11]*External Affairs Documents Relating to Newfoundland and Canada*, 789.

indicated that he might come out publicly. He had also expressed a desire to be appointed to the Newfoundland delegation being selected to go to Ottawa. The responsibility for selecting those delegates lay with the Commission of Government.

Many others stepped away from those in the Responsible Government League who wanted to continue to legally challenge the referendum.

A major source of satisfaction for the Canadian Government was the September 1948 report from External Affairs which stated, that "...it is clear that none of the more responsible men who advocated Responsible Government during the referendum campaign wish to be associated with the League's present activities of continuing the fight against union."

BRADLEY WANTED THE PREMIER'S POSITION

When the victory of the Confederates was assured, not only was the St. John's establishment planning on how they could gain control of the first provincial government, but even Joey's closest confidant throughout the battle, F. Gordon Bradley, was eyeing the Premiership. Smallwood and Bradley had come to an agreement previously that if their cause succeeded, Joey would become Premier and Bradley, Newfoundland's first Federal Cabinet minister. The matter became the only personal quarrel the two ever had. In his autobiography, Smallwood recalled the day when Bradley decided he wanted to be Premier:

> We were out for a walk in the northern suburbs of St. John's, and as we came down Robinson's Hill and approached the Feildian athletic field, we turned in and sat in the empty bleachers to continue our discussion. It happened to be one of the few times when Bradley was not completely pessimistic about the prospects of success for the Confederation cause.

Suddenly, as we sat there, he sprang his surprise. I couldn't become the first Premier of the new province. I wouldn't be acceptable to the people. I didn't have the standing, I was, I inferred him to be thinking, a nobody. Indeed, I was a nobody; but in spite of that I had an altogether different opinion from him on my standing with the people.

Gordon's plan was this: 1) he should get knighthood and an Imperial privy councillorship; 2) he should become the first Premier of the Province, but he would take me into his cabinet; and 3) he would, some months later, enter the Canadian Cabinet, and his last act as Premier of Newfoundland would be to recommend me to the Lieutenant Governor for the premiership. I could scarcely believe my ears, and my response was prompt and categorical. 'Count me out, Gordon. I withdraw. You take it–you carry on the fight for Confederation. You get Confederation, and then you'll deserve your knighthood and imperial councillorship. You'll have earned the right to be called the Rt. Hon. Sir Gordon Bradley, Prime Minister of Newfoundland, Newfoundland's Minister in the Canadian Government. I'm through.' He was alarmed and back-tracked quickly, and that was the last I ever heard of those particular ideas.

Soon after when Bradley was invited to the Prime Minister's Office, he expected to be offered the position of Secretary of State, however, he returned to his hotel fuming and told Smallwood he had not been offered any post. Joey reassured him that he would be invited into the cabinet and after his own private meeting with St. Laurent next day, he came back to the hotel and said to Bradley, "The Premier of Newfoundland greets Canada's Secretary of State!"

Smallwood felt that Bradley felt intimidated by the power of the Prime Minister and was too timid to bring up the question of his role in Confederation. Joey had no such fears and pressed the view that Newfoundland had to have a member in the Federal Cabinet and that man must be Gordon Bradley.

TATTERED REMNANTS OF RGL FOUGHT TO LAST

Those left in the Responsible Government League attempted to overturn the Confederate victory on two fronts. Peter Cashin held a rally at the Star Hall and circulated a petition to the British Parliament to have the referendum overturned. On November, 12, 1948, a three man delegation from the RGL flew to London to deliver their petition. The three included: F.W. Marshall, Peter Cashin and John Higgins.

The next day, six men who had served in the old House of Assembly issued writs in the Newfoundland Supreme Court claiming the National Convention and referendum were unconstitutional and should be overturned. The six were Frank McNamara, John O'Dea, W.C. Winsor, Harold Mitchell, Magistrate William Browne and John Currie. Both efforts failed. The Supreme Court threw out the writs and the British Parliament rejected the RGL petition.

The tattered remnants of the RGL continued their opposition to union right up to the last. On the same day the London delegation (protestors from the RGL) returned to St. John's, and organized a public protest to Government House, Ches Crosbie refused to sign the terms of union and he presented a minority report to the Governor. An effort by Colonel George Drew, leader of the National Progressive Conservative Party, which could have caused a lengthy delay in union, was defeated in the House of Commons by a vote of 192 to twelve. Yet, when the Newfoundland Bill was voted on, it was passed with a vote of 140 to seventy-four. The CCF and the Progressive Conservatives opposed it.[12]

---

[12] Drew wanted the nine provinces to have a say on Newfoundland's entry into Confederation. This would have prolonged and perhaps stopped Newfoundland's entry into Confederation. Duplessis had made it plain later that Quebec could never have agreed to Canada recognizing Labrador as Newfoundland's.

The RGL's final effort came just three days before New-foundland became Canada's tenth province. The League sent a fruitless message to the Speaker of the House of Commons claiming the right in the future to initiate a move to secede from Canada and return to Newfoundland sovereignty.

Gordon Walker, MP, during second reading of the bill in the British Parliament which gave the force of law under the British North America Act 1949 to union between Newfoundland and Canada, addressed the argument, "...that the majority for Confederation was too small, and that a two-thirds majority should have been required." He stated:

> It is better to accept the majority than the minority. Any tricks about a two-thirds majority, mean, in fact, that we would be accepting the minority against the majority. Democratic organizations, and especially our sort of Parliamentary democracy, depend upon clear and simple majorities on clear and simple issues placed before the people.[13]

Walker described Confederation as a treaty between Canada and Newfoundland. He argued that Newfoundland chose between two forms of self-government and chose to become a "...self-governing province within the Confederation of Canada rather than to be a self-governing nation, and a very small one, in a dangerous and difficult world."

IMPORTANCE OF TERM NEGOTIATIONS

Canada wanted Newfoundland, but certainly not at any price. The negotiations for the terms of union were crucial and Smallwood's knowledge of the Canadian system and how far they could be pushed became invaluable. Professor Raymond Blake, author of *Canadians at Last* observed:

---

[13] *Documents on Relation to Canada and Newfoundland*, Vol. 2 pt. 1, pg. 1550.

If Newfoundland had demanded too much in 1948, there might well have been no union in 1949. The dominion would have fared worse on its own than it had with Canada. The delegation fully realized in 1948 that provincial status ensured there would be no repeat of the embarrassing bankruptcy in the 1930s.

A prominent witness to the historic events leading to Confederation was Gordon A. Winter, who served as a member of the delegation that negotiated the final terms for union. He was an interim Smallwood cabinet minister and later served as Lt. Governor of Newfoundland. Winter described Smallwood's role:

> He fought tenaciously and continually for every advantage and benefit that could be obtained. Apart from his interests as a loyal and dedicated Newfoundlander, it was very much in his political interest to persuade the Government of Canada to give every possible concession. The better the plan worked, the more successful he was going to be as provincial leader, a post he coveted at the time.[14]

Winter attested to the difficulties the delegation ran into. He explained:

> The financial arrangements alone posed considerable difficulties. For our part, we had to have sufficient financial resources to make the new province viable, and from Canada's point of view, it was difficult politically for them to treat the new province more generously than other provinces...notably our neighbouring maritime provinces.

An interesting aspect of the final negotiations in 1948 was that the Canadian Government had not yet agreed that Labrador should be part of the new province of Newfound-

---

[14] Ibid.

land. Years later Premier Maurice Duplessis told Winter that if Ottawa had consulted with Quebec at the time, Newfoundland would have to surrender Labrador to Quebec first. Had that happened Newfoundland would not have joined Canada.

It was inevitable that the transition to provincial status would have some negative effects on businesses operating under the old system. In August 1948, Calvin C. Pratt, President of Steers Limited, told J.C. Britton, a former Canadian Trade Commissioner in Newfoundland, that the political situation was already contributing to the chaotic state in some areas of business in the country. Exempted from his criticism were: food, its distribution, and his agencies and wholesale distribution system. Pratt explained:

> The textile distribution has gone to pieces, as the shopkeeper's sole object is to run his stocks down and even the consumers, I am told, particularly in the outports, are expecting almost a free distribution of goods. However, this is purely the psychological reaction from the excitement of the campaign and the perspective of people will become more rational even before the actual consummation of union with Canada.[15]

He blamed this state of affairs on both the Responsible Government advocates as well as the Confederates for the partisanship each generated. Pratt also criticized the Commission of Government which he said could have guided the changes in business to avoid the problems it was causing for a minority.

At this time in Newfoundland history the country had 130 firms which employed about 4000 people. Tariffs on imported goods which the merchants passed on to the consumer contributed to 82% of all Newfoundland Government revenues in 1933, and by 1948 under Commission of Government were still as high as 54%. The coming of

---

[15] Ibid Part 2, 1698.

Confederation saw these being removed from imported Canadian goods and an immediate drop in the cost of living in Newfoundland.[16]

DAYS BEFORE UNION STILL
NO LIEUTENANT GOVERNOR

Although publicly things appeared to be running smoothly in the month leading up to union with Canada, behind the scenes a crisis was developing which was not settled until a few days before Newfoundland entered Confederation. The crisis involved the appointment of a Lieutenant Governor during the interim period while awaiting the holding of a provincial election and the establishment of a legislature. The problem was a political one rather than a legal one, but it remained a festering boil until finally settled.

The initial Canadian plan was to appoint an interim Lieutenant Governor until the first appointment could be made to that position. The problem that emerged was that Newfoundland would have, for a short period of time, a Lieutenant Governor but no legislature. Would the interim Lieutenant Governor be willing to appoint an interim premier and cabinet without a legislature in place, and if not how would the province be governed?

The terms of union had provided for the Newfoundland Chief Justice to act as Lieutenant Governor until the first appointment could be made. However, Chief Justice Edward Emerson developed concerns about following that route and was concerned enough to bring them to the Prime Minister, Louis St. Laurent, on February 22, 1949. Emerson told the Prime Minister that he hoped he would not have to serve. He explained:

It is most desirable, especially in a small community such as this, for the Supreme Court to be free from suspicion of taking sides in partisan politics and so far its history

---

[16] PANL GN 10/1/file 10.

in this respect has been excellent. I feel that no matter what form the caretaker Government takes, its creator runs grave risk of being subjected to accusation of bias.

My brother judges and I felt justified in letting our views on Confederation be known as this question, in our opinion, far transcended any matter purely of party. You will readily see therefore how vulnerable I am to attack.[17]

Despite his expressed concern about his responsibility in the matter, Emerson told St. Laurent that, if necessary, he was willing to undertake the task assigned to him. Informed sources in St. John's had been claiming that St. Laurent had already chosen Sir Leonard Outerbridge as the interim Lieutenant Governor and favoured Joey Smallwood as the interim Premier. However, Canada would not directly appoint the interim Premier that would be the choice of the Lieutenant Governor. But, would the Lieutenant Governor act on a political appointment before the new province had a legislature?

The Prime Minister responded immediately to Emerson and assured him that he would soon decide on the appointment which would spare the Chief Justice any embarrassment. With a little more than a month left before union, Ottawa conducted a secret probe to make sure their new appointment would not have any constitutional concerns about making political decisions without a legislature first being established. This turned out to be more difficult than expected, and with only days before an interim Premier and cabinet was to be sworn in, there was still no Lieutenant Governor.

On March 9, 1949, McEvoy had reported to Mackay that Smallwood had been claiming in Ottawa, Toronto and in Newfoundland that his nominee, Sir Leonard Outerbridge,

---

[17] *Documents on Relations between Canada and Newfoundland*, Vol. 2, pt. 1 pg 1578, 1579.

would be appointed Lieutenant Governor on condition that he would appoint Smallwood as Interim Premier. It turned out that this had been a rumour started by Smallwood's opponents.

Smallwood and Outerbridge had already reached an understanding. Smallwood promoted Outerbridge for the position he wanted, Lieutenant Governor, and Outerbridge would call upon Smallwood to become interim Premier. Although Outerbridge had been offered the position, and the Prime Minister awaited his acceptance, things changed. During a meeting with the High Commissioner in St. John's, Outerbridge said that he would have a problem making a political decision before the legislature was established.

The Canadians then approached Sir Albert Walsh who was planning to resume his legal practice and had no interest in the position of Lieutenant Governor. However, he was a political realist, and when asked the same question put forward to Outerbridge, he replied that he would not have any problem and considered it quite legal. He also explained that whoever held the position would have no choice but to invite Smallwood to serve as interim Premier. At this stage, no political parties had been formed and Smallwood's Confederate organization was the closest thing to a political party and they had won the election.[18]

With just a week left before Confederation, Walsh was persuaded to accept the position for a time limit of five to six months in which period the new province would have its own legislature and Outerbridge would replace him. He reluctantly agreed to this on the condition that Sir Leonard be told that same day of the decision and that the public would be informed that he was staying only for a brief period.

On March 25th, Outerbridge had already written and mailed his acceptance of the office to the Prime Minister

---

[18] Gordon Bradley conducted the conversation with Walsh to determine his views on the position of an interim Lieutenant Governor.

when he received the letter from Ottawa advising him that he had not been selected. It was too late to stop his acceptance letter from going through the mail. Sir Leonard was terribly embarrassed when he learned that Walsh had been given the appointment. On March 26th, the new Lieutenant Governor met with Smallwood and the Chief Justice to work out plans for the ceremonies of union, just five days away.

Despite the efforts to have a candidate from the St. John's establishment invited to become interim Premier, the Canadians had already decided on Smallwood. The Prime Minister was influenced by the report of R.A. Mackay whom he had sent to assess the political situation in Newfoundland. Mackay recommended Smallwood and predicted that he would carry the districts outside St. John's. His report noted:

> He has to have in his Cabinet representatives from St. John's who normally should be Catholic because of the rigid manner of having denominations represented, but if this is impossible he must still have representation from the city and particularly from the business groups who opposed Confederation.[19]

The official position of the Canadian Government was expressed in a secret memo to the High Commissioner in Newfoundland on March 15, 1949, by the Secretary of State for External Affairs who quoted Prime Minister St. Laurent:

> It is our feeling that Bradley and Smallwood are the only personalities who, until elections have been held, can be considered to represent any substantial organized body of opinion. Bradley is not interested in the provincial field and we therefore feel that Smallwood is the person who should be called upon to form a provincial administration, but we do not wish to dictate this view to the new Lieutenant-Governor.[20]

---

[19] *Documents on Relations Between Canada and Newfoundland*, Vol.2 pt.1.
[20] Ibid, p1594.

St. Laurent was also of the opinion that Sir Albert Walsh as Lieutenant Governor offered a measure of stability until the provincial election could be held because the interim Government had no one with any experience in the preceding administration. In regards to Outerbridge, St. Laurent said he understood his concerns about making decisions before the election of the legislature.

Smallwood was not concerned about the choice to appoint Walsh, however, he felt it would be a disappointment to the Anglican Church. He told officials that he intended to inform the Anglican Bishop of the intent to appoint Outerbridge at a later date. The Anglicans had favoured the appointment of an Anglican because historically more Anglicans had served as Governor than those of any other faith.

CHAPTER 13

Establishment Tries to Stop
Joe - and Conspiracy Charges

I have sometimes asked myself whether union would have been possible if Smallwood had taken my polite "No!" for an answer and not ignored me and gone directly to pound on political doors. As one looks back one is compelled to ask...who else could have done it but Joe Smallwood?

- Professor R. A. McKay-Professor of Law, Dalhousie
University and Adviser External Affairs Department

ONE LAST HURDLE

Just three years before Smallwood was sworn in as the first Premier of the Province of Newfoundland, his knowledge of the Canadian system was marginal. In the relative short period from 1946 to 1949, he had emerged as the acknowledged expert on the Canadian system and the advantages Confederation offered Newfoundland, as well as leader of the Newfoundland Confederate movement. He had gathered documents and reports from every federal department of Government, visited Ottawa and gathered more knowledge from bureaucrats and cabinet ministers. He totally absorbed himself in the operations of the National Convention and the negotiations for union.

In the National Convention, he served on four of its ten committees and attended the meetings of the other six. In negotiations with Ottawa, he was the only Newfoundlander to serve on all eleven committees. He played the political game like a master chess player, trying to anticipate every move and developing effective offensive strategies. Yet, after leading his Confederates to victory, he still had a battle to confront. The establishment would make a last ditch effort to keep political power in the hands of the St. John's establishment.

The establishment was reluctant to let go of its power, and sought to replace Joey with someone from the 'upper class' or at least to reduce his role in Confederation. Not all merchants and professionals were in the Responsible Government Party, some went along with the Smallwood movement, while not actually supporting him or the cause he was battling. One of these was John B. McEvoy.

John B. McEvoy was a prominent, respected Newfoundland lawyer, well-connected with the St. John's establishment. While secretly supporting Smallwood, he was actually in favour of a return to Responsible Government as the road to Confederation, a policy repeatedly condemned by Smallwood confederates. Some well-known merchants and professionals were among McEvoy's impressive list of clients and trusted friends.

He also had a powerful friend at a very high level in Ottawa who played a major role in Newfoundland's road to Confederation. The Hon. R.A. Mackay, was a senior adviser to Canada's Secretary of State for External Affairs and often advised the Prime Minister and Federal Cabinet.[1] He had also served as a Professor of Law at Dalhousie University where McEvoy was one of his students. Through this contact, McEvoy expanded his influence with others in Canada's capital, including C.D. Howe, Minister of Trade and Supply.

In the first year of the National Convention, he endeared himself to the Smallwood Confederates. He became Chairman of the National Convention through their backing, and he delivered a devastating blow to Ches Crosbie's Economic Union Party by revealing research he had done in the United States showing that no less a person than a Judge of the World Court had strongly condemned Crosbie's idea.

McEvoy kept in close contact with his Ottawa friend Mckay through visits and personal and secret letters which would have been politically embarrassing for both gentlemen had the contents become public information. He obviously had no idea that his letters, seeking to undermine Smallwood and advance the cause of others, as well as seeking a political appointment for himself, were shared with others, let alone, kept on file at External Affairs. These records, now open to the public, tell an amazing story of the backstabbing deceptions that went on in the last battle Smallwood had to deal with before coming to office.

John McEvoy, who had been Chairman of the National Convention, and a Confederate, claimed he had the backing of some politically prestigious men in St. John's to take over leadership of the Confederates. Just two days after the voting in the first referendum, he indicated to R.A. Mackay that his associates wanted to replace the Confederate leadership and that he had made up his mind to accept the leadership role.

---

[1] It is significant to note that twenty-years after Confederation, Professor Mackay said that Confederation could not have succeeded without Smallwood.

Mackay consulted with Pearson and the two agreed this was a matter that Canada should not become involved with.

Several days later McEvoy sent Mackay another letter informing him he was no longer interested in the planned coup because his wife "Ollie" was ill. Yet, he did have two suggestions for his friend. The first recommendation was that while he was staying out of the political fray, he was willing to accept a senate appointment. The other recommendation was that businessman Calvin Pratt be chosen as the interim Premier.[2] He had no way of knowing it then, but the Canadians had reasoned that the Confederation Movement was a party which fought the battle for union, and if successful, the obvious and only choice for interim Premiership would be its leader, Joe Smallwood.[3]

The Federal Cabinet certainly kept tabs on the key players in the Newfoundland Confederate Movement, as well as its opponents. C.D. Howe, Canada's Minister of Trade and Commerce, enquired about John McEvoy's standing in the movement. McEvoy's secret lobbying for political favours may have been the reason behind Howe's enquiry.

Senator McLean, after consulting with friends in Newfoundland, informed Howe that McEvoy was not part of the Confederate organization which covered the Island, nor was he popular among the Confederates because of the trouble he caused them prior to the first referendum. The Senator was referring to an interview McEvoy gave to *The Evening Telegram* which was published on February 9, 1948. He quoted McEvoy from the interview:

If the office of Commonwealth Relations decides that Confederation is to go on the referendum ballot paper,

---

[2] *Documents on Relations Between Canada and Newfoundland*, Vol. 2. Pt 1

[3] J. R. Smallwood, *I Chose Canada*, 562. At the May 31, 1971, annual meeting of the Canadian Historical Society held at MUN, Smallwood and Jack Pickersgill conducted a lengthy discussion about Newoundland's entry into Confederation. The transcript of that discussion is printed in full in the book's Appendix Two.

it would go on only in principle, and not on the basis of the present terms which are unnegotiated.

The present terms of Confederation were received by a delegation hampered by their lack of power and the people should not be asked to make an irrevocable decision on the unnegotiated terms which this delegation received. Before the people are asked to make a decision for, or against union with Canada, the terms must be negotiated between governments. In other words, before the people are asked to make a decision, a Responsible Government must be elected in Newfoundland and negotiate terms with the Government of Canada.[4]

That choice had long been ruled out by Smallwood and his followers because they did not trust those controlling the Responsible Government Movement. Smallwood and Bradley had asked McEvoy to withdraw his statement, but he refused. Senator McLean told the Minister:

The Confederate leaders took strong objection to Mr. McEvoy's statements for two reasons. Firstly–for McEvoy to say the terms were unnegotiated was entirely unfair to men like Mr. Bradley, Smallwood and others who had come to Ottawa in 1947 and negotiated for months with members of the Federal Cabinet until a basis was arrived at for Confederation. Secondly, the Confederate leaders felt, with good reason, that if Responsible Government was set up first, matters would be dragged along for years before Confederation could be arrived at–and possibly not at all in our time. I know what a hard battle the Confederates had, but they won a real democratic victory. Responsible Government was defeated twice.[5]

---

[4] *Documents on Relations Between Canada and Newfoundland*, Vol. 2 pt.1
[5] Ibid, p1561,1562.

Senator McLean added that the Confederates needed McEvoy during the campaign. They valued his opinions but they were convinced that his statements caused them considerable harm at a critical time.

The Canadian High Commissioner in Newfoundland also refuted charges that the terms of union of 1947 had not been negotiated. He provided some background to the negotiations, pointing out that the National Convention was elected by the people of Newfoundland and the Commission of Government approved the delegation to Ottawa elected by Convention delegates. The terms agreed upon were presented to the National Convention and to the people of Newfoundland. "These terms," he said, "had been known for nine months which gave the Convention ample time to assess their probable impact on Newfoundland."

After reading the Senator's report, Howe remained impressed with McEvoy's ability and prestige and replied, "would like to keep him in the Liberal camp if at all possible. This does not mean that McEvoy is in line for any particular political preferment, as far as I know."

McEvoy's undermining of the Smallwood Confederates negatively affected his relationship with the political powers in Ottawa as the day for union approached.

McEvoy, unaware of the backroom notes he was generating between Newfoundland and Ottawa, still had several strong supporters among the Newfoundland Commissioners and got himself appointed as one of the delegates to finalize the terms of union with Ottawa. In a letter to his friend in External Affairs, Professor Mackay, he lavished praise upon Mackenzie King. He mentioned that he listened to the radio broadcast of the Liberal Convention in Ottawa and commented, "I was particularly impressed by the Prime Minister's Valedictory Address which was a masterpiece and in every way you care to look at it." He added:

When I learned from Joe Smallwood he and Gordon Bradley were attending the [Federal Liberal] Convention, I was somewhat concerned since I felt that the Prime Minister and the Minister might wake up any morning now and find themselves out of jobs, Bradley being Prime Minister and Joe, Minister of External Affairs.[6]

JOEY AND BRADLEY AT FEDERAL LIBERAL CONVENTION

McKenzie King was aware that Smallwood and Bradley were attending the 1949 Liberal Convention, but not that they were scheduled to speak. King finished his own address at 6:00 p.m. and left the building. He returned at 9:00 p.m. When he arrived, Smallwood was speaking and the Prime Minister noted in his diary that Joey had given, "a humorous address." Although Smallwood drew thunderous applause, the Prime Minister felt it was poor political strategy to have the two Newfoundland Confederates appear as speakers.

The Prime Minister sat between them on the platform and was not hesitant in expressing his thoughts. He advised them that it would be better for the Convention if they did not propose any resolutions dealing with Newfoundland. He explained, "It might raise the question of the provinces claiming their right to have a special say." Smallwood and Bradley agreed.

Their conversation touched on other matters and King later wrote, "I quite enjoyed sitting between these two men at the time and felt there was something quite significant about this little feature of the evening."

McEvoy pointed out to Mackay that Joey had decided to remain in Provincial Politics and that he (McEvoy) had pledged his support to him because, he told Joey, "...I have absolutely no interest in Provincial Politics myself." While Smallwood and Bradley were attending the Liberal Convention in Ottawa, McEvoy held a meeting with the remaining

[6] Ibid, p1985.

delegation consisting of Sir Albert Walsh, Ches Crosbie, and Gordon Winter, who were still in St. John's preparing for the forthcoming Ottawa meetings.

SELF-PROMOTING

In January 1949, McEvoy approached Mackay again, but not to help the Newfoundland Confederate cause. He had been invited to be guest speaker at the Canadian Club of Montreal on January 31, 1949, and was seeking information from his friend to help him give credit for Confederation to those he felt deserved it: the Prime Minister, his cabinet colleagues, J. Burchill; and Dean (Vince) MacDonald. He told Mackay, "If there is anything you want done before, please advise me." Then he went on in an attempt to undermine Smallwood:

> As I have feared, I have been approached from many quarters to lead a party but in view of a pending operation and the fact that Ollie [his wife] says she would not tolerate my entering the provincial field for one moment, I have thus far rejected all proposals. My little friend with the "Big Bow Tie" [Joe Smallwood] is, I understand, finding the going pretty tough and I predict, 'He's seen nuthin, yet' as he's sure going to run into a lot of trouble, as I've constantly predicted. Confidentially, I can secure a Lieutenant Governor and a Provincial Leader should it be desired. They are both wealthy men of the highest possible integrity. I say they are my two men because they are both clients of mine and are doing nothing unless approved by me.[7]

To add pressure to the Liberals in Ottawa, McEvoy said that George Drew, leader of the Federal Progressive Con-

---

[7] Ibid, p1986 (2) In predicting 'He's seen nuthin yet' McEvoy and friends were convinced that Joey could not bring together a credible interim cabinet.

servative Party, was scheduled to visit St. John's in late January 1949 and was interested in one of his men. He followed this with a reminder of his on-going soliciting of an appointment to the Senate:

> I hope my ambition to insure against being drafted into political life will be realized by my appointment as one of the six. I thought I would be taken out of circulation insofar as other fields of political endeavour are concerned to which 'Ollie' replied, 'Pray God it happens as I'm afraid it will wear you down and we must not anymore go through anything like we experience in 1947 and 1948.'

McEvoy also reminded Mackay that during a recent visit to Ottawa, he had been promised a senate appointment, and he would appreciate anything Mackay could do to move the promise forward.

Smallwood suspected McEvoy was hatching a plot to take over leadership of the Confederate Movement in order to be involved in the interim government. However, he believed McEvoy was promoting himself and Ches Crosbie for the interim leadership positions, likely with himself as Premier. Joey was not aware that McEvoy had told External Affairs that he, and thousands like him, would not support a Liberal party under Joe Smallwood, and hinted that the PC's would benefit if Joe was appointed interim Premier.

Around mid-November 1948, Joey made his own countermove by confronting Mackay with his concern. After telling Mackay about his suspicions, he warned that if he and Bradley did not get control, the Liberal Government would lose every seat in Newfoundland.

The first public indications that Ottawa had made up its mind on the choice for an interim Premier came early in 1949. The *Daily News* reported on January 31, 1949, "Joseph Smallwood asserted here tonight he would be the first Premier of Newfoundland after Confederation. He said he expected to be appointed by the Governor and that when an election is called, he will campaign as the head of a political party." Smallwood said he would select the interim cabinet.

In March 1949, just three weeks before Joe Smallwood was sworn in with his interim cabinet, McEvoy fired off an angry protest to his Ottawa friend. In it he referred to a *Daily News* story that day in which Smallwood named some members of his interim cabinet. He wrote:

> It may well be that this is pure propaganda on Small-wood's part but should it have any foundation in fact it is going to be difficult to defend for reasons we have already discussed, and, in particular, because I was clearly given to understand that no person entering public politics would be appointed to the Interim Cabinet lest the charge be made that Ottawa did so deliberately with the idea of giving such persons advantages over their opponents in the First Provincial election.[8]

McEvoy warned that if Smallwood's announcement was fact, Ottawa would be setting the scene for one of the most bitter campaigns Newfoundland had ever witnessed. Two days later, McEvoy, still bothered by the closeness of the Confederation date, and the uncertainty of the role he would be accorded, sent a second letter to Mackay. This rather short letter was to the point, it stated:

> As evidenced by the clippings herewith enclosed public opinion here seems to be unanimous on one question, at least, and that is Smallwood's brash announcement that he is to head the Interim Government. Should this materialize, it's going to lead to serious trouble as I've repeatedly warned. I sincerely hope, in the interests of Union, that such will not be the case.[9]

---

[8] Ibid, p1988.
[9] Ibid.

He pointed out that the Progressive Conservatives under the leadership of George Drew had a large following among the anti-Confederates who would be angry at such a move and it would attract much unfavourable publicity for the Liberal Party.

When it became clear to McEvoy that Smallwood was to become the Interim Premier, McEvoy continued to undermine Smallwood. In a mid-March conversation with the High Commissioner in St. John's, which was described in an External Affairs Report to the Prime Minister's Office, he recommended that Ottawa make a special effort to accommodate Calvin Pratt, or he would end up as leader of the Progressive Conservative Party.

The High Commission was taken aback when McEvoy suggested, "We should make Smallwood take him (Pratt) on as Finance Minister, with some kind of promise that Smallwood could not stay long; alternatively, that we should have him [Pratt] run for the Federal House with a similar understanding about Bradley." He was suggesting a Federal Cabinet post for Pratt.

The report pointed out that McEvoy's attitude was always anti-Smallwood, but pro-Confederate. McEvoy boasted that, with the help of Ottawa, he had the influence to get the majority of merchant support to accept Confederation and also control Smallwood and his supporters. By the end of his letter, he was recommending Ches Pippy for Lieutenant-Governor, Calvin Pratt as Premier, and himself and Phil Gruchy, Vice President and General Manager of the Anglo-Newfoundland Development Company. If these appointments could not be arranged, then he, Gruchy and Pratt should be appointed senators. Unknown to McEvoy, many of the old establishment were already mending fences and joining with their opponents.

McEvoy was not the only person wanting to discredit Smallwood's success of 1949. Twenty years after Confederation, Hon. H.A. Winter made the following comments in a letter to Ira Wild, Commissioner of Finance in Newfoundland in 1946:

> Joe Smallwood poses as the 'father' of Confederation, but I preached it, if only on purely economic grounds, years before Joe was heard of. I knew the longstanding feeling against it in Newfoundland, but I knew also that it rested on the shortsighted and penurious view Canada had taken on the question in the past.[10]

Unlike Smallwood, Winter made no effort to convert the Newfoundland people to Confederation.

CONSPIRACY THEORY

The second referendum which resulted in the Confederate win was settled by the democratic principle of majority vote, 50% plus one. The terms of union were made known to the Newfoundland people and the choice for union with Canada won with a 4.6% majority, eleven votes short of 7000 votes. If Newfoundland had voted by districts based on those represented in the National Convention, the outcome would have been a landslide victory of twenty-nine Confederate Districts to nine Responsible Government Districts. There were twenty-five districts in both referendums compared to the twenty-nine in the National Convention.

Another important point, long forgotten, is that thousands of pro-Confederate supporters voted for Responsible Government as the best course to follow in achieving Confederation for Newfoundland. Had they voted directly for Confederation the margin of victory would have been higher.

It seems ironic that the Responsible Government Party[11] would launch petitions and court challenges to stop a

---

[10] Ibid, p1961
[11] The most respected members of the RGP disassociated themselves from these efforts. Ches Crosbie called upon Newfoundlanders to unite and move forward.

majority decision which the Confederates won while accepting its own win in the first referendum without question. After winning the first referendum, the RGP organized a campaign, founded the *Independent* newspaper and raised money to contest the second referendum.

A British MP ridiculed the idea by pointing out that to overturn the election outcome would be to award victory to the minority. He added, "It was a shameless disregard for the right of the Newfoundland people by the St. John's Establishment."

An argument repeated, incredibly, by writers over the years was that massive voting fraud took place. One author even claimed that Britain had instructed the Newfoundland Commission of Government to make sure, regardless of the outcome of the election, that Confederation won. Consequently, 7000 votes were shaved off the total numbers to fix the outcome. Shaving 7000 votes could not have escaped the attention of the Responsible Government Party's own scrutinizers, let alone other scrutinizers and election officials noticing it.

Part of this scenario behind the conspiracy claim was that the turnout for the second vote on July 22nd was 6100 votes less than the first vote on June 3rd. Harold Horwood viewed the whole conspiracy theme as "nonsense." Horwood argued that most knowledgeable people on Newfoundland life in that era would have known that fishermen were at home for the June 3rd vote but on July 22nd an estimated 10,000 fishermen were at sea and very few got back to vote. There were also Labrador fishermen and Newfoundland banking crews who did not get back to vote.

JOEY AND CASHIN CLASH IN FIRST LEGISLATURE

On July 29, 1949, Peter Cashin, who originated the conspiracy theory on his 1946 radio shows and again in the National Convention, continued to spin the theory in Newfoundland's first provincial legislature. By this time, Cashin had claimed that Prime Minister Winston Churchill of England and Prime Minister Mackenzie King of Canada had met in Montreal during the war to plot Newfoundland's entry into Confederation. Joey, then Newfoundland's first Premier, promptly pointed out that even if that claim were true:

> After all that conniving, they only managed to have Confederation put on the ballot paper. They only managed to get to the point where Confederation was competing, that's all. But then, why would I have to fight if it was all cut and dried by these great men and their Governments.[12]

Joey said had there been a conspiracy, he would not have had to work so hard, his role would have been much easier. He continued to attack Cashin's theory:

> If Great Britain was so very anxious to have Newfoundland join Canada, she could really have done something which would have furthered that end a great deal. She could simply have told Newfoundlanders that as far as she was concerned, her aid to Newfoundland was finished.

> She could have said that she was facing the present dollar shortage, and would no longer be able to help Newfoundland, then, that if she voted for the Commission of Government, they would, in effect, be voting for Responsible Government, for the country would be entirely on her own and under a Commission. The 22,000 votes that went for the Commission would then have gone for Confederation and the Confederates would have won in the first referendum.[13]

Joey told the House that bringing about Confederation was the most democratic thing that ever happened in

---

[12] *The Evening Telegram,* July 30, 1949.
[13] Ibid.

Newfoundland. He sparked some laughing in the legislature when he concluded, "It's like Mr Cashin, 'This is my story, that is my song! Talking of plots, all day long'." Cashin answered with a laugh, to which Joey commented, "That's an infectious laugh, worth over a thousand votes any day." The confrontation came during the two week debate in reply to the Speech from the Throne.

Others over the years have disregarded any suggestions of a conspiracy taking place. Twenty years after Confederation, Judge Harold Winter who served as Commissioner of Justice, in a letter to Ira Wild Commissioner of Finance in Newfoundland, recalled an experience to support his statement that no conspiracy had taken place. He referred to a despatch to London the Commission sent years before the referendum which recommended Confederation for Newfoundland, and it was brushed aside by the British. He wrote:

I expected an unfavourable reception, but was not prepared for the crushing rejection we got. Under the polite diplomatese [sic] we were told to behave ourselves, take our books home and study our lessons. Confederation was out: no one in Newfoundland wanted it; and even to mention it would bring them and us into disrepute.

But, I think, I have, at least, shown how absurd the argument is that England wrangled confederation for us. It might be said that her creature, the National Convention, did; but it was precisely because England discounted confederation that the National Convention was formed, or even thought of.[14]

---

[14] *Documents on Relations Between Canada and Newfoundland*, p1961. (2) Twenty years later, Winter had become bitter against Smallwood and in private letters undermined both the Convention and Smallwood.

274

In his book *Dawn Without Light,* Dr. Herbert Pottle, who served in the Commission of Government and who resigned from Smallwood's cabinet halfway through his term, denied any conspiracy had taken place. Harold Horwood, one of Smallwood's top Lieutenant's and MHA for Labrador in Joey's first administration, described the conspiracy claims as "nonsense." A study of the Canadian documents relating to Confederation contains much evidence showing a conspiracy did not exist.

The Hon. R.A. Mackay, one of the key players in the negotiations from the start, concluded that Confederation was not possible without Smallwood. He astutely remarked that if the 48% of voters who supported Responsible Government had remained vigorously opposed, the events of July 22nd would not have proceeded as peacefully as they did. Concerns of civil disobedience were unfounded.

Author Raymond Blake, after researching Newfoundland's entry into Confederation, concluded, "Although the Canadians and the British could limit and influence the choices to be made in the long summer of 1948, Newfoundlanders alone decided their constitutional future."

Several other writers arrived at similar conclusions. There had been no conspiracy, but both Britain and Canada tried to influence Newfoundlanders towards choosing Confederation in the same way that, at a later time, the Canadian Federal Government and provinces tried to influence Quebecers to vote "No" in its referenda to secede. In the end, the Newfoundlander marking an "X" on a ballot sheet made the final decision.

In addition to Smallwood's argument against the "Conspiracy Theory" hatched by Peter Cashin, there is a powerful legal argument against conspiracy. If Britain and Canada were determined to force Newfoundland into union with Canada, it could have been achieved legally without the uncertainty of a National Convention and referendum.

All was needed was for Britain to establish Newfoundland as a territory of Canada. This would be followed by the

Canadian Parliament passing an Act to incorporate the territory of Newfoundland into Confederation. The entire process could have been carried out legally with an amendment to the BNA Act (34-35), Chapter 28, Section 2.

It is interesting to note that while Cashin alleged that Roosevelt and Churchill had met in Canada to bargain away Newfoundland to the Canadians, there is no mention of such an encounter in Churchill's memoirs. Churchill would certainly have recorded such an event. His war time memoirs were comprehensive and even revealed political intrigue regarding St. Pierre.

Newfoundlanders believed that political corruption had caused Newfoundland's bankruptcy and loss of independence in 1933. They had little appetite for returning to a Responsible Government, controlled by St. John's merchants and might very well, for the sake of stability, gone along with this process.

Smallwood had changed attitudes and increased enthusiasm towards Confederation for Newfoundland in Ottawa by impressing the powerful with his knowledge of Newfoundland and Confederation and his conviction that Confederation could win.

ENGLAND'S MOTIVE

When England announced that a national referendum would be held in Newfoundland in 1946, she was carefully concealing a secret from the public. This was not the course of action its politicians wanted to follow but economic circumstances made it necessary. It is little wonder then that Peter Cashin sensed that Britain was not being straight forward with Newfoundlanders and it is also understandable that one might suspect a conspiracy was in operation.

England's decision to create an atmosphere in which Newfoundland would join Canada was an alternative dictated by its own dire economic position as the war drew to a close. At the source of its decision was the needed funding of $100 million for development and reconstruction of

Newfoundland after the war.[15] Simply put, England did not have the money, and its politicians had been warned by its Treasury Department as well as economist John Maynard Keynes it could not borrow the funds without jeopardising its own financial position and its place as a world power.

British politicians wanted to restore Responsible Government after the war and finance a development and reconstruction program. In response to Britain's request in 1944, the plans were prepared by the Commission of Government and the total cost estimated at $100 million was to be spread over a ten year period. The plans were submitted to London. The proposal was favoured by British politicians but condemned by its financial advisers.

After much debate, Britain decided that the financial stability of Newfoundland would be best served in a new unpredictable world as a province of Canada. They could not force that choice upon Newfoundlanders, but they wanted to assure that when the time came for Newfoundlanders to choose their own future, they would have that choice.

To make this matter public would have jeopardised Britain's own ability to raise finances for reconstruction after the war.

CANADA'S VIEW

In 1945, Canada felt that Newfoundland some day in the future, and only after a political or economic disaster, would turn towards union with Canada. They recognized that the Newfoundland people disliked Canadians and would turn towards the United States before seeking Confederation with Canada. Canada's interest in Britain's intentions towards Newfoundland in 1945 had nothing to do with any plan to move Newfoundland towards union, as some writers later claimed. The Canadian concern was over the pending

---

[15] The Newfoundland development plan was part of an overall program England was following to help finance the reconstruction of all nations of the British Empire in addition to rebuilding Great Britain.

large amount of borrowing from Canada that England was to undertake and the effect of Britain's Newfoundland policy on that borrowing.

Why was Canada concerned about Britain's borrowing? While the war was still ongoing, Britain was developing plans to rebuild its own war-torn country after the war as well as financing the same throughout its Empire. This ambitious program had a high price tag and was to require a great deal of borrowing. The British consulted with Canada over its role in helping Britain to finance its own country's reconstruction. The agreement between the two nations was that Canada would loan Britain money to purchase its needs from Canada. British politicians were happy with the deal. The Canadians had not been aware of the Newfoundland Redevelopment program.

In considering Newfoundland, the British intended to add the $100 million needed to its Canadian borrowing. In that decision lay the seeds for Britain's change of heart towards Newfoundland, and the expressed interest in Newfoundland by the Canadian Government in 1945. The sequence of events that became the base for conspiracy theorists over the years.

Canadians wanted to know Britain's plan for Newfoundland because it was not prepared to lend money beyond what was needed to cover purchases from Canada

When the British Government prepared to put its program before Parliament, opposition immediately rose from the Treasury. Historian Peter Neary explained:

> Great Britain could not pay for what was being proposed. The expenditures contemplated in Newfoundland would be mainly in Canadian dollars [Newfoundland's currency was tied to Canada's] and London was already borrowing massively from Ottawa. Great Britain's own financial situation in the post-war world would be perilous, and she would hardly look credible in negotiating loans for herself with the United

States and Canada if she was simultaneously attempting to prop up Newfoundland. Great Britain had to look to her own concerns lest financial weakness endangered her position as a great power.[16]

Britain recognized that Newfoundland's prosperity was due to the war and within a few years after the war ended would be turning to England for help which would be very limited. After Smallwood's 1946 visit to Ottawa, the Canadians took a more active interest in Newfoundland, and were forced to decide whether they wanted Newfoundland or not. Like Britain, Canada recognized and respected the right of the Newfoundland people to choose the form of government it wanted. At several pivotal points in the campaign as demonstrated earlier, it was Smallwood's presence and leadership that saved the day for the Confederates.

Britain was not in a position to come out and publicly declare its decision to favour Confederation for Newfoundland and to explain the financial circumstances that forced it to that decision. It did its best to indirectly let Newfoundlanders know that England had little to offer them financially after the war and lobbied Canada to pursue union with Newfoundland. In that respect, it is significant to remember that when Britain asked for Canadian input on making the final decision as to whether to include the choice of Confederation on the ballot paper, after it had been turned down at the National Convention, Canada replied that this issue was strictly a matter between Newfoundland and Britain.

However, nothing done by Britain or Canada in their efforts to influence Newfoundlanders diminished the effectiveness and integrity of Joey Smallwood's Confederate campaign.

---

[16] Dr. Peter Neary, *Newfoundland's Union With Canada, 1949: Conspiracy or Choice?*

CHAPTER 14

Why Joey Chose the Liberal Party

"I was a Liberal because I felt that Liberalism in Newfoundland, with its roots set deeply down in the fishing and working
classes generally, and its honourable record of taking always
the side of the people, was as close as it was reasonable or
practical to think the Island could get to Socialism."

- Joe Smallwood, 1973

Newfoundland had no political parties from 1933-1949. By the election date in 1949, the two traditional parties, the Liberals and Progressive Conservatives had been re-established. However, in 1949 Joe Smallwood, through the aggressive and successful campaign he waged to reverse Newfoundlanders decades of dislike and distrust of their Canadian neighbours, had raised his personal popularity far above any political party. His choice of the Liberal Party could not be taken for granted in 1948 and early 1949.

Smallwood realized through his relentless community-to-community campaigning in the two elections held a year before just where he stood with the Newfoundland people. He had delivered fifty to sixty speeches a day and met large crowds everywhere he visited. Often the entire population of a community would be anticipating his visit.

In the early part of 1949 when the St. John's Establishment was lobbying behind the scenes to persuade Canada to appoint one of their own as interim Premier, Smallwood heard of it, and was determined not to be cheated out of a victory he had earned. He was not prepared to let the reins of power fall back into the hands of the merchants even for the interim period, while awaiting a general election. He let Ottawa officials know that he was aware of the backroom manoeuvrings and that he intended to, "...lead a party in the general election and become Premier."

Smallwood's concern at that time was hardly warranted because the matter had been discussed by top bureaucrats and the federal cabinet, and the consensus was that Smallwood, who had just won a national election, best represented the Newfoundland people. Meanwhile Smallwood, a socialist himself, had carefully considered his choice of political affiliation.

Although the CCF party, which later became the New Democratic Party, never gained a toe-hold in Newfoundland, they were a powerful force in Canadian politics in 1949. In Saskatchewan, under the leadership of Tommy Douglas, they controlled the provincial government;

formed the opposition in three provincial legislatures; and had elected thirty members to the Canadian Parliament.

The CCF's national leader, M.J. Caldwell, was impressed with Smallwood's background as a socialist and labour organizer and, prior to the second referendum, invited him to join the CCF. He suggested to Smallwood that he and the CCF were fighting the same forces that had exploited Newfoundland for generations.

Smallwood declined an invitation from the CCF leader to attend the 1948 CCF Convention in Winnipeg. In his book *Joey*, Harold Horwood said, "Although Smallwood's sympathies were with the CCF, he realized they could not finance an election." Other socialist leaning prominent Newfoundlanders abandoned their CCF leanings to join Smallwood, and were elected to Newfoundland's first legislature, including Horwood. Several of these resigned in the first years of Confederation over policy disagreements.

The party had targeted many prominent labour leaders and organizers in Newfoundland whom they expected to join them, but they were disappointed to find that most had already committed to Smallwood and the Liberal party. Caldwell visited Newfoundland from December 11-16, 1948, but found little enthusiasm and support for the CCF for the 1949 provincial election.

Caldwell had expected that Ted Russell, teacher, magistrate, director of Cooperatives with the Commission of Government and later a popular author, to lead the CCF in Newfoundland, but Russell declined and accepted an invitation from Smallwood to serve in Newfoundland's first cabinet.[1]

Other possible candidates for the CCF included: Greg Power; Charles Ballam; Sam Hefferton; Irving Fogwell; Charles Horwood; Nish Jackman, President of the Wabana Mines Workers Union; and Ron Fahey, President of the Newfoundland Federation of Labour; Harold Horwood;

---

[1] JRS MUN Collection 4.03.002 , April 18, 1949

and Bill Gilles. Gilles was the only one who actually ran for the CCF in 1949 but was unsuccessful.

It was ironic that Prime Mackenzie King's first interest in Newfoundland was sparked in Parliament in 1943 by J. W. Noseworthy, a Newfoundland born CCF Member of Parliament from Ontario. In response to Noseworthy's question regarding the likelihood of Newfoundland joining the Canadian union, King said, "The door for Newfoundland is opened should they make their decision clear and beyond all possibility of misunderstanding; Canada would give most sympathetic consideration to the proposal."

In 1984, Peter Fenwick became the first NDP (previously CCF) to be elected in Newfoundland.

WHY JOEY CHOSE THE LIBERAL PARTY

Joey considered and weighed the arguments both pro and con of which party to align with. He found strong reasons to support the Liberal Party. He explained his choice:

> In my politics, I was a Liberal because I felt that Liberalism in Newfoundland, with its roots set deeply down in the fishing and working classes generally, and its honourable record of taking always the side of the people, was as close as it was reasonable or practical to think the Island could get to Socialism. It was Liberalism that had, through the great Dr. William Carson, waged that original battle for the right merely to live in Newfoundland, to put a chimney in your house; the historic fight to make the English appointed governors of Newfoundland live on the Island all year long; the fight to force the Governor to have a small advisory council of local people; the fight for sweeping reform of the Supreme Court; the fight for Representative Government. It was Liberalism that had brought in manhood suffrage and the secret ballot. It was Liberalism that had built the railway across Newfoundland; Liberalism that had built the great pulp and paper industry at Grand Falls, and

again at Corner Brook. All down through the years, it
seems to me, Liberalism had done those things that Socialism would have done, except for the impossible so-
cialization of industry. I found no difficulty whatsoever,
as a Socialist, in being a Newfoundland Liberal, and indeed a Canadian Liberal when I became a Canadian.[2]

In private, Smallwood often expressed admiration for the
fervour and dedication of the rank and file members of the
New Democratic Party. He frequently used the words "passionate campaigners" in his descriptions.

ORGANIZING THE LIBERAL PARTY-1949

The provincial Liberal Party of Newfoundland was not
formed until after Joey Smallwood was sworn in as the new
province's first Premier on April 1, 1949. In the election that
followed, the Liberals won twenty-two seats, the PC's five
and Major Peter Cashin was elected as an independent.

One of Aubrey MacDonald's most popular anecdotes
about Smallwood was his story about being alone with
Smallwood on the day he was to be sworn in as the new
province's first Premier. I recall the first time I heard Aubrey
tell the story. It was at a private lunch with Mayor Dorothy
Wyatt, Jim Byrne, businessman; Frank 'Toe' Byrne, and
Henry Hutchings, businessman, at a downtown restaurant.

According to Aubrey, one hour before Joey Smallwood
was to be sworn in as Newfoundland's first Premier he had
some moments of deep thought as he looked out through
a radio studio window on the top floor of the Newfoundland Hotel. Aubrey MacDonald, was the only other person
in the studio and he often described that historic moment
in his own very popular radio broadcasts. Aubrey recalled:

His dreams and plans had been followed, his battles
fought gallantly and won, he stood on the verge of a

[2]Joseph R. Smallwood, *I Chose Canada*, p164.

truly great moment in the history of his country. What great thoughts must be going through his head. Just as I was thinking that I'd give anything to know his feelings at that momentous moment and was just about to break the silence and ask him, Joe turned to me, as though he was reading my mind. I tensed up a little in expectation of being given an insight into the thinking of Canada's newest father of Confederation as he was about to make history, and reverently listened to him say, 'You know Aubrey, if I was two inches taller, I'd be Prime Minister of Canada.'

MacDonald, in a more serious mood, described Smallwood saying, "He was the last of a vanishing breed of dynamic, magnetic, flamboyant politicians. Devil or saint, dictator or demigod, call him what you will, he is still a child of the ages. Joey Smallwood belongs to an era, and the era belongs to Joey Smallwood."

Almost 1500 people from all over Newfoundland came to St. John's for the founding convention of the Newfoundland Liberal Party. Smallwood had chartered a train to bring delegates into St. John's. Others made their way to St. John's by way of trucks, cars, and horse and buggies. The three day convention was held at the CLB Armoury on Harvey Road. Smallwood was officially made leader of the provincial Liberal Party and F. Gordon Bradley became leader of the federal wing of the party.

The event was not without humour. Joey recalled later that one man had brought a truck load of delegates to the convention from his hometown with the expectations of becoming the Liberal candidate in his district. When he learned that Smallwood had already appointed one of his newly sworn in cabinet ministers as the candidate in this man's district, he took it in good stride. He confided to his friends, "But for a trick of fate today, I'd be the 'onable Arvey'."

As leader of the Liberal Party, Smallwood's message to Newfoundlanders was that any attempt to persist in isolation would condemn Newfoundlanders for all time to a very low standard of living and a bitter struggle for existence. He warned of the dangers of nursing delusions of grandeur. He reminded voters that Newfoundland was a small country, an island country, and it had a population of 350,000 people and most of them were very poor people. He described the daily stresses Newfoundlanders faced:

> Most of them lived on a very low standard of physical life and material life. They were remote from each other. They were isolated from each other and from the rest of the country. They were unconnected by roads and unconnected by telephone. They were completely out of touch with each other. Their school system was very poor. Their hospital system was very poor. The great majority of them lived with kerosene oil lamps.[3]

SMALLWOOD INFLUENCES CHANGE

For the average Newfoundlander the complexities of the Canadian federal system of government were not easy to grasp, especially after fifteen years of no democracy and their government being run by a commission of six men. In 1945, very few people would have predicted that Newfoundland would ever choose to join with Canada. In the 1946 National Convention election only one man had openly declared himself a Confederate. In 1948, the Newfoundland people chose Confederation. How was such a change brought about in such a short period of time?

On July 24, 1948, just two days after the Confederation victory, Paul Bridle, Canada's acting High Commissioner in Newfoundland,[4] sent a dispatch to Ottawa in which he answered this question:

---

[3] Joseph R. Smallwood, *I Chose Canada.*

[4] Canada replaced the High Commissioner with an 'Acting High Commissioner' during the Referendum vote because they feared demonstrations and violence and felt their offices would be less of a target if the High Commissioner was not present.

If one were to single out one Newfoundlander more responsible than others for this development, one would name Mr. J.R. Smallwood. He is known in this country as the "Apostle of Confederation" and unquestionably deserves the major share of the credit for the success which it has achieved at the polls.[5]

Bridle pointed out that there was little doubt that many voted for Confederation out of fear of the consequences of a return to Responsible Government. He said people remembered the depth to which the life of the average person sank in Newfoundland during those days and were filled with alarm for themselves and their children over thoughts of Newfoundland returning to that form of government. He added that many prominent, thoughtful Newfoundlanders shared the same concerns.

Walter R. Harris, Parliamentary Assistant to the Prime Minister of Canada, pointed out, "Confederation with Canada brought Newfoundland into the mainstream of North American life and set in train a revolutionary process."[6]

Aubrey McDonald witnessed Smallwood in action in his early days. He recalled:

In the grinding poverty of the thirties, there were radicals, soapbox orators, raising their voices in rebellion against the rich landlords and merchant princes of Water Street. Joey fell into that category, but he was a voice crying in the wilderness. A poor man himself, he was an apostle of the poor, but he was like a cracky biting at the heels of Great Danes.

Albert Perlin, described by Harold Horwood as "a one man brain trust for the other side," and associate editor of

---

[5] *Documents on Relations between Canada and Newfoundland*, p953
[6] *Documents Relating to Canada and Newfoundland.*

the *Daily News* was among those recognizing Smallwood's work:

> Whatever his current critics or future historians may have to say in the light of hindsight about some of his ideas and his methods, nobody can take from him the credit for launching and directing a revolution which has transformed our Newfoundland way of life.

Perlin added that Smallwood had in less than twenty years, "Repaired the glaring social deficiencies of a deprived past." He noted that although he had access to financial resources as a Canadian province his success was achieved mostly by his own efforts and vision.

Senator Ches Carter recalled the high regard people in his district had for Smallwood, "In 1949, Smallwood was considered a deity, particularly among the generation that had experienced the 1930s. My campaign manager told me that one day he met a person who started talking about "Joey" and pointing his finger up to the sky said, 'Sir! He come right down'. "

According to Carter, the provincial Liberals were in political trouble in 1957 in many outport districts, and Smallwood's handling of the IWA strike changed all that and restored him once again to the pinnacle of popularity.[7]

WHERE JOEY'S SPEAKING STYLE CAME FROM

The Smallwoods were not religious. His father Charles was a Methodist and his mother, a Catholic, both of them had given up attending church. After moving to St. John's, the family was attracted to the new Bethesda Mission that was set up on New Gower Street in the centre downtown and Joey did attend services with them. Harold Horwood was of the opinion that Joey developed his style of speaking from the

[7]See *Crimes That Shocked Newfoundland,* Jack Fitzgerald, Creative Publishers, for the historical account of the IWA Strike.

preachers at this mission. Those experiences may have had an effect on Joey's speaking style, but according to Smallwood, his repetitive style was inspired by Sir Richard Squires.

In 1984, I travelled with Smallwood and Tom Barron, a Liberal activist and organizer, to the Burin Peninsula. We were driving to Lawn where the first students to graduate under the new high school system, which had raised the final grade from eleven to twelve, were graduating. Joey was their guest speaker, and I had an opportunity to speak also and present several of my books to the principal for the school library. I recall well the drive down to Lawn:

Tom and I were taking turns driving, and I was at the wheel when Tom asked Joey if he had developed his repetitious style of public speaking from observing Adolph Hitler during the war. I was impressed by the frankness of the question and most attentive to Joey's answer. He didn't hesitate in his reply. He had developed this style long before WWII. Smallwood pointed out that he had adopted the style from Prime Minister Sir Richard Squires and told us about the occasion he was drawn to Sir Richard's speaking style. It was at dinner with Sir Richard and Lady Helena Squires. Lady Helena was being critical of her husband's speaking style. Joey said:

Lady Helena noted Richard takes so long to make a point, and he repeats himself. If a black cat walked across the stage, It was not enough for him to simply state, 'A black cat has walked across the stage,' he has to say, 'A black cat just walked across the stage. It was not a black and white cat....it was not an orange cat...nor was it a white cat...No, it was not a cat of any of these colours. It was a black cat, no other colour but black, a black cat.

Now, throughout Lady Helena's humorous mimicking of her husband, Sir Richard continued to eat his lunch.

When she finished, he interrupted eating long enough to comment, 'Yes, Helena, but you would have to agree that if there was a thousand people in the audience, by the time I would finish, every single one of them would know that a black cat had crossed the stage.'

Smallwood's skills as an orator were legend. There were many stories of his going into a hostile hall and gaining the confidence of crowds in attendance. Sam Hefferton, a member of Smallwood's first cabinet, explained:

Critics found fault with his repetitious delivery but he had a mastery of language, and ability to marshal facts quickly that made him a doughty advocate and a formidable opponent. The ability to think on his feet; the oratorical skill to gain and to keep the interest of his audience, and when the occasion demanded it he had, if I may borrow a quotation from Allen Drury's political novel Preserve and Protect, 'the flair to use the most gracious phraseology.' Men of action are generally centres of controversy, but these are the people who get things done.[8]

Not long before his passing in 1990, I stopped off at his daughter Clara's dairy bar across the street from his Roache's Line Home. I had not called earlier to say I was coming to visit so I stopped to check with Clara Russell, to see if Mr Smallwood was well enough to have a visitor. She said he was doing well, and that he loved to go for a ride to Bay Roberts. Looking through the window, she commented, "Here he comes now. Would you go over and bring him across the street." She added that he came to the dairy bar every day to get a milkshake. Having a daily milkshake was a routine he followed during his early years as Premier.

[8] James R. Thoms, ed., *Call Me Joey*.

Joey was wearing a black overcoat and a salt and pepper hat. A much frailer and weaker man than when I had last seen him. He was three quarters way down the driveway from his Roache's Line home when I pulled my car alongside and he stepped inside. We had a brief chat before we arrived back at Clara's during which he accepted my offer to drive to Bay Roberts after his milkshake.

Although the stroke he had suffered affected his speech, his mind was sharp and we could carry on a conversation, but he experienced difficulty at times and would stop in the middle of a sentence trying to remember the appropriate word, and I would help him along by guessing it. He seemed frustrated by his problem, and I noticed a tear running down his face. I felt so deeply saddened and helpless. I had seen Smallwood at his best, in the Legislature, in crowded halls and stadiums, privately working the telephones in his room at the Chateau Laurier Hotel wheeling and dealing with the Liberal Party power brokers across Canada, lining up the support that brought success to Pierre Elliot Trudeau's bid for national Liberal party leader and Prime Minister of Canada.

I visited him many times after his resignation from politics, thoroughly enjoying his amazing recollection of history. The ride from Bay Roberts to drop him off at his daughter's dairy bar was a painful and a deeply emotional experience for me. After returning him to the dairy bar, I shook his hand and told him I would drop in again for a visit and left. It was the last visit I had with him. By the end of the year, he had passed away. I know that Joe Ashley, Greg Power and Eric Dawe kept in touch with him to the end, as did Steve Neary and Ron Pumphrey, who also made special visits on his birthday. There may have been a few others whose names I am unaware of, but many of those who had sought his friendship and attention in better days had deserted him in retirement and sickness.

CHAPTER 15

The Rt. Hon. Joseph R. Smallwood, First Premier of the Province of Newfoundland and Labrador

His place in history? It is absolutely secure as a great Newfoundlander and a great Canadian. Like all the rest of us, he didn't do everything perfectly, but I don't know who else ever did everything perfectly. In terms of his overall place in history...quite secure, perhaps as the greatest Newfoundlander that ever lived.

- Hon. Clyde Wells, Premier of
Newfoundland and Labrador, 1990

NEWFOUNDLAND DOMINION OR COLONY?

Prime Minister Walter S. Monroe, showed no enthusiasm towards Britain's decision to award Dominion Status to Newfoundland. His response to the announcement which he gave in the Newfoundland House of Assembly on May 11, 1927 was:

> We are now an autonomous community equal in Status with any other Dominion of the British Empire. We did not ask for it, nor did we want it, and we did not throw our hats in the air when we got it. It is of no value to us.[1]

In 1932, Newfoundland had the opportunity to adopt the Statutes of Westminster, required to give Newfoundland full Dominion status but it did not.

There have been claims over the years that Newfoundland entered Canada as a sovereign nation unlike any other of the nine provinces. That question was the source of some controversy at the time of union, and was even raised in the Canadian Parliament. Harold Horwood, a prominent Confederate in 1949 and later a Canadian author, went as far as to assert that "...the Terms of Union had the force of a treaty, a contractual relationship between Canada and a foreign country,'[2] that once passed into law, could possibly be declared invalid.

Was Sir William Coaker right when he described Newfoundland as a "theoretical Dominion?" In later years constitutional experts examined the question and not all agreed that Newfoundland ever had full Dominion status. Some argued that Newfoundland never did achieve full sovereign Dominion Status because it failed to enact the required Statutes of Westminster. After the Balfour Declaration in

---

[1] Proceedings of the Newfoundland House of Assembly 1927, 4th Session, 26th General Assembly p17.

[2] Harold Horwood, *Joey*.

1926 gave colonies Dominion Status, the British Parliament felt in order for the new Dominions to act internationally, each country had to adopt the Statutes of Westminster.

A year later, Britain's foreign office claimed Newfoundland had no international status at all, and pointed out that Britain represented Newfoundland at the League of Nations which treated Newfoundland as a colony. Neither was Newfoundland interested in negotiating treaties, a function it was happy to leave to Britain.

In 1933, the Statutes of Westminster had been introduced into the Newfoundland Legislature and were on their way to being passed when the Government of the day decided it was not a priority and withdrew it.[3]

The argument that won the day for Dominion Status being recognized in 1949 was the fact that England did not have a written constitution and was governed by convention.[4] Once the colonies were given Dominion Status by convention, with or without the Statutes of Westminster, the status of Dominion, at least within the British Empire was legally recognized.

When the Statutes of Westminster were discussed by the Newfoundland Government in June 1931, there was little interest in pursuing Dominion status. Archival records show that government took the unusual step of holding a secret joint session of both Houses to discuss the question of Dominion and the Statutes of Westminster. Not only was there little interest in the matter on the political level, but also among the press and the general public. In the quarterly report of government for the period ending June 31, 1932, it was stated, "The general feeling appears to be that

---

[3] GN/1/1/17 Box 34

[4] By convention meant that the colonies had already been operating as Dominions, therefore that status would be recognized by British law. However, Newfoundland was represented by Britain in the majority of its international activities prior to the Balfour Declaration, and would have required enactment of the Statutes of Westminster. Other colonies adopted these Statutes.

Newfoundland had no grievance and would have preferred to leave the matters alone being desirous of safeguarding Imperial Unity and close association with the United Kingdom.

In 1949, Newfoundland's Dominion Status was recognized even though questioned in the Canadian Parliament.

OLDEST COLONY BECOMES TENTH PROVINCE

After organizing the Confederate Movement and leading the political battle that resulted in a victory for the Confederates, Joey Smallwood was sworn in as Newfoundland's first Premier on April 1, 1949. However, he did not hold the full status of a Provincial Premier because the first provincial election had not been held, and his position was an interim one until the people elected a government in a general election.

There had been pressure on Ottawa to appoint an interim Premier who had not been involved in politics and the issue was discussed at some length. Considering Smallwood's success in the recent countrywide referendum, Ottawa recognized that it was he who best represented the wishes of the Newfoundland people and therefore would be the most democratic choice.

Just days before April 1st, Smallwood and members of his cabinet were officially informed of their appointments. Smallwood had put together his recommended list for the cabinet. The new government was described as an interim Provincial Council and was comprised of: Joseph R. Smallwood, Premier and Economic Development; Gordon Winter, Finance; Leslie R. Curtis, Justice; Herman Quinton, Public Health; Herbert Pottle, Welfare; Samuel Hefferton, Education; Charles Ballam, Labour; Michael Sinnott, Public Works; Phil Forsey, Home Affairs; and William J. Kehoe, Natural Resources.

During the discussion between Smallwood and the High Commissioner, Smallwood asked if he had any trouble with Outerbridge to which the High Commissioner replied, "I know of none." Joey commented that he saw no particular advantage in the appointment of Sir Albert Walsh over Outerbridge since, "...both were good men and I could work harmoniously with either one."

When the High Commissioner asked if Joey had heard the rumour that Outerbridge had been offered the position and turned it down, Joey answered that he had not and there was no need to worry, "...it won't get outside St. John's." At this stage Smallwood was not aware of the content of the High Commissioner's interviews with Walsh and Outerbridge. Later, Outerbridge explained to Joey that the Canadians had misinterpreted his comments during the interview.

OTTAWA WELCOMES NEWFOUNDLAND

The ceremony on Parliament Hill in Ottawa welcoming Newfoundland as Canada's tenth province was impressive. It was a beautiful hot summer's day with a cool breeze that was more than welcomed by those in attendance. Civil servants had been allowed to have an early lunch so they could attend the historic event which opened with the bells of the Carillon [set of bells sounded from a keyboard] in the Peace Tower playing the "Squid Jigging Ground," written by Newfoundland born Arthur Scammel. This was played by Canada's official Carilloneur; Robert Donnell. Six bars of the Canadian National Anthem were played thirty minutes before the Royal Salute.

THE PEACE TOWER

The Peace Tower in Ottawa has historic significance to Canadians. It arose from the ashes of the old Parliament Building which was destroyed by fire in 1916. Upon completion; it was dedicated to peace and on the arch in the base were carved the coats of arms for the nine provinces of Canada. The architect and stonecutter carrying out the work, however, carved ten shields instead of nine. The tenth one remained blank for the day, which the Fathers of Confederation had foreseen when Newfoundland would join Canada. That day came April 1, 1949 when the arch and union had been completed.

During the ceremony, St. Laurent carved the first letter in the stone of the shield which now bears the Newfoundland Coat of Arms.

The band music was supplied by a composite of the Governor General's Foot Guard led by Major A.E. Wood.

In his welcoming address, Prime Minister Louis St. Laurent said:

> With the pleasure we have in welcoming you of Newfoundland as Canadians, there is mingled a feeling that you could have joined no better nation. The formal union is completed today. But the real union—took place in the recent terrible war in which Canadians and Newfoundlanders were so closely joined.

After describing Newfoundlanders as, "...in adversity and in prosperity, they have developed qualities of heart and spirit for which they are renowned," the Prime Minister quoted the poem written by Newfoundland born E.J. Pratt:

> 'This is their culture, – their master passion
> of giving shelter and of sharing bread.
> Of answering rocket signals in the fashion
> Of losing life to save it. In the spread
> Of time—the Gilbert-Grenfell-Bartlett span—
> The headlines cannot dim their daily story.
> Nor calls like London! Gander! Tehran!
> Outplay the drama of the sled and dory.'

The fact that Newfoundland has become a province of Canada will not cause you to lose your identity, of which you are all so justly pride.[5]

---

[5] *Documents on Relations Between Canada and Newfoundland,* Vol.2 pt.1, pp. 1681, 1683.

Frederick Gordon Bradley was sworn in earlier that day as Newfoundland's first Federal Cabinet Minister.

Smallwood sworn in

The ceremony at Government House in St. John's was broadcast by CBN. A choir under the direction of Bob McLoud stood by in the CBN studios waiting for the signal to begin singing the "Ode to Newfoundland." It had been pre-arranged by officials for the choir to sing only the first two verses of the Ode which were heard by radio at Government House and was part of the ceremony. The announcer began:

> I am speaking to you now from Government House in St. John's, the official residence of all governors of Newfoundland since about 1832 [sic], when responsible government was first introduced into the island. In this building all our governors and administrators of government since that time have taken their oaths of allegiance and office, and it is eminently fitting that here should be sworn in also the first Lieutenant Governor of the new province of Canada.

Sir Albert Walsh was sworn in as interim Lieutenant Governor by Chief Justice Sir Edward Emerson. Representing the Canadian Government was Hon. Colin Gibson who presented Walsh with Canadian citizen's papers recognizing Newfoundlanders as Canadian citizens. The ceremony was witnessed by Justices of the Newfoundland Supreme Court and representatives from Canada, United States, France, Portugal, and the Mayor of St. John's. Following the National Broadcast from Ottawa welcoming Newfoundland into Confederation, Lt. Governor Walsh swore in the new interim Premier and Cabinet.

The instant availability of Canada's social programs to Newfoundlanders had an obvious impact on voters. Within a month after becoming a Canadian province, Newfoundlanders had more money in their pockets to deal with the necessities of life which they so often lacked prior to 1949. The Port Union Fishermen's Advocate reported on May 16, 1949:

> It is notable that some little children have shoes to wear; the first time since birth, and the ever present cast of hopelessness on the countenance of the very poor, who could not give the little ones even a piece of ribbon is now being received with the mellowness of hope.

Not only was this reaction happening in the outports, in St. John's the *Evening Telegram* on May 14, 1949 reported, "The difference can already be noticed in the shoes, etc. worn by little children and by the extra cans of milk one sees being passed across the counter in the stores. The Family Allowances are a godsend."

The passing of this kind of poverty did not escape the Irish wit along the Southern Shore. A fisherman who had campaigned for the Tory candidate in the district said to his neighbour who had supported the Liberals, " The women got the baby bonus yesterday and I see, yer little Pater got his first pair of shoes today." His neighbour quipped, "Indade he did! And bejasus if yer little Paddy didn't ask 'em what they were."

The family allowance (baby bonus) and other Canadian social programs, so important to the working class in Newfoundland at the time of Confederation, were mocked by anti-Confederates for decades afterwards.

RECONCILIATION

Among the first tasks tackled by Smallwood after coming to power was to mend fences with his opponents, in particular, the Water Street merchants. Harold Horwood, a socialist, and the only insider in the Confederate Movement to write a book about Smallwood, disliked that idea. He observed, "In fact, no effort at reconciliation was needed in that quarter. The merchants came flocking in droves."

In July 1948, when some prominent supporters of Responsible Government were crossing over to the Confederates, they came under bitter criticism from their former friends. Smallwood went on the offensive and in a radio broadcast said, "If it were not for these mendacious tactics many more highly respected members of the community would by now have made their views known publicly."[6]

Other opponents, witnessing the immediate financial benefits of union, soon discovered that Joey had been telling the truth about Confederation. In the first provincial General Election that followed in June 1949, the Liberal Party led by Smallwood recorded 65.5% of the vote, a 13% increase over the Confederate vote one year before. This would not have been possible if the 47.66% vote the Responsible Government Party obtained in the referendum had been a solid anti-Confederate vote. The truth is that thousands in that party were actually Confederates who adhered strongly to the belief that Newfoundland should first return to Responsible Government and then negotiate terms with Ottawa. The true percentage of anti-Confederates was much lower than the recorded Responsible Government vote suggested.

FIRST BENEFITS

The impact of Confederation upon Newfoundlanders was immediate. The federal bureaucracy had begun work in December 1948 to make sure that eligible Newfoundlanders would receive social program entitlements in April 1949. Consequently, family allowance cheques were delivered to Newfoundlanders on the same day in April that other Canadians received them. Newfoundlanders became eligible for Canada's unemployment assistance and insurance programs followed by remarkable improvements in Old Age Assistance and Veterans Pensions.

---

[6]*Documents on Relations Between Canada and Newfoundland*, part 1 Vol. 2.

These programs put dollars into the pockets of families that often went as long as six months without any money. Newfoundland's Old Age Pension system was a disgrace. The qualifying age was set at seventy-five years, but not guaranteed at that age. It depended on the availability of money in the government treasury. Some did not get the pension until seventy-seven, and seventy-eight. The pension was paid quarterly with thirty-six dollars for a couple and eighteen dollars for a single person. By the day Newfoundland became a province, the never-to-be forgotten six cents per day dole had increased to twenty-five cents a day.

The flow of money from the Federal Treasury benefited families as well as business. Newfoundlanders had more money to spend on food, clothing and other necessities than ever before. Confederation eliminated the tariffs, an added windfall to the people, which resulted in a drop in commodity prices by as much as 30% to 40%. To compete with Canadian products, Newfoundland merchants were forced to drop prices even lower. Some merchants reduced the number of ships they owned and invested in retail stores to avail of the improving economy brought on by Confederation.

Term 29 Debate

The success of Newfoundland's delegation to Ottawa in 1948 to have Term 29 included in the terms of union proved its value when ten years later Prime Minister John Diefenbaker ignored the entitlement given to the tenth province by this term. This resulted in the battle-line being marked between Newfoundland and Ottawa.

The political confrontation that resulted between Diefenbaker and Smallwood began when Prime Minister Diefenbaker introduced the Atlantic Development grants for all the Atlantic Provinces, excluding Newfoundland.

Senator Ches Carter recalled, "Diefenbaker argued that Newfoundland was amply taken care of by the grants available under Term 29. It was Mr. Smallwood's forceful and masterly presentation of Newfoundland's case that forced Mr. Diefenbaker to change his mind."

In the Lion's den, where Diefenbaker made the announcement, Smallwood eloquently pointed out that the Term 29 grants were merely to ensure maintenance of Newfoundland public services at the existing level reached in 1957, whereas the purpose of the Atlantic Development grant was to improve services beyond the existing level. His eloquence and the force of his argument convinced the other provincial premiers that Newfoundland too was entitled to a share in grants allocated for improvement of services and Mr Diefenbaker had no choice but to concede.

DID JOEY WANT CONFEDERATION ON ANY TERMS?

Opponents of Smallwood, in later years, claimed that he went to Ottawa prepared to agree to Confederation on any terms. A merchant member of the delegation which negotiated the terms strongly disagreed with that position. Hon. Gordon Winter, who was also a former Lt. Governor and member of the interim provincial cabinet, responded:

Nothing could have been further from the truth. He fought tenaciously and continually for every advantage and benefit that could be obtained. Apart from his interests as a loyal and dedicated Newfoundlander, it was very much in his political interests to persuade the Government of Canada to give every possible concession. The better the plan worked, the more successful he was going to be as a provincial leader...a post he coveted and had his eye on at the time.

His boundless energy was perhaps his most outstanding characteristic. He worked without ceasing, night and day, often depriving himself of rest and sustenance. He certainly fascinated the members of the Canadian cabinet...at times some of them didn't quite know what to make of him.

In 1974, twenty-five years later, the Prime Minister of Canada wrote a confidential letter recognizing Smallwood's contribution to the Newfoundland people and to Canada. Prime Minister Pierre Elliott Trudeau sent this letter to

Smallwood which he prefaced with the words "Private and confidential."

The letter meant a great deal to the former Newfoundland Premier and he shared a copy with me with the stipulation that it be kept from the press. He said at the time, "I doubt that many Canadians ever received so gracious a letter from the leader of the Canadian nation." That was almost forty years ago. The writing of this book offers an opportune time to share that letter with the public. In it Trudeau wrote:

I cannot think of a single living Canadian who has accomplished so much for his people as you have. Not only did you re-shape Confederation, and the destiny of Newfoundlanders as full-fledged partners in that union, but you were also the chief architect of a social and economic revolution of massive proportions in the province you have loved and served so well. It is given to few people in this life to make a real difference in the lives of their fellow men. You are a man who has made an historic difference of unique quality—a difference which will continue to have a beneficial impact upon your province and your country long after you and I have departed from the scene.

The full letter is included as an appendix to this chapter.

BISHOP O'NEILL SURPRISED SMALLWOOD

While campaigning for Confederation, Smallwood attempted to attract the Roman Catholic Bishop of Harbour Grace, Reverend John O'Neill to his cause. The two debated the issue for more than an hour, but in the end O'Neill was not the least convinced. Some years later, while Smallwood was Premier, he attended a public reception honouring the Bishop's service to his church which was held in the Catholic Cathedral at Grand Falls.

Smallwood was seated with official guests in the front row and was surprised when the Bishop began talking about Confederation. He was startled when the Bishop told the crowd that he had opposed Confederation when approached by Smallwood in 1946 and admitted he had been wrong to do so. He went on to point out that union with Canada was good for Newfoundland and that Smallwood had been right from the start.

Among the finest public tributes paid to Joe Smallwood was that given by former Newfoundland Premier Clyde Wells in 1990 when he said:

> History will record Mr. Smallwood made a far greater contribution to the people of this province, and I suppose to the people of Canada, than any person before him in Newfoundland or any person that is presently alive. I just don't see any prospect of anyone else making a contribution to the well-being of the people of this province that comes even remotely close to measuring up to the size of the contribution Mr. Smallwood made. I've said that on a consistent basis for the last twenty years. I happen to believe it to be the truth. The fact I had political differences with Mr. Smallwood doesn't blind me from recognizing the good that the man did, and giving him the credit he deserves for it.

His place in history?

It is absolutely secure as a great Newfoundlander and a great Canadian. Like all the rest of us, he didn't do everything perfectly, but I don't know who else ever did everything perfectly. In terms of his overall place in history...quite secure, perhaps as the greatest Newfoundlander that ever lived. [7]

Liberal Senator Ches Carter, who, as Senator, had his differences with Smallwood, described Smallwood's contribution to Confederation:

> Almost single-handedly he brought Newfoundland into Confederation with Canada in the face of formidable

---

[7] Jim Thoms, *Call Me Joey.*

opposition that to lesser men would have been insurmountable. I doubt if, at that time, there was any other person alive who could have done it. This was a tremendous blessing for Newfoundlanders and in itself would be sufficient to assure him an honoured place in history. He opened up a new way of life for them and provided almost unlimited opportunities for their children and generations yet unborn. He cut away the chains of poverty that had bound our people for 500 years.

He brought Newfoundland into the 20th century, abolished their isolation from the outside world and provided roads to abolish isolation from each other within the province. Next to Confederation, his greatest achievement was Memorial University.

Smallwood came from a working class family in pre-Confederation Newfoundland at a time when the merchants controlled the country. It was beyond the imagination of the merchant class that such a man could challenge and change their century old system and rise to the highest office in the country. Joey Smallwood did just that!

APPENDIX

Confidential letter sent by Prime Minister Pierre Elliot Trudeau to the Hon. Joseph R. Smallwood in 1974.

Ottawa
November 15, 1974
Personal and confidential

Dear Joey,

I am writing this letter not to congratulate you on a battle well fought, because with millions of Canadians I simply take it for granted that any battle you are in will be well fought; nor do I intend to offer my sympathy at the outcome, because I know you to be a man who has no time to listen to sympathy when there is a future full of further challenges to be faced.

I am writing simply as any man would to a friend who has encountered a turning point in his life. I am writing to reaffirm that friendship, to express my admiration for you as a prodigious benefactor of Newfoundland and of Canada as a whole, and, finally, to express once again a deeply felt sense of personal gratitude.

I will never forget a major turning point in my own life— the national leadership campaign in 1968—a time when I needed support without reservation, and at a time when your support could influence convention delegates all across Canada. I have no hesitation in acknowledging the great debt I owe you. Indeed, I willingly share with you the credit for whatever good I and other members of the government have been able to accomplish for Canadians since 1968.

But you do not need the warmth of reflected credit, when you have earned so much in your own right as Premier of Newfoundland. I cannot think of a single living Canadian who has accomplished so much for his people as you have. Not only did you re-shape Confederation, and the destiny of Newfoundland as full-fledged partners in that union, but you were also the chief architect of a social and economic revolution of massive proportions in the province you have loved and served so well.

It is given to few people in this life to make a real difference in the lives of their fellow men. You are a man who has made an historic difference of unique quality—a difference which will continue to have a beneficial impact upon your province and your country long after you and I have departed from the scene.

And so I am doubly grateful: to you as a friend who has helped me; and to you as a Canadian who helped our country to become greater than it would have been without you.

Long-standing tradition, rooted in the principle of non-interference of national leaders in the affairs of provincial political parties, persuaded me to take no part, directly or indirectly, in the recent Newfoundland Liberal Leadership Convention. I want to assure you that neither I, nor anyone acting on my behalf, exercised any concerted influence for or against any of the leadership candidates.

Now that the convention is over, only those who do not know you very well will believe that you are ready to retreat to a well-earned retirement. I know that, despite your unique record of achievement in public service, you still have much to contribute to Newfoundland and to Canada. I will watch with great interest and continuing fascination, the new chapters you will write in a life story which has few equals in our history.

With personal good wishes and
warm regards, to you and to your family,
Pierre E. Trudeau

Almost 40 years after sharing a stage during an American Presidential election with Eleanor Roosevelt, wife of US President Franklyn D. Roosevelt, Premier Smallwood welcomes Mrs. Roosevelt to St. John's for the official opening of Memorial University in 1961. (PANL)

Premier Smallwood welcomes Prime Minister John Diefenbaker to St. John's for the opening of Memorial University in 1961. (PANL)

Joseph R. Smallwood at the fulfillment of a dream he had as a young student at Bishop Feild College to one day become Premier of Newfoundland. Sir Albert Walsh, sworn in as Governor on the same day, administered the oath of office to the new Premier. (Daily News)

Major Peter Cashin (centre) led the three-man delegation from the Responsible Government League to London in a last-minute effort to stop confederation. (PANL)

Activity at the Polling Station located at the Star Hall, Henry Street, St. John's. (PANL)

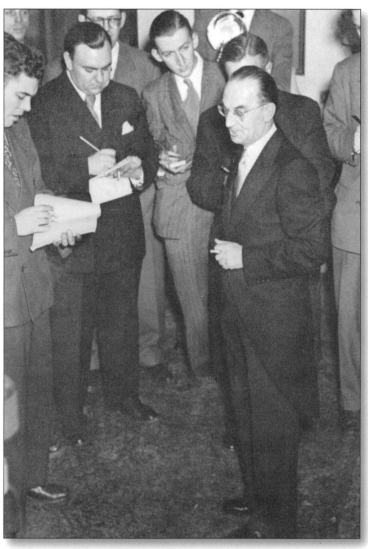

After being sworn in as Newfoundland's first provincial premier, Smallwood met with the press. (Evening Telegram)

Premier Smallwood working at his home office in Canada House on Circular Road in the first years of Confederation. (Evening Telegram)

Three generations of Smallwoods. Premier Joey Smallwood, his grandson Joey and great grandson Joey. (PANL)

Smallwood introducing Jack Pickersgill to voters in Bonavista, Trinity Conception. The two travelled througout the district by boat, and road when possible. (PANL)

Premier Smallwood during his last term as Premier. (L-R) Hon. Jim McGrath, Premier Smallwood and Hon. Ed Roberts, later leader of the liberal party of Newfoundland and Labrador, and Lt. Governor of Newfoundland. Small-wood once described Roberts as one of the most brilliant men he had encountered in Newfoundland Politics. (Evening Telegram)

Acknowledgements

The researching and writing of *1949 The Twilight Before the Dawn* spanned a decade throughout which I had the support and encouragement of friends. Ten years ago Richard 'Dick' Hartery provided valuable help in tracking down records dealing with the topic. This led me deeper into the subject and culminated in the writing of this book. Bob Rumsey provided on-going feedback and editing of material, as he has been doing, for all my books over the past decade; Don Morgan's long background in the publishing business and his accumulate knowledge of Newfoundland history has been invaluable in the final editing of this book. The management and staff at Creative Publishers, as always have been 'terrific.' Donna Francis, marketing manager, has been a constant source of help and moral support. Joanne Snook-Hann and Todd Manning take over after the final editing and bring their expertise to the final stage of preparing and publishing of the finished product. I am grateful to Pam Dooley, for her energy and efforts in acting as intermediary between me and the publisher in bringing *1949* to publication.

I am especially thankful to my son Maurice Fitzgerald who for more than twenty-years has been designing my book covers and providing photography work and advice all of which have contributed to the popularity of my books.

I am deeply grateful to Dale Russell Fitzpatrick, granddaughter of the Hon. Joseph R. Smallwood for her cooperation and permissions given for use of Mr. Smallwood's biographical material.

I also thank the staff members of the several archives throughout St. John's for their cooperation, courtesies and advice. These centres include : the Provincial Archives of Newfoundland and Labrador, the MUN Archives, The Centre for Newfoundland Studies, the Hunter Library (Newfoundland Collection), the Queen Elizabeth II Library at MUN, and the Archives of the City of St. John's.

BIBLIOGRAPHY

Connors, William. *The Barrelman (1938-1940)*. St. John's, Newfoundland: Creative Publishers, 1998.

Blake, Raymond B. *Canadians at Last, Canada Integrates Newfoundland as a Province*. Toronto, Buffalo and London: University of Toronto Press Incorporated, 1994.

Galgay, Frank. *The Life and Times of Sir Ambrose Shea Father of Confederation*. St. John's Newfoundland: Harry Cuff Publications Limited, 1986.

Fitzgerald, Jack. *Battlefront Newfoundland, Britain's Oldest Colony at War 1939-1945*. St. John's, Newfoundand: Creative Publishers, 2010.

Gilmore, William C. *Newfoundland and Dominion Status: the external affairs competence and international law status of Newfoundland, 1855-1934*, 255-266. Agincourt, Ont: Carswell Publishers, 1988.

Gwyn, Richard. *Smallwood the Unlikely Revolutionary*. Toronto: The Canadian Publishers, McClelland & Stewart Ltd., 1968.

Horwood, Harold. *The Life and Political Times of Joey Smallwood*. Toronto: Stoddart Publishing Co. Ltd., 1989.

Moore, Christopher. *1867, How the Fathers Made a Deal*. Toronto: The Canadian Publishers, McClelland & Stewart Ltd., 1997.

Neary, Peter. *Newfoundland in the North Atlantic*. Kingston and Montreal: McGill& Queen's University Press, 1988.

Pearson, Lester B., *The Memoirs of the Right Honourable Lester B. Pearson*. Toronto University Press, 1971-75.

Pickersgill, J. W. *My Years With Louis St. Laurent, a Political Memoir*. Toronto: University of Toronto Press, 1975.

Pottle, Herbert L. *Newfoundland Dawn Without Light*, St. John's, NL: Breakwater Books, 1979.

Prowse, D.W. *A History of Newfoundland*. Macmillan, 1895.

Robinson, Houston T. *Newfoundland's Surrender of Dominion Status in the British Empire*, microfilm, 1918-1934.

Rowe, Frederick W. *The Smallwood Era*. Toronto: McGrath-Hill Ryerson Limited, 1985.

Smallwood, Joseph R. *I Chose Canada, the Memoirs of the Honourable Joseph R. ("Joey")*. Toronto: Macmillan of Canada.
    -To You With Affection
    -No Apology From Me
    -The Time has Come to Tell, self published.

Smallwood, Joseph R. Editor in Chief and Pitt, Robert D. W., Managing Editor. *The Encyclopedia of Newfoundland and Labrador Vol.1*. Newfoundland Book Publishing Ltd, 1967.

Thoms, James R. *Call Me Joey*. St. John's, NL, Harry Cuff Publications, 1990.

Who's Who, St. John's, Nl. Boone Advertising.

Wheare, Kenneth Clinton. *The Statutes of Westminister, 1931*. Clarendon Press, 1938.
    The Statute of Westminister and dominion status. Oxford University Press, 1949.

DOCUMENTS, NEWSPAPERS, MAGAZINES

Neary, Peter. "Newfoundland's Union With Canada, 1949-Conspiracy or Choice?"Centre of Newfoundland Studies, MUN.

McCann, Phillip. "Confederation Revisited: New Light on British Policy," 1983. CNS MUN

PANL GN/10/A. Box 1, file 8.
PANL File GN 158.100
PANL MG 285.10
PANL MG 285.26, 27, 28.
PANL Fonds MG 285
PANL GN 38.7.1, Boxs 7-1-3- File 5
Series, File MG 285.10 (1947-1948) Speeches to the National Convention
PANL GN/1/17 Box 34
MUN Archives, Collection 285, 2.07.010
MUN Archives- 2.07.11
MUN Archives- 2.08.039-.41

Documents on Relations Between Canada and Newfoundland. Vols. 1 and 2. Department of External Affairs.

The Evening Telegram, St. John's, 1946 to 1950.
Daily News, St. John's, 1941- 1950.
Newfoundland Herald, St. John's, 1948.
MacKay, R.A., editor. *Newfoundland: economic diplomatic and strategic studies.* Toronto: Oxford University Press, 1946.

INTERVIEWS

Tom Barron, St. John's, NL, June 2011.
Michael Critch, Journalist. Last living journalist who covered the National Convention, 2011.
Conversations with Joseph R. Smallwood, 1968 -1988.